❧ Contemplating Historical Consciousness ☙

MAKING SENSE OF HISTORY
Studies in Historical Cultures
General Editor: Stefan Berger
Founding Editor: Jörn Rüsen

Bridging the gap between historical theory and the study of historical memory, this series crosses the boundaries between both academic disciplines and cultural, social, political and historical contexts. In an age of rapid globalization, which tends to manifest itself on an economic and political level, locating the cultural practices involved in generating its underlying historical sense is an increasingly urgent task.

Recent volumes:

Volume 36
Contemplating Historical Consciousness: Notes from the Field
Edited by Anna Clark and Carla L. Peck

Volume 35
Empathy and History: Historical Understanding in Re-enactment, Hermeneutics and Education
Tyson Retz

Volume 34
The Ethos of History: Time and Responsibility
Edited by Stefan Helgesson and Jayne Svenungsson

Volume 33
History and Belonging: Representations of the Past in Contemporary European Politics
Edited by Stefan Berger and Caner Tekin

Volume 32
Making Nordic Historiography: Connections, Tensions and Methodology, 1850–1970
Edited by Pertti Haapala, Marja Jalava, and Simon Larsson

Volume 31
Contesting Deregulation: Debates, Practices and Developments in the West since the 1970s
Edited by Knud Andresen and Stefan Müller

Volume 30
Cultural Borders of Europe: Narratives, Concepts and Practices in the Present and the Past
Edited by Mats Andrén, Thomas Lindkvist, Ingmar Söhrman, and Katharina Vajta

Volume 29
The Mirror of the Medieval: An Anthropology of the Western Historical Imagination
K. Patrick Fazioli

Volume 28
Evidence and Meaning: A Theory of Historical Studies
Jörn Rüsen

Volume 27
Sensitive Pasts: Questioning Heritage in Education
Edited by Carla van Boxtel, Maria Grever, and Stephan Klein

For a full volume listing, please see the series page on our website:
http://berghahnbooks.com/series/making-sense-of-history

CONTEMPLATING HISTORICAL CONSCIOUSNESS

Notes from the Field

Edited by Anna Clark and Carla L. Peck

berghahn
NEW YORK • OXFORD
www.berghahnbooks.com

First published in 2019 by
Berghahn Books
www.berghahnbooks.com

© 2019, 2020 Anna Clark and Carla L. Peck
First paperback edition published in 2020

All rights reserved. Except for the quotation of short passages
for the purposes of criticism and review, no part of this book
may be reproduced in any form or by any means, electronic or
mechanical, including photocopying, recording, or any information
storage and retrieval system now known or to be invented,
without written permission of the publisher.

Library of Congress Cataloging-in-Publication Data

Names: Clark, Anna, 1978- editor. | Peck, Carla L., editor.
Title: Contemplating Historical Consciousness: Notes from the Field / Anna Clark and Carla L. Peck.
Description: First edition. | New York: Berghahn Books, 2018. | Series: Making Sense of History; volume 36 | Includes bibliographical references and index. |
Identifiers: LCCN 2018048855 (print) | LCCN 2018049913 (ebook) | ISBN 9781785339301 (ebook) | ISBN 9781785339295 (hardback: alk. paper)
Subjects: LCSH: Collective memory. | Historiography—Social aspects. | Public history—Social aspects. | History—Study and teaching—Social aspects.
Classification: LCC D16.9 (ebook) | LCC D16.9 .C6343 2018 (print) | DDC 907.2—dc23
LC record available at https://lccn.loc.gov/2018048855

British Library Cataloguing in Publication Data

A catalogue record for this book is available from the British Library

ISBN 978-1-78533-929-5 hardback
ISBN 978-1-78920-837-5 paperback
ISBN 978-1-78533-930-1 ebook

Contents

List of Illustrations and Tables   vii

Acknowledgments   viii

Introduction
    Historical Consciousness: Theory and Practice   1
    Anna Clark and Carla L. Peck

Part I. Historical Consciousness, Curriculum, and Pedagogy

Chapter 1. Schools, Students, and Community History in Northern Ireland   19
    Alan W. McCully and Keith C. Barton

Chapter 2. "Orientation to the Past": Some Reflections on Historical Consciousness Research from England   32
    Arthur Chapman

Chapter 3. History Education Research into Historical Consciousness in Flanders   46
    Karel Van Nieuwenhuyse and Kaat Wils

Chapter 4. Historical Consciousness: A Learning and Teaching Perspective from the Netherlands   61
    Carla van Boxtel

Chapter 5. Historical Consciousness and Representations of National Territories: What the Trump and Berlin Walls Have in Common   76
    Mario Carretero

Part II. Historical Consciousness within and beyond Borders

Chapter 6. Mothers' Darlings of the South Pacific 91
Angela Wanhalla

Chapter 7. Looking Back at *Canadians and Their Pasts* 103
Peter Seixas

Chapter 8. *Private Lives, Public History*: Navigating Australian Historical Consciousness 113
Anna Clark

Chapter 9. "Chinese and their Pasts": Exploring Historical Consciousness of Ordinary Chinese—Initial Findings from Chongqing 125
Na Li

Chapter 10. "They Fought for Our Language": Historical Narratives and National Identification among Young French Canadians 142
Stéphane Lévesque and Jocelyn Létourneau

Part III. Historical Consciousness and Cultural Identity

Chapter 11. What is Black Historical Consciousness? 163
LaGarrett J. King

Chapter 12. "There Are Current Lessons from the Holocaust": Making Meaning from Jewish Histories of the Holocaust 175
Jordana Silverstein

Chapter 13. The "Realness" of Place in the Spiral of Time: Reflections on Indigenous Historical Consciousness from the Coast Salish Territory 185
Michael Marker

Chapter 14. Intergenerational Family Memory and Historical Consciousness 200
Anna Green

Chapter 15. Researching Identity and Historical Consciousness 212
Carla L. Peck

Epilogue
Why Historical Consciousness? 224
Maria Grever

Index 233

Illustrations and Tables

Figures

9.1.	Historical activities	131
9.2.	Trustworthiness of source of information about the past	132
9.3.	Connectedness to the past	134
9.4.	The importance of various pasts	135

Maps

5.1.	Territories lost by Mexico and obtained by the US after their war (1846–1848)	81
5.2.	Territorial development of the US	83

Tables

10.1.	Key historical figures: total frequency and per province	147
10.2.	Key words: total frequency and per province	150
10.3.	Key words in relation to sense of belonging to province (Québec or Ontario), in percentage of total frequency	154

Acknowledgments

The inspiration for this edited volume can be traced to a meeting between Anna Clark, Carla Peck, and Peter Seixas in March 2015. During the meeting, Anna noted that it had been ten years since the publication of Peter's foundational book, *Theorizing Historical Consciousness,* and suggested that it would be interesting to ask—ten years later—how scholars working in history and history education have applied their understanding of "historical consciousness" in their research. Peter encouraged us to pursue the idea, and provided thoughtful advice, critique, and commentary as the book began to take shape. We are indebted to him for his help in conceptualizing the purpose and scope of this volume.

We would also like to thank each of the contributors to this volume, who took up the challenge of reflecting on their work in meaningful and thought-provoking ways. In terms of the book's production, we would like to thank Stefan Berger, editor of the *Making Sense of History* series, for his encouragement of this collection, along with Chris Chappell, Amanda Horn, and Elizabeth Martinez at Berghahn Books for their editorial assistance and advice during publication. Lastly, we extend our sincere thanks to Burcu Cevik-Compiegne, whose editorial and research assistance was indispensable.

INTRODUCTION

Historical Consciousness

Theory and Practice

Anna Clark and Carla L. Peck

In recent decades there has been considerable international research into the meanings, uses, and consumption of the past among various peoples around the world. These memory studies have been fuelled not only by the nationally oriented work of Pierre Nora and David Lowenthal, among others, but also by the exploration of commemoration, trauma, and genocide as sites of history. Holocaust, and then postcolonial, studies precipitated an expansive research interest that was less nationally bound and more defined by ethnicity and experience. Both of these closely related fields have seen a wealth of theoretical speculation, semiotic analysis, and investigation of representations of the past and of those who produce them.[1]

With that burgeoning field of research also began the important interpretive work of interrogating and making meaning from history sites, such as monuments, textbooks, remembrances, and exhibitions. The result of such scholarly attention meant these markers in effect became "works" of history, as laden with meaning as any text, and demanded critique accordingly: memorial architecture was analyzed and interrogated, syllabuses and textbooks were rigorously combed, commemorations and museum exhibits were re-read from critical perspectives, family histories were interpreted with a scholarly lens.[2] Building on the scholarship into these public historical iterations, feminist and postcolonial scholars also revealed the embodied power of the past, as memories of slavery, colonization, Indigenous histories, the Holocaust, and motherhood registered corporeally. Archaeologists and

---

Notes for this section begin on page 11.

ethnographic and family historians documented archives and material culture produced in the most vernacular of settings. Even "silences" became important historic sites—as gaps in the record that warranted interpretation and research.[3]

Taken together, this corpus of work into history-making, from the most powerful public narrative to the most intimate memoir, has come to be defined as "historical culture."[4] The term encompasses histories produced by public institutions, bureaucracies, curriculum developers, governments, and professional and academic historians, as well as quotidian historical discourses of the everyday. And, its defining has meant that a diversity of historical productions—public and private histories as well as academic historical scholarship—has come to be seen as legitimate areas and moments for examination and research.

In turn, analysis of this history-making plethora required new methodologies—such as oral history, memory studies, museum studies, environmental history, history education or didactics, public history, and heritage studies—to begin to make sense of it. This included shifting the interpretive lens towards the public themselves, the "readers," "consumers," and "users" of that historical abundance. Along with those interrogations of history-making, then, came empirical studies into the significance of historical culture to the people who consume it.[5] Such research asked implicitly, what does the history around us mean? How do peoples and communities engage with and produce history? In other words, can we read from historical culture a *historical consciousness*?

Thus, the concept of historical consciousness refers both to the ways people orient themselves in time, and how they are bound by the historical and cultural contexts which shape their sense of temporality and collective memory.[6] "Human beings are history-makers," as the late Australian ethnographic historian Greg Dening ruminated. "Of all the systems that are expressions of who a people are, the sharpest and clearest is their historical consciousness."[7] Jörn Rüsen, one of the most influential of historical philosophers, described historical consciousness as *making sense* of the past, where the "past is interpreted for the sake of understanding the present and anticipating the future."[8] More than simply understanding how people think about history, this interpretation of historical consciousness also reveals history as fundamental to the ways we think about ourselves. The study of "historical consciousness makes it possible to understand how people *use* the past," contends Canadian historian Stéphane Lévesque.

So the term is a useful but slippery one, describing not only humanity's changing interest in its past, but also how people learn and engage with historical knowledge and practice over time.[9] Historical consciousness covers "every form" of thinking about the past, Rüsen insists, from "historical studies" to the "use and function of history in private and public life."[10] What unifies that breadth is the capacity of historical consciousness to recognize humanity's "historicity," insists Paul Riceour, "the fundamental and radical fact that we make history, that we are immersed in history, that we are historical beings."[11]

Yet tracing the development of the concept, as John Lukacs stated in 1968, is deeply problematic: "historical consciousness (like the remembered past) is in itself a historical phenomenon and not only a psychological one (like memory)."[12] Historical consciousness "is always filled with a variety of voices in which the echo of the past is heard," elaborated the German philosopher Hans-George Gadamer. "Only in the multifariousness of such voices does it exist."[13] Family and community histories, formal education, historical scholarship, public history, and popular uses of the past may be equal shapers of historical consciousness, but how they interact in its formation is surely up for debate.[14] (Hence the diversely-themed chapters in this book.) We would also add that *socio-cultural context* and *the politics of identity* are equally significant in the ways people connect with and make history—and the question of whether historical consciousness can be used cross-culturally, such as its capacity to engage with Indigenous temporal relationships, is a guiding concern of this collection.

Despite the fluidity of the term, and mounting questions about its universal application, "historical consciousness" has become a critical area of research in historical and memory studies, especially in relation to the field of history didactics. And Jörn Rüsen's now famous typology of historical consciousness not only indicates the different ways people use and think about history but also implies a certain ontogeny. The four categories of historical consciousness he defines can be read as points on an increasingly sophisticated historical spectrum:

1. *traditional* history recognizes the continuity of tradition—historical inheritance becomes a sort of prescription
2. *exemplary* history uses the past to instruct contemporary action and belief
3. *critical* history deconstructs any necessary continuity of tradition
4. *genetic* history historicizes difference across time

Significantly, however, none of these categories is mutually exclusive, and Rüsen himself emphasizes his model should be interpreted as a sketch of different modes of historical consciousness, rather than a prescriptive hierarchy.[15]

Indeed, the notion of ranking historical consciousness is problematic since it has important implications for the vernacular, multicultural, and subaltern history-making that researchers continue to study around the world.

"As long as we fail to acknowledge this intrinsic connection between the most sophisticated historical theory and the procedures of historical memory most deeply embedded in the culture and the everyday lives of people, we will remain caught in an ideology of linear progress," argues Rüsen, "which considers cultural forms of memory simply as interesting objects of study, rather than recognizing them as examples of 'how to make sense of history.'"[16]

Rather than a hierarchy of historical consciousness that elevates some forms of historical engagement and connection over others, what is important here is the exploration of how they relate to one another, and how they might change over time. Rüsen's schema is no crude didactic prescription for developing historical consciousness, insists Peter Lee: "We are not being offered a ladder-like progression in which we move from one stage to the next, leaving the first behind."[17] Indeed, people may hold different types of historical consciousness in tension simultaneously, thus the importance of *trying* to understand its complexity. After all, writes Australian historian Tom Griffiths, history "can be constructed at the dinner table, over the back fence, in parliament, in the streets, and not just in the tutorial room, or at the scholar's desk."[18]

Nevertheless, Rüsen and others are unambivalent about the potential of historical consciousness to develop over time. And they see formal history education and learning in schools, universities, museums, and curated heritage sites, for example, as a means to facilitate that development.[19] Catherine Duquette, Peter Lee, and Andreas Körber have gone even further, each developing pedagogical frameworks of attainment in historical consciousness, with their own models of curriculum design and assessment.[20] Such theoretical work reveals the pedagogical possibilities of historical consciousness, argue Carlos Kölbl and Lisa Konrad: models "help to clarify what is meant by the term historical consciousness," and they "help in assessing historical consciousness in a more transparent and a more methodologically consistent way."[21] Meanwhile, in jurisdictions such as Sweden and Germany, the development of historical consciousness is already a stated curriculum goal.[22]

Such theorizations about the dimensions and potential of historical consciousness—pedagogically, psychologically, and disciplinarily—continue to shape discussion of the term and its applications. These were addressed by Peter Seixas in a compelling volume, *Theorizing Historical Consciousness,* published in 2004, which gathered leading thinkers such as Rüsen himself, along with James Wertsch, Roger Simon, and Chris Lorenz. That collection, motivated by leading theorizations of historical consciousness, in turn motivated important work in the field, and this volume is no exception.

Moreover, the utility of "historical consciousness" as a theoretical term has been mapped out *on the ground,* as it were, in research projects across a variety of comparative and transnational sites, national settings, and familial or community contexts. Such scholarship explores the importance of history and history-making in human society, identifying markers and expressions of historical culture and practice (the "historical"); it is also driven by a desire to understand the ways history forms part of our collective and individual identities (the idea of "consciousness").

Pedagogical interest, in particular, has shaped several leading research projects in historical consciousness over the last twenty-five years. An ambitious study of the historical consciousness and political attitudes of nearly 32,000 teenagers, initiated by Magne Angvik and Bodo von Borries in 1991, surveyed students in twenty-five European countries, as well as in Israel and Palestine. While subsequent educational research has not replicated that impressive scale, it has continued to expand our knowledge of historical consciousness in diverse educational contexts and settings—from the historical views and perspectives of high school students in the Netherlands, England and France, for example, to a qualitative study of Indigenous histories and history education in Australian and Canadian high schools.[23]

Indeed, several chapters in this collection reflect in detail on the relationship between personal and pedagogical historical questions. These include important projects to explore the formation and limits of historical consciousness in the classroom in Northern Ireland (Keith C. Barton and Alan W. McCully) and Québec (Stéphane Lévesque and Jocelyn Létourneau), the experiences of black students in the US (LaGarrett J. King), and a study of multiculturalism in Canada (Carla L. Peck).

Other national-based studies, such as Roy Rosenzweig and David Thelen's groundbreaking inquiry into the historical attitudes of "everyday Americans," have helped to extend some of those discussions about the formation of historical consciousness into domestic and community life. Their exploration of vernacular histories, what they termed "popular history making," was prompted by a powerful social paradox: a sense of crisis in national historical knowledge dominated public and political discussions about US history, all while an explosion of historical production and consumption was equally apparent. Rosenzweig and Thelen's qualitative and quantitative investigation of around 1,400 Americans in turn influenced two subsequent national studies in Australia and Canada, which were completed using similar methodologies.[24]

These national projects had several distinguishing features. First, by locating their research within the boundaries of a nation-state, they were able to contextualize their findings within national historical discussions and historiographies, as well as unsettle parochial public debates about the state of history in each of those jurisdictions. Second, by extending the survey groups beyond the classroom, the responses yielded rich data about the ways historical consciousness changes over time, and how it is mediated through communities, social generations, and families, as well as by formal and public historical contexts.

Critically, those national projects challenged professional understandings about the ways history is practiced, and by whom. The research confirmed the distinct lack of community engagement with "official" national narratives and history education: participants in all three national studies often found it difficult to engage directly with the history they learned at school, for example, confirming public anxiety about historical knowledge being in a state of perpetual "crisis."[25] On the other hand, their own stories and experiences generated very strong connections with the past, which revealed the power of collective and intergenerational memory in these communities and a flourishing popular contemplation of history.[26] Respondents kept objects to pass on to their own children or grandchildren, participated in family reunions, and compiled genealogies; they visited museums, heritage trails, and historical societies; they talked about the past with their friends and families; and they avidly consumed history in the form of historical fiction, documentaries, video games, and popular history books.[27]

Taken together, such research noted uneasiness between disciplinary and vernacular historical practice. That distinction, between the tactile, familial, and experiential inheritance we get from local, personal histories, and the relative detachment seen in disciplinary or official History (with a capital "H"), has been widely noted in memory studies and public history.[28] In turn, this growing body of work into historical consciousness also demonstrated the variety and scale of popular engagement with the past that operated outside the boundaries of academic scholarship.[29]

The ubiquity of these studies into memory, historical culture, and historical consciousness provided some scholars with a basis to their claim that we had entered a new "regime of historicity." Where previously the distance between past and present was widely recognized in the modern era (both by historians and the public), we now discovered that relationship no longer functioned in the same way. Were we now in an era of "the presence of the past"? And, if so, what might the consequences of that proximity to the past actually mean?

For several scholars, the profusion of contemporary history-making and identification, effectively merging ourselves with our pasts, is troubling. "Increasingly, the popular embrace of history is an emotional embrace, one that runs counter to the more critical understanding brought to the past by historians," noted the Australian historian Mark McKenna.[30] In a review of Rosenzweig and Thelen's *Presence of the Past,* moreover, the late historian Michael Kammen argued that despite the pressure to democratize the discipline of history, everyday historical understandings are not equivalent to scholarly expertise: "family and pastness are clearly not the same as history and should not be casually conflated with it."[31] The British historian John Tosh made a similar claim when he insisted that "thinking *about* history" and "thinking *with* history" are not the same thing.[32] Such comments reveal an inherent tension in the ways "historical consciousness" is understood: whereas the scholarly need to understand and incorporate everyday "past-mindedness" into the corpus of the history discipline is imperative, it should not signal a retreat from understanding the distinctive skills of historical cognition.

Such critique does not mean that researchers themselves are oblivious to the tensions and challenges of historical consciousness in the field. Far from it. This collection includes some powerful and revealing reflections on the practice and articulation of that research. In his chapter, Peter Seixas revisits the *Canadians and Their Pasts* project, and gives compelling insight into some of the questions and tensions raised by such large-scale, collaborative, and grounded social research. Anna Clark's chapter into Australians' historical consciousness explores the intersection of personal and public narratives in that country, and notes some of the limitations of trying to map that at a community level. Na Li's chapter on the state of historical consciousness in China, expanding on the survey model originally applied by Rosenzweig and Thelen, similarly discusses the emerging impact of popular histories and a historically-minded public for the fields of public and disciplinary history.

Karel Van Nieuwenhuyse and Kaat Wils recount how an initial examination of Flemish history standards led to a number of rich studies into various aspects of historical consciousness, including the role of history education in shaping one's sense of belonging to national and supranational communities. This is a particularly interesting question in Belgium, a country with two dominant cultural and linguistic regions. Arthur Chapman similarly focuses on the role of history education and asks, "What modes of relationship to the past are enabled and developed through historical teaching and learning?" Through analysis of history curricula and studies with secondary school students and student teachers, Chapman argues that researchers must attend to the interplay between curriculum and pedagogy to better understand how historical consciousness is expressed in curricula and how this gets taken up by teachers and students in the classroom. Carla van Boxtel's chapter draws on her extensive research with secondary school students to explore how the development of students' historical reasoning can lead to a more sophisticated historical consciousness.

Researchers now find themselves at a difficult, but promising conjuncture. What sense can be made of the explosion of increasingly diverse collections of research and researchers? Can we begin to sketch the patterns that emerge from the empirical studies that have flowed from the theorizations of Jörn Rüsen, Roger Simon, and Jürgen Straub? Using Seixas's edited collection, *Theorizing Historical Consciousness,* as a starting point for our own, we conceived this book to tease out that intersection between the theory and practice, between research and reflection.

Contemplating Historical Consciousness asks leading scholars from around the world to reflect on their research and their practice—as historians, ethnographers, history educationists, social scientists, and demographers—to explore the possibilities and limitations of research into historical consciousness. It draws on three decades of research into historical consciousness— comparative, national, and local/intimate—to survey the field. What do we understand about historical consciousness? And what is still to be learned?

The volume is structured into three sections. Part I encompasses one of the vital fields of international research into historical consciousness— its implications for curriculum and pedagogy—and draws on the experiences of researchers working within and across nations and communities. Alan W. McCully and Keith C. Barton contemplate their own research *in conversation,* reflecting on years of collaboration into history education in Northern Ireland. Arthur Chapman (England), Karel Van Nieuwenhuyse and Kaat Wils (Flanders, Belgium) and Carla van Boxtel (the Netherlands) similarly explore the meaning and implications for historical consciousness in the classroom. Meanwhile, Mario Carretero's chapter reflects on research into historical consciousness at the beginning of an important project, rather than retrospectively.

Part II includes commentary on notable national and comparative studies in Canada (Peter Seixas), Australia (Anna Clark), the Pacific (Angela Wanhalla), and Francophone Québec (Stéphane Lévesque and Jocelyn Létourneau), as well as an emerging study of historical consciousness in China (Na Li). These chapters reflect on the process of doing work in national, comparative, and transnational contexts. They also reveal important continuities and contrasts of that large-scale research, and give compelling accounts of historical identities and communities, implicitly asking: what makes a national historical community? How do they compare? And how has the historical consciousness of those communities been examined? These case studies allow for reflection not only on the research projects themselves but also their reception in national and international communities; namely, how research into historical consciousness compares with public and official historical discourses in those jurisdictions.

Part III includes evaluations by Michael Marker and LaGarrett J. King on research into cultural and regional groups such as Indigenous and Black historical consciousness in North America. It also includes investigations by Anna Green and Carla L. Peck into diverse collective or social generations' understanding of history, as well as the ways historical consciousness is formed by the historical experience of events such as the Holocaust, as

Jordana Silverstein explores. In this final part of the book, the potential (and limitations) for researchers to understand the historical consciousness of particular cultural groups is particularly prescient: how is historical consciousness formed and passed on? And what is its relationship to broader national or collective memories? Does such research offer insight into the radical potential for historical consciousness studies?

Each contributor was asked to consider and evaluate the aims and conceptualization of their research, their methods, and their findings, as well as some of the tensions it raised. They were given five questions to guide their responses and research reflections.

1. What is your conception of memory, history, and historical consciousness?
2. What were the motivations for your research into historical consciousness? Who do you want to speak with and investigate? Why?
3. What research method did you employ?
4. What were the possibilities and limitations of this research?
5. What's left unanswered?

Some, like Keith C. Barton and Alan W. McCully, took these as the literal guides for their chapter, which results in a beautifully honest discussion about their still influential collaboration in Northern Ireland. Anna Green used her site of the family to explore these questions as distinctly generational, tying the practice of historical consciousness into the practice of family history itself. Mario Carretero interrogates the potential of the concept itself by exploring the place of historical context in present-day global politics. Others (such as Angela Wanhalla's piece on the Mothers' Darlings project) did not set out to conduct explicit research into historical consciousness. Yet they found that the questions their projects raised—in terms of historical inheritance, remembering and forgetting, and the ways histories are used and forgotten in the formation of identity—offer a rich sense of the potential of historical consciousness in the field.

Critically, the book also delves into the limits of historical consciousness. How does this western concept work in Indigenous contexts? Michael Marker's probing essay helps us think about this important question. Reflections by several contributors (Carla L. Peck, LaGarrett J. King, Arthur Chapman, Stéphane Lévesque and Jocelyn Létourneau) on the question of how minoritized groups in multicultural societies develop historical consciousness also provide important commentary on whether the term can be deployed in culturally diverse contexts. And does the concept have utility in non-western societies, such as China, which has its own strong sense of historical culture? Na Li's chapter offers some discussion here.

As you read on, you will see that each of the chapters is both scholarly and reflective, discussing and evaluating each contributor's own research of historical consciousness in the context of wider writings and theorizations in the field. Our aim was to provide readable, engaging, and thoughtful discussions into the range of research undertaken in historical consciousness, as well as the impact of that research. Western-centric research is counterposed with Indigenous contemplation, as well as projects in China and the Pacific. The results of small-scale qualitative projects are discussed alongside larger quantitative studies. Transnational and comparative research rubs, sometime uneasily, alongside research into local and family studies. Research on Holocaust memory is presented alongside everyday family historical engagement. The combination and the relationships between the projects show that the sum of this collection is more than its parts.

Taken together, these essays offer useful and engaged reflection on a burgeoning field of scholarship that is rarely synthesized or examined as a whole. Space and time obviously limited the scope of this collection—including chapters on historical consciousness in Africa, for example, or South America, or even a reflection on the concept's development in Germany, inevitably would have prompted further consideration. Nevertheless, we have thoroughly enjoyed seeing this book take shape, contemplating both the possibilities and limitations of research in the field of historical consciousness, as well as posing important questions about future directions. We hope it generates some useful discussion, as well as questions for further research and reflection.

Anna Clark holds an Australian Research Council Future Fellowship at the Australian Centre for Public History, University of Technology Sydney. She has written extensively on history education, historiography, and historical consciousness, including: *Private Lives, Public History* (2016), *History's Children: History Wars in the Classroom* (2008), *Teaching the Nation: Politics and Pedagogy in Australian History* (2006), and the *History Wars* (2003) with Stuart Macintyre, as well as two history books for children, *Convicted!* and *Explored!* Reflecting her love of fish and fishing, she has also recently finished a history of fishing in Australia.

Carla L. Peck is Professor of Social Studies Education in the Department of Elementary Education at the University of Alberta. Her research interests include students' understandings of democratic concepts, diversity, identity, citizenship, and the relationship between students' ethnic identities and their understandings of history. She has held several major research grants and has authored and co-authored numerous journal articles, book chapters, and books related to this work, including *Education, Globalization and the Nation*

(2016) and *Teaching and Learning Difficult Histories in International Contexts* (2018).

Notes

1. Nora, "Between Memory and History"; Lowenthal, *The Past Is a Foreign Country*; Novick, *The Holocaust in American Life*; Silverstein, *Holocaust Historiography, Anxiety and the Formulations of a Diasporic Jewishness*; Banivanua Mar and Edmonds, "Introduction"; Wolfe, *Traces of History*.
2. Inglis, *Sacred Places*; Wertsch, *Voices of Collective Remembering*; Winter, *Sites of Memory, Sites of Mourning*; Loewen, *Lies My Teacher Told Me*.
3. Butler, "Overcoming Terra Nullius"; Chakrabarty, "Empire, Ethics, and the Calling of History"; Green, "Intergenerational Family Stories"; Haebich, "Forgetting Indigenous Histories"; Sear, "A Thousand Different Hands"; Veracini, "Historylessness"; Wolfe, "Islam, Europe and Indian Nationalism"; Winter, "Thinking about Silence"; Welzer, "Collateral Damage of History Education."
4. Ahonen, "Historical Consciousness"; Grever, "Fear of Plurality."
5. Carretero, Berger, and Grever, eds., *Palgrave Handbook of Research in Historical Culture and Education*.
6. Rüsen, "Historical Consciousness"; Seixas, "What Is Historical Consciousness?", 15.
7. Dening, *Performances*.
8. Rüsen, "Tradition," 45–7. See also Lee, "Walking Backwards into Tomorrow"; Megill, "Jörn Rüsen's Theory of Historiography."
9. Straub, ed., *Narration, Identity, and Historical Consciousness*, 50–51.
10. Rüsen, "The Didactics of History in West Germany," 284.
11. Ricoeur, *Hermeneutics and the Human Sciences*, 274.
12. Lukacs, *Historical Consciousness*, 15.
13. Gadamer, *Truth and Method*, 285. See also Clark and Grever, "Historical Consciousness."
14. Ahonen, "Historical Consciousness," 698.
15. Seixas, "Introduction," 3–24. See also: Taylor, "Trying to Connect," 175–90; Taylor and Young, "Making History"; Wineburg, "Making Historical Sense"; Wineburg, *Historical Thinking and Other Unnatural Acts*; Rüsen, "Tradition"; Rüsen, "Forming Historical Consciousness."
16. Rüsen, "Preface," viii.
17. Lee, "Walking Backwards into Tomorrow," 5, 33.
18. Griffiths, *Hunters and Collectors*, 1. See also Trouillot, *Silencing the Past*, 3, who writes: "The vernacular use of the word history thus offers us a semantic ambiguity: an irreducible distinction and yet an equally irreducible overlap between what happened and that which is said to have happened."
19. Rüsen, "Historical Consciousness," 80–82. See also Ahonen, "Historical Consciousness," 699.
20. Duquette, "Relating Historical Consciousness to Historical Thinking Through Assessment"; Körber, "Historical Consciousness, Historical Competencies—and Beyond?," 42; Lee, "Walking Backwards into Tomorrow."
21. Kölbl and Konrad, "Historical Consciousness in Germany," 26.
22. Seixas, "Historical Consciousness and Historical Thinking."
23. Grever, "National Pride and Prejudice"; Grever, Pelzer, and Haydn, "High school students' views on history"; Clark, "Teaching the Nation's Story."

24. Angvik and von Borries, *Youth and History*; Rosenzweig and Thelen, *Presence of the Past*; Conrad et al., *Canadians and Their Pasts*; Ashton and Hamilton, *History at the Crossroads*.

25. Sears and Hyslop-Margison, "Crisis as a Vehicle for Educational Reform"; Clark, "Teaching the Past"; Clark, *History's Children*; Nash et al., *History on Trial*; Symcox, *Whose History?*; Morton, "Teaching and Learning History in Canada"; Morton, "Canadian History Teaching in Canada"; Wineburg, *Historical Thinking and Other Unnatural Acts*.

26. Ashton and Hamilton, *History at the Crossroads*, 10.

27. Rosenzweig and Thelen, *Presence of the Past*; Ashton and Hamilton, *History at the Crossroads*; Rosenzweig and Thelen, "How Americans Use and Think About the Past."

28. Hamilton, "Memory Studies and Cultural History"; Jensen, "Usable Pasts: Comparing Approaches to Popular and Public History"; Lowenthal, "History and Memory"; Lowenthal, *The Heritage Crusade and the Spoils of History*; Nora, "Between Memory and History"; Samuel, *Theatres of Memory*.

29. Welzer, "Collateral Damage of History Education"; Glassberg, *Sense of History*; Griffiths, *Hunters and Collectors*; Rüsen, "Preface"; Ribbens, "A Narrative that Encompasses Our History."

30. McKenna, "The History Anxiety," 580.

31. Kammen, "Carl Becker Redivivus," 234.

32. Tosh, *Why History Matters*, 6–7.

Bibliography

Ahonen, Sirkka. "Historical Consciousness: A Viable Paradigm for History Education?" *Journal of Curriculum Studies* 37, no. 6 (2005): 697–707.

Angvik, Magne, and Bodo von Borries, eds. *Youth and History: A Comparative European Survey on Historical Consciousness And Political Attitudes Among Adolescents*. Hamburg: Körber-Stiftung, 1997.

Ashton, Paul, and Paula Hamilton. *History at the Crossroads: Australians and the Past*. Ultimo, NSW: Halstead Press, 2010.

Banivanua Mar, Tracey, and Penny Edmonds. "Introduction." In *Making Settler Colonial Space*, edited by Tracey Banivanua Mar and Penny Edmonds, 1–24. Basingstoke: Palgrave Macmillan, 2010.

Butler, Kathy. "Overcoming Terra Nullius: Aboriginal Perspectives in Schools as a Site of Philosophical Struggle." *Educational Philosophy and Theory* 32, no. 1 (2000): 93–102.

Carretero, Mario, Stefan Berger, and Maria Grever, Maria, eds. *Palgrave Handbook of Research in Historical Culture and Education*. London: Palgrave Macmillan, 2017.

Chakrabarty, Dipesh. "Empire, Ethics, and the Calling of History: Knowledge in the Postcolony." In *Unsettling History: Archiving and Narrating in Historiography*, edited by Alf Lüdtke and Sebastian Jobs, 63–88. Frankfurt: Campus Verlag, 2010.

Clark, Anna. "Teaching the Past." *Australian Cultural History* 22 (2003): 191–201.

———. *History's Children: History Wars in The Classroom*. Sydney: UNSW Press, 2008.

———. "Teaching the Nation's Story: Comparing Public Debates And Classroom Perspectives On History Education In Australia And Canada." *Journal of Curriculum Studies* 41, no. 6 (2009): 745–62.

Clark, Anna, and Grever, Maria. "Historical Consciousness: Conceptualizations and Educational Applications." In *International Handbook of History Education*, edited by Scott Metzger and Lauren Harris, 177–201. New York: Wiley Blackwell, 2018.

Conrad, Margaret, Kadriye Ercikan, Gerald Friesen, Jocelyn Létourneau, Delphin Muise, David Northrup, and Peter Seixas. *Canadians and Their Pasts*. Toronto: University of Toronto Press, 2013.

Dening, Greg. *Performances*. Melbourne: Melbourne University Press, 1996.
Duquette, Catherine. "Relating Historical Consciousness to Historical Thinking Through Assessment." In *New Directions in Assessing Historical Thinking*, edited by Kadriye Ercikan and Peter Seixas, 51–63. New York: Routledge, 2015.
Gadamer, Hans-Georg. *Truth and Method*. London: Continuum Impacts, 2006.
Glassberg, David. *Sense of History: The Place Of The Past In American Life*. Amherst: University of Massachusetts Press, 2001.
Green, Anna. "Intergenerational Family Stories: Private, Parochial, Pathological?" *Journal of Family History* 22 (2013): 387–402.
Grever, Maria. "National Pride and Prejudice. Teaching History in Societies with Many Nationalities." *Canadian Issues* (Fall 2008): 44–51.
———. "Fear of Plurality: Historical Culture and Historiographical Canonization in Western Europe." In *Gendering Historiography: Beyond National Canons*, edited by A. Epple and A. Schaser, 45–62. Frankfurt: Campus Verlag, 2009.
Grever, Maria, Ben Pelzer, and Terry Haydn. "High school students' views on history." *Journal of Curriculum Studies* 43, no. 2 (2011): 207–29.
Griffiths, Tom. *Hunters and Collectors: The Antiquarian Imagination in Australia*. Melbourne: Cambridge University Press, 1996.
Haebich, Anna. "Forgetting Indigenous Histories: Cases From The History Of Australia's Stolen Generations." *Journal of Social History* 44, no. 4 (2011): 1033–46.
Hamilton, Paula. "Memory Studies and Cultural History." In *Cultural History in Australia*, edited by Richard White and Hsu-Ming Teo. Sydney: UNSW Press, 2003.
Inglis, Ken. *Sacred Places: War Memorials in the Australian Landscape*. Carlton, Vic.: Melbourne University Press, 2001.
Jensen, Bernard Eric. "Usable Pasts: Comparing Approaches to Popular and Public History." In *People and Their Pasts: Public History Today*, edited by Paul Ashton and Hilda Kean, 42–56. Basingstoke: Palgrave Macmillan, 2009.
Kammen, Michael. "Carl Becker Redivivus: Or, Is Everyone Really a Historian?" *History and Theory* 32, no. 2 (2000): 230–42.
Kölbl, Carlos, and Lisa Konrad. "Historical Consciousness in Germany: Concept, Implementation, and Assessment." In *New Directions in Assessing Historical Thinking*, edited by Kadriye Ercikan and Peter Seixas, 17–28. New York: Routledge, 2015.
Körber, Andreas. "Historical Consciousness, Historical Competencies—And Beyond? Some Conceptual Development Within German History Didactics." Deutsches Institut für Internationale Pädagogische Forschung, 2015. Retrieved 20 June 2016 from www.pedocs.de/volltexte/2015/10811/pdf/Koerber_2015_Development_German_History_Didactics.pdf.
Lee, Peter. "'Walking Backwards into Tomorrow': Historical Consciousness and Understanding History." *International Journal of Historical Learning, Teaching and Research* 4, no. 1 (2004): 1–46.
Loewen, James W. *Lies My Teacher Told Me: Everything Your American History Textbook Got Wrong*. New York: The New Press, 1995.
Lowenthal, David. *The Past Is a Foreign Country*. Cambridge: Cambridge University Press, 1985.
———. "History and Memory." *The Public Historian* 19, no. 2 (1997): 31–43.
———. *The Heritage Crusade and the Spoils of History*. Cambridge: Cambridge University Press, 1998.
Lukacs, John. *Historical Consciousness: The Remembered Past*. 3rd ed. New York: Schocken Books, 1985.
McKenna, Mark. "The History Anxiety." In *The Cambridge History Of Australia*, edited by Alison Bashford and Stuart Macintyre, 561–80. Port Melbourne: Cambridge University Press, 2013.

Megill, Alan. "Jörn Rüsen's Theory of Historiography: Between Modernism And Rhetoric Of Inquiry." *History and Theory* 33, no. 1 (1994): 39–60.

Morton, Desmond. "Teaching and Learning History in Canada." In *Knowing, Teaching and Learning History: National and International Perspectives*, edited by Peter N. Stearns, Peter Seixas, and Sam Wineburg, 51–62. New York: New York University Press, 2000.

———. "Canadian History Teaching in Canada: What's The Big Deal?" In *To the past: History education, public memory, and citizenship in Canada*, edited by Ruth Sandwell, 23–31. Toronto: University of Toronto Press, 2006.

Nash, Gary B., Charlotte Crabtree, and Ross E. Dunn. *History On Trial: Culture Wars And The Teaching Of The Past*. New York: Alfred A. Knopf, 1997.

Nora, Pierre. "Between Memory and History: *Les Lieux de Mémoire*." *Representations* 26 (1989): 7–24.

Novick, Peter. *The Holocaust in American Life*. Boston: Houghton Mifflin, 1999.

Ribbens, Kees. "A Narrative that Encompasses Our History: Historical Culture and History Teaching." In *Beyond the Canon: History For The Twenty-First Century*, edited by Maria Grever and Siep Stuurman, 63–78. Basingstoke: Palgrave Macmillan, 2007.

Ricoeur, Paul. *Hermeneutics and The Human Sciences*. Cambridge: University of Cambridge Press, 1981.

Rosenzweig, Roy, and David Thelen. *The Presence of The Past: Popular Uses Of History In American Life*. New York: Columbia University Press, 1998.

———. "How Americans Use and Think About The Past." In *Knowing, Teaching and Learning History: National and International Perspectives*, edited by Peter N. Stearns, Peter Seixas, and Sam Wineburg, 262–83. New York: New York University Press, 2000.

Rüsen, Jörn. "The Didactics of History In West Germany: Towards A New Self-Awareness Of Historical Studies." *History and Theory* 26, no. 3 (1987): 275–86.

———. "Historical Consciousness: Narrative Structure, Moral Function, and Ontogenetic Development." In *Theorizing Historical Consciousness*, edited by Peter Seixas, 63–85. Toronto: University of Toronto Press, 2004.

———. "Preface." In *Narrative Identity, and Historical Consciousness*, edited by Jürgen Straub, vii–xii. New York: Berghahn Books, 2005.

———. "Forming Historical Consciousness: Towards a Humanistic History Didactics." *Antíteses* 5, no. 10 (2012): 519–37.

———. "Tradition: A Principle of Historical Sense-Generation and its Logic and Effect in Historical Culture." *History and Theory* 51 (2012): 45–59.

Samuel, Raphael. *Theatres of Memory: Past and Present in Contemporary Culture*. London: Verso, 1994.

Sear, Martha. "A Thousand Different Hands: History in Communities." In *Australian History Now*, edited by Anna Clark and Paul Ashton, 198–214. Sydney: New South, 2013.

Sears, Alan M., and Emery J. Hyslop-Margison. "Crisis as a Vehicle for Educational Reform: The Case of Citizenship Education." *Journal of Educational Thought* 41, no. 1 (2007): 47–62.

Seixas, Peter. "Introduction." In *Theorizing Historical Consciousness*, edited by Peter Seixas, 3–24. Toronto: University of Toronto Press, 2006.

———. "What is Historical Consciousness?" In *To The Past: History Education, Public Memory, And Citizenship In Canada*, edited by Ruth Sandwell, 11–22. Toronto: University of Toronto Press, 2006.

———. "Historical Consciousness and Historical Thinking." In *Palgrave Handbook of Research in Historical Culture and Education*, edited by Mario Carretero, Stefan Berger, and Maria Grever, 51–72. Basingstoke: Palgrave Macmillan, 2017.

Silverstein, Jordana. *Holocaust Historiography, Anxiety and the Formulations of a Diasporic Jewishness*. New York: Berghahn Books, 2015.

Straub, Jürgen, ed. *Narration, Identity, and Historical Consciousness.* New York: Berghahn Books, 2005.

Symcox, Linda. *Whose History? The Struggle for National Standards in American Classrooms.* New York: Teachers College Press, 2002.

Taylor, Tony. "Trying to Connect: Moving from Bad History to Historical Literacy in Schools." *Australian Cultural History* 22 (2003): 175–90.

Taylor, Tony, and Carmel Young. *Making History: A Guide for the Teaching and Learning of History in Australian Schools.* Canberra: Department of Education, Science and Training, 2003.

Tosh, John. *Why History Matters.* Basingstoke: Palgrave Macmillan, 2008.

Trouillot, Michel-Rolph. *Silencing the Past: Power and the Production of History.* Boston: Beacon Press, 1995.

Veracini, Lorenzo. "Historylessness: Australia as a Settler Colonial Collective." *Postcolonial Studies* 10, no. 3 (2007): 271–85.

Welzer, Harald. "Collateral Damage of History Education: National Socialism and the Holocaust in German Family Memory." *Social Research* 75, no. 1 (2008): 287–314.

Wertsch, James V. *Voices of Collective Remembering.* Cambridge: Cambridge University Press, 2002.

Wineburg, Sam. *Historical Thinking and Other Unnatural Acts: Charting the Future of Teaching the Past.* Philadelphia: Temple University Press, 2001.

———. "Making Historical Sense." In *Knowing, Teaching and Learning History: National and International Perspectives,* edited by Peter Stearns, Peter Seixas, and Sam Wineburg, 306–25. New York: New York University Press, 2002.

Winter, Jay. *Sites of Memory, Sites of Mourning: The Great War in European Cultural History.* Cambridge: Cambridge University Press, 1995.

———. "Thinking about Silence." In *Shadows of War,* edited by Ben Ze'ev, Ruth Ginio, and Jay Winter, 3–31. Cambridge: Cambridge University Press, 2010.

Wolfe, Patrick. "Islam, Europe and Indian Nationalism: Towards a Postcolonial Transnationalism." In *Connected worlds: History in transnational perspective,* edited by Ann Curthoys and Marilyn Lake, 233–65. Canberra: ANU E-Press, 2005.

———. *Traces of History: Elementary Structures of Race.* London: Verso, 2016.

Part I

HISTORICAL CONSCIOUSNESS, CURRICULUM, AND PEDAGOGY

CHAPTER 1

Schools, Students, and Community History in Northern Ireland

ALAN W. MCCULLY AND KEITH C. BARTON

Although we have each conducted a number of studies of history education in Northern Ireland, we focus here on our most extensive joint project, which involved an investigation of the historical ideas of 253 young people, across the first three years of secondary school, and the relation of their ideas to both school and community influences. That study resulted in three principal publications, each of which approached the data in a different way.[1] A study of this magnitude and complexity required systematic and ongoing collaboration between the two of us, as we worked together to develop questions, interview techniques, data analysis, and theoretical explanations. Rather than writing this chapter jointly, however, we have chosen to approach it as an exchange, because each of us brought our own interests and perspectives to the research. In the sections below, we each respond to the questions posed by this volume's editors in hopes of providing useful insights into how we thought about and conducted this work.

What were the motivations for your research into historical consciousness? Who do you want to speak with and investigate? Why?

Alan: It is important to state that the work we are reporting on was not initiated or framed by the concept of historical consciousness. Indeed, work on historical consciousness was only gaining momentum in the period we

---

Notes for this section begin on page 30.

were conducting our analysis and writing up our findings and conclusions. Thus, while not being central to our thinking, it is relevant to the ideas that emerged. Indeed, our work has been frequently referenced by those writing through an historical consciousness lens.

In truth, the starting point for our study lay in the practical challenges of teaching history in a deeply divided society emerging from conflict. During thirty years of violence it had been clear to educators that there were connections between people's understanding of the past in Northern Ireland and the attitudes they voiced on contemporary cultural and political issues. This included the way Unionists and Nationalists expressed their respective sense of national identities—a process that frequently was exclusive and antagonistic to the other group. Our interest was particularly centered on how history learned in school interacts with history encountered in families and in the community. In Northern Ireland, families often have traditional patterns of religious and cultural loyalties that are passed down generationally, and these are reinforced through symbolic representations in their respective communities. Marches, banners, commemorations, and wall murals display sectional loyalty through the use of imagery associated with historical events and figures from the past.

From the 1970s, history teaching made a distinctive response to the conflict in Northern Ireland. Previously, the absence of a prescribed curriculum at primary and junior secondary level had allowed schools the opportunity to follow programs that fit in with their cultural outlook. In turn, this meant that there was considerable unevenness as to children's exposure to, and experience of, Irish history. Considerably influenced by the disciplinary approach of the Schools Council History Project in England,[2] a statutory curriculum emerged in 1991 that placed emphasis on inquiry, the investigation of evidence, and a recognition that historical knowledge is open to alternative perspectives and interpretations. In the 1990s this approach was gaining wider international recognition as a viable strategy for teaching history in contested societies, but little empirical evidence existed as to its impact on the popular understanding of the past. Thus, our research was interested in examining the interface between formal school history and that learned informally outside school—and how each influenced the other in shaping young people's application of their historical learning.

Keith: As Alan notes, the connection between school and family/community history was a particularly important part of this research, and it related not only to academic questions but also to very practical issues that history teachers in Northern Ireland face. We cannot stress strongly enough how different the Northern Ireland curriculum is from that of most nations, both in its official and enacted forms. We often hear scholars from other countries claim—or simply assume—that every nation imparts an officially sanctioned narrative of the past to its young people through school textbooks and other means. That is manifestly not the case in Northern Ireland; there is no attempt to present a single narrative of national development, because interpretation of the region's past is precisely what is at issue in contemporary conflicts. The curriculum, as Alan explains above, is grounded in inquiry, the interpretation of evidence, and consideration of multiple perspectives.

This is evident beginning with students' initial exposure to history in the primary grades. During my first study there, my own eight-year-old daughter was enrolled in a local school, and her first history lesson consisted of looking through the school's rubbish bin to see what conclusions could be reached about the day's activities. Later in the year, around the time of the Thanksgiving holiday in the United States, she was studying how archaeological remains could be used to understand the settlement patterns of Mesolithic people—a far cry from the Pilgrim origin myth she would have been studying back home. At neither primary nor secondary level does the Northern Ireland curriculum attempt to initiate students into a consensual narrative of national origins and development, as is done in many countries. Thus, the conflict between school and community history is not between one narrative and another, but between two very different ways of understanding the past.

Teachers, meanwhile, are conscientious in their delivery of this curriculum. Here, too, we are sometimes met with incredulity from scholars in other countries, who assume that teachers must invariably impose their own political interpretations on the curriculum. Teachers in Northern Ireland certainly impose their own interpretations on history, but based on our experience, that of our colleagues, and the evidence of inspectorate reports, these interpretations are not partisan narratives of the past; rather, teachers aim to instill in students a respect for inquiry, evidence, and multiple perspectives—precisely what the curriculum requires.[3] History teachers who did otherwise would be considered unprofessional by their colleagues.

Teachers are well aware that this approach to history conflicts with what many students learn in their schools and communities. Unfortunately, this sometimes leads to pessimistic conclusions about their own ability to influence students' thinking; some secondary teachers say quite openly, "There's nothing we can do by the time they get to us." And yet, my own study of primary students' understanding of history revealed no deeply entrenched historical identifications at that age.[4] Alan and I wondered, then, whether the idea that secondary school history has limited effect was really true. Do students enter secondary school clinging to such strong narratives that educators can do nothing to change them? This was the motivation for doing more than a single snapshot of secondary students' understanding, and instead looking at their ideas after each of the three required years of secondary history education. Did their ideas change, or not?

What is your conception of memory, history, and historical consciousness?

Keith: I want to focus not so much on how we *could* situate ourselves in this theoretical landscape but how we actually *do* situate ourselves. I think that we have been guided not so much by particular theories of history, memory, or historical consciousness as by the practical work of teaching young people to understand and relate to the past. Both of us are teacher educators. Our day-to-day work involves helping teachers learn how to engage children and adolescents with the school subject of history, as well as providing guidance to curriculum developers, fellow teacher educators, and others involved in the work of schools, museums, and similar educational institutions. Through our research, we hope to do this in a more informed way, and we situate ourselves with respect to those goals rather than specific theories of history or "memory."

My point is not that our work is theoretically naïve; I certainly hope that it is not. Both of us recognize that historical accounts are necessarily interpretive and invariably are permeated with contemporary social, cultural, and political purposes and assumptions, and that narrative structures are imposed on the past rather than derived from it. We also recognize that people's ideas about history arise not just from the results of formal historical scholarship but from a variety of influences that circulate in families, communities, the media, and elsewhere, and that these ideas serve social functions, such as community identification or justification of contemporary social arrangements. These are our guiding theoretical perspectives, and in general terms, they are so well established among scholars that they hardly need justification.

These ideas can be explained and elaborated in a variety of ways, and it is these distinctions that make up the theoretical landscape of history and historical consciousness. Such distinctions, however, have contributed little to our own research, because they rarely help us think through how we can or should influence students' educational experiences. We are reminded of Marx's observation that, "The philosophers have only described the world in various ways; the point, however, is to change it." When the two of us discuss our findings with each other, we do not spend much time worrying about theories of historical consciousness; we are much more likely to talk about how educators can guide students in thinking about history in more complex ways. The theories that have contributed to these discussions are those that call attention to the link between external influences and the ideas that learners develop. These include Wertsch's idea of "cultural tools," Bakhtin's understanding of "internally persuasive dialogue," and Halpern's suggestions about how to increase empathetic understanding.[5] Each of these, we think, holds promise not only for understanding how young people think about the past but also for providing them with more meaningful educational opportunities.

Alan: Keith's response above captures the essence of what we are about. Both of our initial careers have been shaped by practical challenges we have encountered in classrooms when teaching history to children and young people of all ages and abilities. We come to the issues from a learning and teaching perspective, but as teacher educators we understand that practice gains insight from being theorized, and once conceptualized these insights can be transferred to different contexts. In order to make sense of data, it is useful to take account of theoretical work on ideas such as "collective memory," "imagined communities," and "historical consciousness," work which is of value in providing insight into how environment influences students' thinking. However, our aim is not to deepen theoretical understanding of the concepts themselves but to use the insight to contribute to the better design of curriculum and teaching tools to overcome obstacles and take students' learning forward.

So how do we change things? Several years ago, I accompanied my teacher education students on a field trip to Kilmainham Jail in Dublin, the site of the execution of the Irish Nationalist leaders of the Easter Rising against the British. The group was encouraged to "feel" the atmosphere of the courtyard where the shootings took place and to encounter the personal stories of those who were killed. Afterwards the students shared their thoughts, both face-to-face and online. The response of one young woman from a Unionist/Protestant background illustrates how emotional engagement can interplay with historical criticality to produce new understandings. Subsequent to the visit she became aware that even as an honors history graduate her interpretation of the past was shaped by her background:

> The visit to Kilmainham really challenged me. I have to admit I had some inbred feelings . . . I realized how much historical events like this get distorted as a result of the current political situation. My views of the Easter Rising were totally tainted by my opinions on the situation in Northern Ireland and, I guess, this was the lens I used to view the past. But Kilmainham really shattered that lens.

Through the realization of how family and community have influenced her own study of the emotive past, I would argue that this young teacher is now in a stronger position to work with students, such as the ones our research uncovered, who are wrestling to establish veracity from their encounters with historically connected material.

Thus, one aim for teaching, arising from our research in a divided society, is to involve students in a meta-cognitive process whereby they can take account of the variety of factors shaping their ideas. Another is to challenge entrenched and unsubstantiated positions, to "myth-bust" and expose the use of history for political and social purposes. A third is not to shy away from the discipline's complexity but to demonstrate that historical knowledge is provisional and discursive and that teachers have a responsibility to introduce students to the full spectrum of past actions, including those of people in the past who acted differently from the majority within their communities. Fourth, history teaching should involve students in a constant dialogue between historical events and the present to enable them to make connections between past and contemporary situations and attitudes. This should include an exploration of the relation between national identity and history. Students should be given opportunity to de-construct their own, and their community's, sense of identity in order to understand how history has contributed to the evolution of identity over time—and to see that identity is neither fixed nor immutable.

What research method did you employ?

Alan: Exploring the relationship between national identity and the learning of history presented methodological challenges. An orthodox approach to ascertain political and cultural allegiances in Northern Ireland has been to survey participants and ask them to categorize themselves using labels such as Irish, British, or Northern Irish. We deemed this inappropriate for our work, in that self-categorization would not reveal the nuances of how encounters with history specifically influenced students' understanding of who they were. Nor would it give insight into ways that history shaped other, less contentious, dimensions of their identity—such as local associations or personal interests. It was important, then, that participants were given stimuli to articulate historical connections in their own words. Hence, data collection was qualitative, using established elicitation techniques for working with children and young people.[6]

Keith: I really only have one method, and I've used it in nearly all my research: Give participants a set of items, ask them to make some kind of choice, and then have them explain their choices. I probably imposed this method on Alan without much discussion, since I don't recall considering any alternatives. But I think it's a good method, and one that is used in multiple fields of the social sciences (and that has been used extensively in research on students' understanding of history). In the research Alan and I conducted together, we gave students a set of images related to the history of Ireland, Britain, and the world, and we asked them to arrange them into groups; we then asked them to explain which groups or images had the most to do with them or who they were.

Despite the advantages of this method, we still faced numerous choices about how to adapt it to the complicated issue of history and identity in Northern Ireland. One of the most important issues involved our selection of images. Some choices perhaps reflected our own attempts to be too clever. We thought that a photo of Irish soldiers wearing Nazi-style helmets might inspire comment about how Ireland's neutrality during World War II provided tacit support for the Axis powers, but no student made this connection. We may have learned the most, however, from one of our most glaring omissions. Although we made sure that we included iconic images representing both Unionist and Nationalist perspectives, these all came from the period before Partition (which is the end of the period that students studied in school). Although Protestant students readily identified with Unionist icons, Catholic students were less enthusiastic in their choices. Early in the project, then, we decided to ask which images we should have used but did not, and Catholic students quickly told us we should have included one of Bobby Sands, the hunger striker.

Alan: The early indication we had of the hunger strike omission came with the responses of Catholic students in West Belfast to a wall mural picture depicting the Irish Famine. The gaunt skeletal figures copied from contemporary images taken from the *London Illustrated News* of the time were interpreted as related to the 1981 Hunger Strike. Once we included an image of a Bobby Sands mural, it was instantly recognized not only by those from Nationalist backgrounds but by many Protestants as well. In Nationalist areas, responses that resulted from the picture provided valuable insight into how the Republican "armed struggle" had been internalized by students as a campaign for social justice—and indicated the impact of community politicization on their thinking as they moved through high school.

There was a further methodological consideration that had to be taken into account if the data we collected was to stand up to scrutiny and give genuine insight into the impact of historical learning on students: the sample had to reflect a variety of settings. Northern Ireland may be a small territory, but the types of schools found there reflect not only the cultural and religious divide but differing backgrounds of academic achievement, which in turn often reflects socioeconomic levels. Also, demographically, the distribution of the region's Unionist and Nationalist populations results in significant local variation, and during the Troubles some areas saw endemic violence while others were much less affected. Thus, if the study was to capture the relation between school and community history across Northern Ireland, it had to account for local differences and avoid the trap of focusing only on those most likely to be politicized by conflict. Ultimately, a strength of our research was that we sampled a wide enough variety of school types that we were able to include students of varied regional origin, achievement level, cultural/political background, and gender.

What were the possibilities and limitations of this research?

Alan: Though our study is not reported within the framework of historical consciousness, its exploration of the inter-connectedness of students' sense of identity with historical learning in school and communities is informative for scholars pursuing its understanding. Seixas, for example, accepts the succinct *History and Memory* definition of historical consciousness as "the area in which collective memory, the writing of history and other modes of shaping images of the past in the public mind merge."[7] That formal historical study is just one source of historical knowledge for young people, and that it often struggles to make an impact against more dominant (and emotive) narratives in the community, is borne out by our research experience in Northern Ireland. Young people were not simply accepting or rejecting either school history or community history but were drawing from both to construct their own understanding. They wanted to reach their own conclusions rather than being compelled to follow what others believed, but in doing so they were still likely to remain loyal to their original cultural and political allegiances.

Yet, community influences should not be seen as uniformly pervasive. In fact, students' identifications varied by school type, gender, geographical location, and individual context. Political and religious issues were important for many, but for many others, factors linked to family and local heritage came to the fore—even if the former became more influential as students got older. Above all, students were interested in history's usefulness in helping them understand the origins and nature of contemporary conflict. Thus, the application of the concept of historical consciousness is useful in that our research supports the view that students' experience of history in a symbolically charged, divided, and conflict-affected environment involves the "merging" of past images (in the minds of individual students at least).

Rather than being shocked that history learned in the home and the street was an important influence on the students we interviewed, we were encouraged that many also demonstrated that they valued school history because it promoted a critical attitude and gave them insight into viewpoints that they were unlikely to encounter elsewhere. This led us to consider why history teaching was helping young people to reflect on aspects of the dominant narratives of their respective communities but not necessarily leading them to overturn those narratives. In doing so, we came to acknowledge more clearly the role for formal history teaching. As context influences the capacity to see beyond the partisan, so effective teaching must have insight into the wider forces acting on students beyond the classroom. While it is not history teaching's role to impose its perspective on students to the exclusion of their own sense of identity, history at school certainly should nevertheless inform, challenge, and clarify students' thinking and provide them with opportunities to test their provisional understanding through engagement with others. That way, they might be better equipped to make critical judgments on all the representations of the past they encounter in their lives. Thus, they would be better placed to understand the impact of the past on the present—an understanding that students in our study saw as the reason for studying the subject in the first place.

Keith: But how far do students' willingness and ability to deepen their thinking extend? A fundamental limitation of this research—indeed, of any research—is that it only captures students' responses in a particular setting. In this case, that setting was somewhat formal interviews, conducted in schools, by adults whom students undoubtedly associated with their history teachers. This is not a matter of students telling us "what we wanted to hear," because our interview methods did not point in any obvious substantive direction, and we think students recognized that we really did want to understand their thinking. But "what people think" is influenced by context. In this context, students explained their thinking in ways that reflected open-mindedness, tolerance, and respect for the historical record. We have little doubt that students' explanations sincerely reflected how they were thinking about history and their identities at that moment. But one student pointed out to us what many others were no doubt aware of: that they could not express the same open-mindedness outside of school, among their peers or in other community settings. It is quite likely that when students encounter emotive depictions of history in these other contexts, the way they think about history and identity will be different than in our interviews.

Attempting to uncover what students "really" think is a pointless endeavor. It is not that students misled us, and in other contexts they express what they really think; nor is it the case that their academic explanations reflect their authentic ideas, which are otherwise suppressed and distorted by social pressures. Both kinds of thinking are authentic, and both reflect social pressures. The important question is how these different kinds of thinking interact. Our interviews provided some evidence of how students bring in ideas and interests developed outside of school as they consider more academic approaches to the past, and we have described this process in terms of "internally persuasive dialogue." But we have little insight into how students' learning of history at school influences how they think elsewhere. When they encounter historical images in a wall mural or parade, do they still engage in this process of constructing an internally persuasive dialogue? Or do they forget and ignore what they learned at school? Or do they keep their understandings side-by-side, as parallel but unconnected ways of approaching the past? It is likely that not all students react in the same way, and this suggests still other questions, about the social or personal characteristics that lead them to respond in one way or the other.

What's left unanswered?

Alan: If good research raises more questions than it answers, then for me the study opened up a couple of avenues of interest. One was the tendency to present history in divided societies in the form of binary perspectives which, our research suggests, leads to students' identifying with "our" and "their" stories, despite efforts at critique and synthesis. The danger is that students come to accept stereotypes and to see conflict as between monoliths with little hope of a solution. This highlights the importance of teaching genuine multi-perspectivity, in which the spectrum of opinion in the past is addressed—and where students can understand the thinking of those in the past who acted differently to the majority within the community with which they identify.

The second avenue of interest involves the part played by emotion in students' receptiveness to history. How far is this explained by environment and how far by individual differences? I have become interested in exploring the contribution that social psychology can make toward understanding why some students allow sacrosanct positions held by families and communities to close down their critical faculties when facing sensitive history. In other cases—as with the student teacher above—emotional engagement can open up previously unconsidered alternatives. As theories and evidence in relation to the social cognition processes involved in prejudice become better understood, so too will understanding of how best to intervene in these processes—and this can have benefits for teaching history.

Keith: Like Alan, my further interests are primarily pedagogical ones, and I agree that a fuller engagement with theory and research from outside the fields of history and education are likely to be beneficial.[8] As Alan implies, knowing more about the social psychology of students may help us design better interventions, not only in history but throughout the social sciences. A great deal has been written about the teaching of controversial issues in recent years, but this work typically emphasizes teachers' broad pedagogical and curricular choices rather than the impact of those choices on students.[9] We need a better understanding of what pedagogical strategies have specific effects, on specific students, in specific settings. What exactly can a teacher do to encourage students to engage with historical evidence or the viewpoint of the other community, and how many such encounters are necessary to affect students' thinking in a deeper way? This kind of nuanced, microethnographic research, linking pedagogical practices and student learning, would be of significant practical use for teachers and other educators.

A related issue involves how to convince teachers to engage in such pedagogy. Teachers in Northern Ireland and elsewhere tend to "play it safe," either by avoiding controversy altogether, or by approaching controversial topics in noncontroversial ways. In the Northern Ireland context, for example, this involves teaching in a way that fails to connect historical issues to their contemporary consequences, or by declining to challenge students' thinking directly.[10] But not all teachers do this; many choose to take the risks necessary to engage students in discussion of difficult topics. Yet, although we know a great deal about why teachers say they avoid controversy, we know much less about why some are so different than their peers.[11] Do they have different motivations? Different personalities? Different levels of knowledge? Different personal or institutional support structures? We know even less about how teacher educators can prepare teachers for the challenges of teaching controversy. Our research points to some of the problems of engaging students in consideration of alternative historical perspectives, but it does little to solve those problems. That's a research agenda worth pursuing.

Alan W. McCully is now an Honorary Research Fellow at Ulster University. During forty years as a teacher, teacher educator, and researcher spanning the period of conflict and post-conflict transformation in Northern Ireland, he has engaged with interventions in the fields of history and social studies seeking to contribute to better community relations in the province. Recently, he worked with the Consortium for Education and Peacebuilding (Ulster, Sussex, and Amsterdam) on a four-country study (Myanmar, Pakistan, South Africa, and Uganda) to strengthen educational policy and practice which promote sustainable peace.

Keith C. Barton is Professor of Curriculum and Instruction and Adjunct Professor of History at Indiana University. He prepares history and social studies teachers and educational researchers, and he has conducted research on the teaching and learning of history in the United States, Northern Ireland, New Zealand, and Singapore. He is co-author, with Linda S. Levstik, of *Doing History: Investigating with Children in Elementary and Middle Schools*; *Teaching History for the Common Good*; and *Researching History Education: Theory, Method, and Context*. He is also the editor of *Research Methods in Social Studies Education: Contemporary Issues and Perspectives*.

Notes

1. Barton and McCully, "History, Identity, and the School Curriculum"; Barton and McCully, "Internally Persuasive Discourse"; Barton and McCully, "Trying to 'See Things Differently.'"
2. Schools Council, *A New Look at History*.
3. Kitson, "History Education and Reconciliation."
4. Barton, "Social Contexts of Children's Historical Understanding."
5. Wertsch, *Mind as Action*; Bakhtin, *The Dialogic Imagination*; Halpern, *From Detached Concern to Empathy*.
6. Barton, "Elicitation Techniques."
7. Seixas, *Benchmarks of Historical Thinking*, 10.
8. Barton and Avery, "Research on Social Studies Education."
9. Claire and Holden, *The Challenge of Teaching Controversial Issues*; Hess, *Controversy in the Classroom*; Misco and de Groof, *Cross-Cultural Case Studies*. For an example of research that addresses student data, see Hess and McAvoy, *The Political Classroom*.
10. Kitson and McCully, "Avoiding, Containing and Risk-Taking."
11. This research is reviewed in Barton and Avery, "Research on Social Studies Education."

Bibliography

Bakhtin, Mikhail M. *The Dialogic Imagination: Four Essays*. Austin: University of Texas Press, 1982.

Barton, Keith C. "'You'd Be Wanting to Know about the Past': Social Contexts of Children's Historical Understanding in Northern Ireland and the United States." *Comparative Education* 37, no. 1 (2001): 89–106.

———. "Elicitation Techniques: Getting People to Talk about Things They Don't Usually Talk about." *Theory and Research in Social Education* 43, no.2 (2015): 179–205.

Barton, Keith C., and Patricia G. Avery. "Research on Social Studies Education: Diverse Students, Settings, and Methods." In *Handbook of Research on Teaching*, edited by Courtney A. Bell and Drew Gitomer, 985–1038. Washington, DC: American Educational Research Association, 2016.

Barton, Keith C., and Alan W. McCully. "History, Identity, and the School Curriculum in Northern Ireland: An Empirical Study of Secondary Students' Ideas and Perspectives." *Journal of Curriculum Studies* 37, no. 1 (2005): 85–116.

———. "'You can Form Your Own Point of View': Internally Persuasive Discourse in Northern Ireland Students' Encounters with History." *Teachers College Record* 112, no. 1 (2010): 142–181.

———. "Trying to 'See Things Differently': Northern Ireland Students' Struggle to Understand Alternative Historical Perspectives." *Theory and Research in Social Education* 40, no. 4 (2012): 371–408.

Claire, Hilary, and Cathie Holden. *The Challenge of Teaching Controversial Issues*. Stoke on Trent, UK: Trentham Books, 2007.

Halpern, Jodi. *From Detached Concern to Empathy: Humanizing Medical Practice*. New York: Oxford University Press, 2001.

Hess, Diana. *Controversy in the Classroom: The Democratic Power of Discussion*. New York: Routledge, 2010.

Hess, Diana, and Paula McAvoy. *The Political Classroom: Evidence and Ethics in Democratic Classrooms*. New York: Routledge, 2014.

Kitson, Alison. "History Education and Reconciliation in Northern Ireland." In *Teaching the Violent Past: History Education and Reconciliation,* edited by Elizabeth A. Cole, 123–54. Lanham, MD: Rowman & Littlefield, 2007.

Kitson, Alison, and Alan W. McCully. "'You Hear about It for Real in School': Avoiding, Containing and Risk-Taking in the History Classroom." *Teaching History* 120 (2005): 32–37.

Misco, Thomas, and Jan de Groof. *Cross-Cultural Case Studies of Teaching Controversial Issues: Pathways and Challenges to Democratic Citizenship Education.* Oisterwijk, Netherlands: Wolf Legal, 2014.

Schools Council. *A New Look at History.* Edinburgh, UK: Holmes McDougall, 1976.

Seixas, Peter. *Benchmarks of Historical Thinking: A Framework for Assessment in Canada.* Vancouver, BC: Centre for the study of historical consciousness, University of British Columbia, 2006.

Wertsch, James W. *Mind as Action.* New York: Oxford University Press, 1998.

CHAPTER 2

"Orientation to the Past"

Some Reflections on Historical Consciousness Research from England

Arthur Chapman

Introduction: Historical Consciousness Raising

The term "historical consciousness" first came to my notice in a history education context around 2002, in conversations with my doctoral supervisor, Peter Lee. Peter participated in the symposium launching Peter Seixas's Centre for the Study of Historical Consciousness (CSHC), subsequently reported in *Theorizing Historical Consciousness,* and introduced me to Jörn Rüsen's work.[1] At the time, I was a full-time history teacher, the head of a history department working with sixteen- to nineteen-year-old history students, and a very part-time history education researcher, working on a doctoral thesis on my students' understandings of "historical accounts" or "interpretations."[2]

In some respects, historical consciousness was rather alien to the pedagogic traditions in which I was working—a variant of the English New History, which focused on developing an understanding of history as form of knowledge.[3] As my colleagues and I explained it to our students at the time, in their course guide, learning history was about:

    Understanding and applying knowledge
    Interpreting and evaluating documents
    Applying concepts
    Understanding the historical process

Notes for this section begin on page 41.

Constructing historical arguments
Doing historical research[4]

Historical consciousness, in Rüsen's model, comprehended all of this—Rüsen's "disciplinary matrix," for example, included historical "concepts" and "method"—and there were aspects of an historical consciousness approach to history that aligned very clearly with my teaching and research interests, as, for example, when historical consciousness is understood in a historiographic sense, as mapping differences in the ways historians approach the past.[5] Rüsen's matrix proved a powerful tool in helping me interpret data arising from my doctoral studies and in subsequent work theorizing historical interpretation in curricular terms.[6]

Historical consciousness, however, comprehended a great deal more than "concepts," "methods," and "historiography"; it posited a focus on "interests," on the "need for orientation in time," and "functions," including the development of concepts of "identity."[7] It also understood the issue of how people look at the past in a broad sense, that is as relating to people in general, not just historians, and explored: "individual and collective understandings of the past, the cognitive and cultural factors which shape those understandings, as well as the relations of historical understandings to those of the present and the future."[8]

These issues appealed to me in principle but exploring them was not directly linked to the explicit focus of my day-to-day history teaching. This was driven by a curriculum that was focused on the past (on why slavery was abolished in the British Caribbean in 1834, on the differences between Nazism and Italian fascism, on the nature and interpretation of the Chartist movement, and so on), and not on the uses and functions of the past at the "level of practical life" in the present.[9]

Rüsen's work stopped me in my pedagogic tracks and made me reflect on my teaching and on the wider framing of history in our curriculum and pedagogy from a meta-historical level. What were my students learning *by* learning history and *through* learning history? What tacit and explicit assumptions about the functions of history were shaping the sense that they did (and did not) make of what they were learning?

I began to be interested in questions like these and to explore them with colleagues in curriculum evaluation work and, some years later, in work exploring trainee history teachers' ideas about the aims and purposes of teaching history.[10] Cognate questions—looking at ideas about the purpose and function of history embodied in curriculum documents—have come increasingly to the fore in my more recent work.[11] I will review the forms and limits of this research in later sections of this chapter. First, I will explore the meanings of historical consciousness a little further.

Memory, History, and Historical Consciousness

As I have said, historical consciousness set new agendas for me, by asking meta-historical questions about the nature of students' learning *about* history that I was not accustomed to asking when focusing on students' thinking *in* history (their causal reasoning, evidential reasoning, understandings of historical accounts, and so on).

Although these questions were not a key focus in day-to-day history education, many of the issues were central to debates on historical culture in Britain and elsewhere in the 1980s and subsequently.[12] The British debate on these issues focused on "heritage" and on the extent to which the contemporary boom in interest in the past was a symptom of cultural health or malaise.[13] Writers such as Tony Hewitson, Patrick Wright, and Frank Furedi took the latter position, tending, to one degree or another, to regard heritage-consciousness as a form of consolatory *kitsch* and nostalgic escapism linked to "Victorian values," Thatcherism, and the abandonment of postwar progressivism. On the other hand, Raphael Samuel argued forcefully against "heritage-baiting" and celebrated multiform popular "retrochic" and "retrofitting," treating "history" as "a social form of knowledge" and "an activity rather than a profession." He saw popular enthusiasm for history in museums, re-enactment, interior design, fashion, and so on, as democratizing popular-cultural appropriations of the past to be mapped and celebrated.[14] The heritage debate was about modes of relationship to the past and about historical ethics—about virtuous and vicious forms of relationship to the past. It also fed into discussions, in the late 1980s and subsequently, about the history curriculum and about the return to subjects that the introduction of a National Curriculum presaged.[15] English debates about heritage were, of course, one aspect of a wider phenomenon—the growth of concerns with "Memory" and "Collective Memory" globally since the 1970s.[16]

Historical consciousness seemed to me to be a more useful way of framing the issues than talk of "heritage" and "collective memory"—terms which are both problematic in a number of senses. Heritage sets up strong contrasts with history, capturing something important—the methodological basis of history as a discipline—whilst tending to obscure the rootedness of all appropriations of the past in particular presents and to minimize the rigor of non-academic modes of constructing the past.[17] "Collective memory" seems to me to be doubly problematic—in positing a collective social subject and in understanding the social construction of the past by analogy with individual psychological processes. Memory can also have a naturalizing effect—missing the extent to which invoking collective memory is a *performative* political enterprise in identity engineering.[18] Both terms tend also to understate the extent to which the representation of the past is a *generative* act—not simply a matter of passing on heritage or curating existing memory but, rather, a mode of meaning-making resulting, as often as not, in new understandings of the past that were not available to those who lived through it.[19]

More importantly, perhaps, historical consciousness has a number of affordances that the history/memory and heritage/history oppositions do not have. Historical consciousness posits a field—*consciousness of* the past—and provides an analytical optic and set of conceptual tools that enable different modes of consciousness of the past to be modelled, compared, and contrasted. For Rüsen—as for Barton and Levstik, Day, Paul and others—our relationships to the past take a number of analytically distinguishable forms.[20] We can approach the past "analytically" and "epistemically," treating it as an object to be interrogated and explored critically. And we can also approach it from an identification stance, looking for roots or for a mirror through which to stabilize identity and a sense of personal or collective self.[21] Relationships to the past can be mediated aesthetically, materially, politically, and ethically; on Rüsen's account, our modes of orientation to the past can be classified structurally and by mode, as "traditional," "exemplary," "critical," and "genetic," in ways that can be differentiated in terms of their understandings of continuity, time, and change.[22] To relate to the past in traditional and in exemplary terms is to assume strong continuity between past and present—for tradition, the present should simply reiterate and continue the past with which it is essentially identical and on the exemplary model both past and present share fundamental features that mean that "lessons" can be learned from one and straightforwardly applied to the other. To relate to the past critically is to assert discontinuity—to seek to distantiate past lifeways by negating them as alien to the needs and values of the present. To relate to the past genetically, by contrast, is to think in historicist terms about both past and present—to foreground change and historicity and to recognize past and present states of affairs, practices and values as *sui generis* and of their time.[23]

Motivations for Research into Historical Consciousness: Orientation *to* the Past

The aspect of historical consciousness that has come to have greatest salience for my work has been orientation *to* or *towards* the past.[24] Much English work on historical consciousness has tended to focus on orientation *in* time, that is to say, on questions about students' abilities to form large-scale representations of the past and to use these "to locate themselves in time and see the past as both constraining and opening up possibilities for the future."[25] To ask about orientation *to* the past is to focus on a related but distinct type of question, for example, the question, "What *modes of relationship* to the past are prominent in the thinking of history students (or history teachers' or history curriculum makers)?"

My interest in orientation *to* the past arose from my research into students' thinking about historical interpretations. Consideration of contrasts in historiography leads, very readily, to the consideration of similarities and differences between historiographic and non-historiographic constructions of the past, a question that is frequently posed in contemporary philosophical reflections on history and historical thinking—for example, in postmodern critiques of "History."[26] The stimulus for my first appropriation of Rüsen's concepts, however, was largely accidental. Inspired by my doctoral supervisor's piloting of instruments exploring orientation in time, my colleagues and I added some additional questions to our end-of-course evaluations and surprised and discomfited ourselves in the process.[27]

Orientation *to* the Past: Three Approaches

In 1999–2000, my colleagues and I decided to review and revise the courses that we offered our Advanced Level (sixteen- to nineteen-year-old) students. We devised a course that tried to move away from the Anglocentrism and Eurocentrism that was then typical of Advanced Level history.[28] This course—"People, Power and Protest"—looked at some British history (the Suffragettes and the Chartists) but also at slavery and the slave trade in the British Caribbean, the British empire in India, and Civil Rights in the US. Students had the option to study this course or another more conventional one focused on dictatorship and democracy in the first half of the twentieth century. In 2003, we added questions to our annual course evaluation questionnaires that asked students in both courses to reflect on the "use" of studying the topics that they had studied, and we also asked them if the things that they had learned had influenced their thinking about: "a) world affairs b) Britain and c) current news stories."[29]

Students' open text answers were coded thematically and compared. There were some clear contrasts in how students on the two courses answered the first question—for example, students in our more innovative course made reference to a wider range of ways in which their studies had been useful.[30] A particularly striking feature of students' answers was what they revealed of how they were relating *to* history—an issue that we had not really considered before. Most of the students' answers indicated exemplary or critical orientations to the past. These orientations are exemplified in the following two extracts from answers to our second question:

'Iraq—I was actually scared that there seem to be parallels and huge similarities between history and the present day, and in fact irritated that governments seem to be making the same mistakes over and over again.'
—Student response, 'People, Power and Protest' course

'How America and the West in general are using Nazi-style propaganda to stop dissenting views, whether they be from religious or left wing groups . . . Dictatorship and Democracy shows how the establishment is making victims and targets of certain groups, such as Muslims, the poor and left-wingers'.
—Student response, 'Dictatorship and Democracy' course[31]

Responses like these surfaced aspects of our students' thinking at the end of their two-year courses that were not revealed in the conventional historical tasks they were usually asked to complete. It was encouraging to see our students using history, and apparent that history was engaging their passions. How they were using their history, however, was somewhat unsettling. Responses such as these suggested that they were thinking about the past in markedly unhistorical ways—treating the past and the present as essentially identical and continuous, in the first response, and reading the past into the present on the basis of superficial and partial analogy, in the second. Their responses raised fundamental questions about the modes of orientation to the past that our students had developed during their studies.

The value and importance of interrogating modes of orientation and asking questions informed by an historical consciousness problematic were confirmed in a subsequent study, conducted in a different context.[32] In 2009/10 I was working with trainee history teachers, rather than with history students. At this time, questions about the purpose of school history arose in somewhat polarized forms in public debates in England, in response to criticisms of the school history curriculum made by Conservative government ministers which resulted, in 2013, in dramatic reconfigurations of our curriculum.[33] My colleagues and I wanted our students to be aware of the full range of positions taken in these debates and to develop their own rationales for their practices as teachers. We asked them to debate the question, "What is school history for?" using an online discussion forum and to make reference to key positions in contemporary debates as they did so.

We developed a coding system to analyze the ideas that forty students advocated and criticized, and we drew on a number of resources in the literature as we developed our analytical categories—including Barton and Levstik's "analytical" and "identification" stances and Rüsen's work.[34] Our students made reference to a wide range of ideas about the purpose of school history—analyzed, for example, using "aesthetic" ("The purpose of school history should be to pursue the past for pleasure"); "disciplinary" ("Developing increased awareness of the nature of how evidence is used to support a claim . . . and other meta historical concepts and processes"); and "group identity" codes ("I think young people should be proud to be British and of this country's past"). Some of our students' responses were coded as advancing "historical consciousness" rationales for school history that explicitly focused on understanding temporality, for example the following case:

> School history is . . . about giving students opportunities to investigate, interpret and develop understandings of human experience within time . . . [I]t should be about demonstrating the value of the enduring over the ephemeral, the truly significant over the immediately pressing (whatever else our everyday culture might suggest); the weight and heft of human action, inaction and chance.

The majority of the student-teachers whose rationales for school history we analyzed were either explicitly critical of the rationales for school history that were prominent in policy makers' thinking or offered contrasting rationales, drawing on ideas that were not prominent in national policy discourse. "Understanding the present" was the most common rationale (advocated by 65 percent of our sample), "citizenship rationales" were positively advocated by a minority (22 percent of our sample), and building "group identity" was the least popular rationale (12.5 percent of our sample). Historical consciousness rationales and disciplinary knowledge rationales were more prominent than either of these last two categories (advocated by 37.5 percent and 32.5 percent of our sample, respectively). Whereas the 2004 study had revealed unexpected dimensions of school students' orientation to the past, with implications for classroom teaching, this study surfaced the kinds of orientation to the past exhibited by history graduate and postgraduate teachers-in-training—orientations likely to have consequences for the kinds of teaching and learning they would develop in classrooms.

My recent and ongoing work is focused on critical exploration of the ways in which school curricula and policy documents and discourses construct representations of history and orientations towards the past.[35] Some curricula—such as the Finnish 2004 curriculum—present rationales for school history redolent of historical consciousness approaches to history didactics, arguing that school history should enable students to reflect on identity in temporal perspective, developing historicized understandings of the past-present-future:

> The task of history instruction is to guide the pupils in becoming responsible players who know how to treat the phenomena of their own era and the past critically. The instruction guides the pupils in understanding that their own culture and other cultures constitute the result of a historical process . . . The task of instruction is to provide pupils with materials for building their identities, for familiarizing themselves with the concept of time, and for understanding human activity and the value of mental and material work.[36]

Other curricula, by contrast, can be understood as aiming to build identity through the transmission of "tradition" and by interpolating students into a particular heritage and set of values, as, for example, in the 2003 Massachusetts *History and Social Science Curriculum Framework*:

> [W]e are convinced that democracy's survival depends upon our transmitting to each new generation the political vision of liberty and equality that unites us as Americans. It also depends on a deep loyalty to the political institutions our founders put together to fulfill that vision.[37]

A focus on modes of orientation to the past can foreground contrasts within, as well as between, individual countries' curricular constructions of history. The English National Curriculum, for example, demonstrates striking contrasts over time in its constructions of history—the 2007 iteration presenting the most and the 2013 iteration the least explicitly "disciplinary" articulation of the curriculum in the series of five documents mandated between 1991 and 2013.[38] The 2013 document also demonstrates some incoherence in its aims, very probably reflecting tensions in the thinking of the various groups that co-constructed it, as can be seen in the contrast between the first "aim" that the curriculum articulates, presenting the history of the British Isles as a single given story to be learned (students are to come to "know and understand the history of these islands as a coherent, chronological narrative"), and the fifth aim, that requires the development of an understanding of the probative and plural nature of historical accounts (students are to come to "understand the methods of historical enquiry, including how evidence is used rigorously to make historical claims, and discern how and why contrasting arguments and interpretations of the past have been constructed").[39]

What Were the Possibilities and Limitations of this Research?

The studies that I have discussed in this chapter all have very clear limits—in sample size and in methodology—and, in contrast to the studies of orientation in time that have been referenced above, they represent initial steps towards a research program only. The limitations of a sample are particularly apparent in the studies of students: both studies are of students in one institutional context only and, in both, validity issues and task effects arise.[40] Responding to a questionnaire administered by your teachers and contributing to a discussion board organized by your lecturers are performances and self-presentations as much as they are windows into students' developed thought-processes. A different task and a different context of completion might yield very different responses.

Limitations of method arise in analyses of curriculum documents which tell us as much about the questions and theoretical frameworks adopted by the analysts as they do about the texts themselves—different questions and different interpretative frameworks would yield different descriptions and categorizations. Perhaps more fundamentally, such analyses raise problems of text and context. Curriculum documents are performances also, addressed to multiple audiences, and, as often as not, like the script of *Casablanca*, the work of many hands, making it particularly difficult to construe what such documents attempt clearly and univocally.[41] Perhaps more fundamentally still, as policy sociology has shown, we cannot learn very much about what curriculum texts mean unless we trace them through their contexts of use, which are, always and inevitably, contexts of re-interpretation and re-constitution.[42] We can learn very little about what an effective curriculum means without exploring the sense that teachers make of it and the sense that students make of the sense that their teachers have made.

What is Left Unanswered?

Despite their limitations, the studies I have reported here highlight the value of asking the question, "What modes of relationship to the past are enabled and developed through historical teaching and learning?" A fruitful research question is one whose answer has the potential to surprise and/or to illuminate theory and practice. As I have said, asking questions about my students' understandings of the uses of the past in 2003 illuminated problems in their thinking that were not surfaced in standard assessments and that had implications for their understanding of history were revealed by doing so. The findings from 2010 were informative also, in drawing attention to potential tensions between the understandings of history that appeal to authors of curriculum documents and those developed through degree-level studies in history. What none of these studies do, however, is allow us to observe these various dimensions of historical learning in dynamic interaction with each other. What happens when the orientations to the past expressed in curricula are interpreted and mediated by teachers, drawing on their own assumptions about what history is and what it is for? How are teachers' intentions reflected in the sense that their students make of what they are taught, drawing on their own tacit and explicit orientations to the past that they are learning about? What difference might teachers make to these outcomes, if sensitized to the differing ways in which their students can read and re-contextualize what they are taught? These are questions that more holistic, sustained, and systematic explorations of orientation to the past might answer.

Arthur Chapman is Associate Professor in History Education at the UCL Institute of Education, University College London. He was a history teacher for twelve years prior to taking a university post in history education and has worked at the universities of Cumbria and Edge Hill as well as London. He is a series editor of the *International Review of History Education,* an associate editor of the *London Review of Education* and of the *History Education Research Journal,* and he co-edited *Teaching History* in 2007–2013. His main research interest is in developing historical thinking, and, in particular, in young peoples' understandings of historical argument, historical explanation, and conflicts of historical interpretation.

Notes

1. Seixas, ed., *Theorizing Historical Consciousness*; Rüsen, ed., *Western Historical Thinking*; Rüsen, *History, Narration*; Rüsen, "History: Overview."
2. Chapman, "Towards an interpretations heuristic."
3. Lee, "Fused Horizons?"; Lee and Chapman, "Learning History."
4. Esher College History Department, *History Course Guide,* 13–14. We presented historical "concepts" to our students as both "general" (e.g., "cause and effect") and "specific" (e.g., "revolution")—our rephrasing of the "first" and "second-order" distinction—and "the historical process" as "understanding the variety of sources available to historians, the different methods historians use in research, the kinds of historical perspectives that exist, and the reasons why historians disagree."
5. Rüsen, *History: Narration,* 133; Megill, "Jörn Rüsen's Theory."
6. Chapman, "Towards an interpretations heuristic"; Chapman, "Using Jörn Rüsen's Disciplinary Matrix"; Chapman, "Historical Interpretations."
7. Rüsen, *History: Narration,* 133.
8. Centre for the Study of Historical Consciousness, "Definition of Historical Consciousness."
9. Rüsen, *History: Narration,* 133.
10. Chapman and Facey, "Placing History"; Chapman et al., "What is School History For?"
11. Chapman, "Grammars of School History"; Chapman, "Changing LUK"; Chapman, "The changing identities"; Chapman, "On the diagnosis."
12. Hewitson, *The Heritage Industry*; Furedi, *Mythical Past*; Wright, *On Living in an Old Country*; Niethammer, *Posthistoire*; Lowenthal, *The Past is a Foreign Country.*
13. Mandler, *History and National Life.*
14. Samuel, *Theatres of Memory,* 6, 17; Samuel, ed., *Patriotism*; Samuel, *Island Stories*. Samuel's work was pioneering also in modelling analyses of how different groups used understandings of the past-present-future to shape both identities and action—Samuel, *The Lost World.*
15. Cannadine et al., *The Right Kind of History.*
16. Nora, "Between History and Memory"; Lowenthal, *The Heritage Crusade*; Lowenthal, *The Past is a Foreign Country*; Niethammer, *Posthistoire*; Wertsch, *Voices of collective remembering*; Todorov, *Hope and Memory*; Assmann, *Cultural Memory.*
17. Wertsch, *Voices of collective remembering*; Danto, *Narration and knowledge*; Rüsen, "History: Overview"; Kansteiner, "Of Kitsch, Enlightenment, and Gender Anxiety"; Kansteiner, "Alternate Worlds." My arguments, in this and the paragraphs that follow, have been shaped by conversations with Peter Lee and many are more eloquently expressed in Lee and Chapman, "Learning History."
18. See, for example, Field, "Frank Field MP."

19. Danto, *Narration and knowledge.*
20. Barton and Levstik, *Teaching History*; Day, "Our Relations with the Past"; Paul, *Key Issues*; Rüsen, *History: Narration.*
21. Barton and Levstik, *Teaching History*; Paul, *Key Issues*; Rüsen, *History: Narration.*
22. Day, "Our Relations with the Past"; Paul, *Key Issues*; Rüsen, *History: Narration.*
23. Beiser, *The German Historicist Tradition*; Rüsen, *History: Narration.*
24. Chapman, "Historical Interpretations," 100.
25. Lee, "Historical Literacy," 65. There is an extensive literature on orientation in time—for example: Shemilt, "The Caliph's Coin"; Shemilt, "Drinking an Ocean"; Lee, "Walking backwards"; Lee, "Historical Literacy"; Lee and Howson, "Two Out of Five"; Howson and Shemilt, "Frameworks of Knowledge"; Rogers, "Raising the bar"; Rogers, "Frameworks for Big History."
26. Jenkins, "Introduction."
27. Lee, "Historical Literacy."
28. Chapman and Facey, "Placing History."
29. Chapman and Facey, "Placing History," 38.
30. Chapman and Facey, "Placing History," Figure 3.
31. Chapman and Facey, "Placing History," 41.
32. Chapman et al., "What is School History For?"
33. Department for Education, *National curriculum*; Evans, "The Wonderfulness of Us"; Cannadine, "The Future of History."
34. Barton and Levstik, *Teaching History*; Rüsen, *History: Narration.*
35. Chapman, "Grammars"; Chapman, "Changing LUK"; Chapman, "The changing identities"; Chapman, "Narrative vices"; Brant et al., "International instructional systems."
36. Finnish National Board of Education, *National Core Curriculum,* 220.
37. Massachusetts Department of Education, *History and Social Science,* 1.
38. Qualifications and Curriculum Authority, *History Programme*; Department for Education, *National curriculum.* Chapman, "The changing identities" reports a crude page-count analysis of all iterations of the curriculum, 1991 to 2013: on this measure, 45.5 percent of the 2007 curriculum and 10.4 percent of the 2013 curriculum are devoted to disciplinary curricular concepts—the highest and the lowest figures in the series.
39. Department for Education, *National curriculum,* 1.
40. Chapman and Facey, "Placing History"; Chapman et al., "What is School History For?"
41. Eco, *Faith in Fakes,* particularly the essay, "Casablanca: Cult Movies and Intertexual Collage," 197–211.
42. Ball, "Policy Sociology."

Bibliography

Assmann, Aleida. *Cultural Memory and Western Civilization: Arts of Memory.* Cambridge: Cambridge University Press, 2011.
Ball, Stephen, J. "Policy Sociology and Critical Social Research: a personal review of recent education policy and policy research." *British Educational Research Journal* 23, no. 3 (1997): 257–74.
Barton, Keith, C., and Linda Levstik. *Teaching History for the Common Good.* London: Lawrence Erlbaum Associates, 2004.
Beiser, Frederick C. *The German Historicist Tradition.* Oxford: Oxford University Press, 2011.
Brant, Jacek, Arthur Chapman, and Tina Isaacs. "International instructional systems: social studies." *The Curriculum Journal* 27, no. 1 (2016): 62–79.

Cannadine, David. "The Future of History." *The Times Literary Supplement*, 13 March 2013. Retrieved 15 November 2016 from http://www.the-tls.co.uk/articles/public/the-future-of-history/.

Cannadine, David, Jennifer Keating, and Nicola Sheldon. *The Right Kind of History: Teaching the past in twentieth century England*. Basingstoke: Palgrave Macmillan, 2011.

Centre for the Study of Historical Consciousness. "Definition of Historical Consciousness." Retrieved 15 November 2016 from http://www.cshc.ubc.ca/about/.

Chapman, Arthur. "Towards an interpretations heuristic: A case study exploration of 16–19 year-old students' ideas about explaining variations in historical accounts." EdD diss., Institute of Education, University of London, 2009.

———. "Historical Interpretations." In *Debates in History Teaching*, edited by Ian Davies, 96–108. London: Routledge, 2011.

———. "But it Might Just be their Political Views: Using Jörn Rüsen's Disciplinary Matrix to develop understandings of historical interpretation." *Caderno de Pesquisa: Pensamento Educacional* 9, no. 21 (2014): 67–85. Retrieved 15 November 2016 from http://universidadetuiuti.utp.br/Cadernos_de_Pesquisa/pdfs/cad_pesq_21/art_3.pdf.

———. "On the Grammars of School History: Who Whom?" *Public History Weekly* 4, no. 11 (2016). Retrieved 15 November 2016 from doi: dx.doi.org/10.1515/phw-2016-5759.

———. "Changing LUK: Nation and narration in the 2004 and 2013 editions of *Life in the United Kingdom*." Paper presented at the international workshop Analyzing Historical Narratives: Theory and Practice, Institute for Social Movements, Ruhr-University Bochum, 7–9 July 2016.

———. "The changing identities of the English history curriculum: recalibrating the national canon, 1991–2013." Paper presented at the annual meeting for the British Educational Research Association (BERA), Leeds, 13–15 September 2016.

———. "On the diagnosis and treatment of narrative vices." *Public History Weekly* 4 (2016). Retrieved 15 November 2016 from doi: dx.doi.org/10.1515/phw-2016-7659.

Chapman, Arthur, Katharine Burn, and Alison Kitson. "What is School History For? British Student-teachers' Perspectives." *Arbor, Revista de Ciencia, Pensamiento y Cultura* 194, no. 788 (2018): 1–14.

Chapman, Arthur, and Jane Facey. "Placing History: Territory, Story, Identity—and Historical Consciousness." *Teaching History* 116 (2004): 36–41.

Danto, Arthur. *Narration and knowledge*. New York: Columbia University Press, 2007.

Day, Mark. "Our Relations with the Past." *Philosophia* 36, no. 4 (2008): 417–27.

Department for Education. *National curriculum in England: history programme of study—key stage 3*. London: Department for Education, 2013. Retrieved 16 November 2016 from https://www.gov.uk/government/publications/national-curriculum-in-england-history-programmes-of-study.

Eco, Umberto. *Faith in Fakes*. London: Minerva, 1986.

Esher College History Department. *History Course Guide: People, Power and Protest*. Unpublished course materials, 2002.

Evans, Richard J. "The Wonderfulness of Us (the Tory Interpretation of History)." *London Review of Books* 33, no. 6 (2011): 9–12. Retrieved 15 November 2016 from http://www.lrb.co.uk/2011/08/19/history-panel/the-wonderfulness-of-us.

Field, Frank. "Frank Field MP: All young people deserve a collective memory of the highs and lows, dangers, failures as well as the triumphs of Britain." *Conservative Home*, 31 August 2009. Retrieved 15 November 2016 from http://www.conservativehome.com/platform/2009/08/frank-field-mp.html.

Finnish National Board of Education. *National Core Curriculum for Basic Education 2004*. Helsinki: Finnish National Board of Education, 2004.

Furedi, Frank. *Mythical Past, Elusive Future: History and Society in an Anxious Age*. London: Pluto Press, 1992.

Hewitson, Robert. *The Heritage Industry: Britain in a Climate of Decline*. London: Methuen, 1987.
Howson, Jonathan, and Denis Shemilt. "Frameworks of Knowledge: Dilemmas and Debates." In *Debates in History Teaching*, edited by Ian Davies, 73–83. London: Routledge, 2011.
Jenkins, Keith. "Introduction: On Being Open about our Closures." In *The Postmodern History Reader*, edited by Keith Jenkins, 1–33. London: Routledge, 1997.
Kansteiner, Wulf. "Of Kitsch, Enlightenment, and Gender Anxiety: Exploring Cultural Memories of Collective Memory Studies." Review of *Theorizing Historical Consciousness*, edited by Peter Seixas. *History and Theory* 46 (2007): 82–91.
———. "Alternate Worlds and Invented Communities: History and Historical Consciousness in the Age of Interactive Media." In *Manifestos for History*, edited by Keith Jenkins, Sue Morgan, and Alun Munslow, 121–48. London: Routledge, 2007.
Lee, Peter. "Walking backwards into tomorrow: Historical consciousness and understanding history." *International Journal of Historical Learning, Teaching and Research* 4, no. 1 (2004). Retrieved 15 November 2016 from http://centres.exeter.ac.uk/historyresource/journal7/7contents.htm.
———. "Historical Literacy: Theory and Research." *International Journal of Historical Learning, Teaching and Research* 5, no. 1 (2005). Retrieved 15 November 2016 from http://centres.exeter.ac.uk/historyresource/journal9/9contents.htm.
———. "Historical Literacy." In *Debates in History Teaching*, edited by Ian Davies, 63–72. London: Routledge, 2011.
———. "Fused Horizons? UK Research into Students' Second-Order Ideas in History: A Perspective from London." In *Researching History Education: International Perspectives and Disciplinary Traditions*, edited by Manuel Köster, Holger Thüneman, and Meik Zülsdorf-Kersting, 195–217. Schwalbach: Wochenschau Verlag, 2014.
Lee, Peter, and Arthur Chapman. "Learning History as Seeing the World Differently. Some Thoughts from a Small Island." In *Subject-orientierte Geschichts-didaktik*, edited by Heinrich Ammerer and Thomas Hellmuth, 341–66. Schwalbach: Wochenschau Verlag, 2015.
Lee, Peter, and Jonathan Howson. "'Two Out of Five Did Not Know That Henry VIII had Six Wives': History Education, Historical Literacy and Historical Consciousness." In *National History Standards: The Problem of the Canon and the Future of Teaching History*, edited by Linda Symcox and Aries Wilshcut, 211–61. Charlotte, NC: Information Age Publishing Inc., 2009.
Lowenthal, David. *The Heritage Crusade and the Spoils of History*. Cambridge: Cambridge University Press, 1998.
Lowenthal, David. *The Past is a Foreign Country: Revisited*. 2nd ed. Cambridge: Cambridge University Press, 2015.
Mandler, Peter. *History and National Life*. London: Profile Books, 2002.
Massachusetts Department of Education. *History and Social Science Curriculum Framework*. Malden, MA: Massachusetts Department of Education, 2003.
Megill, Allan. "Jörn Rüsen's Theory of Historiography between Modernism and Rhetoric of Inquiry." *History and Theory* 33, no. 1 (1994): 39–60.
Niethammer, Lutz. *Posthistoire: Has History Come to an End?* London: Verso, 1994.
Nora, Pierre. "Between History and Memory: *Les Lieux de Memoire*." *Representations* 26 (1989): 7–24.
Paul, Herman. *Key Issues in Historical Theory*. London: Routledge, 2015.
Qualifications and Curriculum Authority. *History Programme of study for key stage 3 and attainment target*. London: Qualifications and Curriculum Authority, 2007.
Rogers, Rick. "Raising the bar: developing meaningful historical consciousness at Key Stage 3." *Teaching History* 133 (2008): 24–30.
———. "Frameworks for Big History: Teaching History at its Lower Resolutions." In *Masterclass in History Education: Transforming Teaching and Learning*, edited by Christine

Counsell, Katharine Burn, and Arthur Chapman, 59–76. London: Bloomsbury Academic, 2016.
Rüsen, Jörn. *History: Narration, Interpretation, Orientation.* New York: Berghahn Books, 2005.
———. "History: Overview." In *International Encyclopedia of the Social and Behavioural Sciences,* 2nd ed., edited by James D. Wright, 114–19. Oxford: Elsevier, 2015.
———, ed. *Western Historical Thinking: An Intercultural Debate.* New York: Berghahn Books, 2000.
Samuel, Raphael. *Theatres of Memory.* Vol. 1, *Past and Present in Contemporary Culture.* London: Verso, 1994.
———. *Island Stories: Theatres of Memory,* Vol. 2. London: Verso, 1998.
———. *The Lost World of British Communism.* London: Verso, 2006.
———, ed. *Patriotism: The Making and Unmaking of British National Identity.* 3 vols. London: Routledge, 1989.
Seixas, Peter, ed. *Theorizing Historical Consciousness.* Toronto: University of Toronto Press, 2004.
Shemilt, Denis. "The Caliph's Coin: The Currency of Narrative Frameworks in History Teaching." In *Knowing, Teaching & Learning History, National and International Perspectives,* edited by Peter N. Stearns, Peter Seixas, and Sam Wineburg, 83–101. New York: New York University Press, 2000.
———. "Drinking an Ocean and Pissing a Cupful: How Adolescents Makes Sense of History." In *National History Standards: The Problem of the Canon and the Future of Teaching History,* edited by Linda Symcox and Arie Wilshcut, 141–209. Charlotte, NC: Information Age Publishing Inc., 2009.
Todorov, Tzvetan. *Hope and Memory: Reflections on the 20th Century.* London: Atlantic Books, 2003.
Wertsch, James. *Voices of Collective Remembering.* Cambridge: Cambridge University Press, 2002.
Wright, Patrick. *On Living in an Old Country: The National Past in Contemporary Britain.* 2nd ed. Oxford: Oxford University Press, 2009.

CHAPTER 3

History Education Research into Historical Consciousness in Flanders

Karel Van Nieuwenhuyse and Kaat Wils

From Amazement to Research

In Flanders, the Dutch-speaking part of Belgium, students holding a Master's degree in history and who wish to become secondary school teachers (grades 9–12) can become certified to teach history following an additional one-year academic program. In 2001, I (Kaat Wils) was appointed Head of the Academic Teacher Training Program in History at the University of Leuven.[1] Even though I had a teaching degree and some teaching experience in a secondary school, the fields of teacher education and research into the teaching and learning of history were new to me. Moreover, there was no academic research tradition (in terms of history education) in Leuven or elsewhere in Belgium to which I could connect. Being trained and academically socialized as an intellectual historian, my first encounter with the history education field made me realize the considerable gap that existed between academic history and history as it was conceptualized within the Flemish field of secondary education. To become acquainted with the field, I started to study its legal, normative framework, the so-called history standards. These were developed and implemented between 1991 and 2000 by the regional Flemish government, delineating the minimum targets that history education should meet.

The standards were established at a moment when the field of history education in Flanders had gone through an exhausting "struggle for sur-

---

Notes for this section begin on page 58.

vival." During the 1970s and 1980s, critical voices had pleaded in favor of a drastic reduction of the school subject, since it was, in their opinion, too often antiquated in its approach and of little social and civic use. They proposed, with some success, to replace history with a new subject titled societal education, which was expected to provide a better understanding of contemporary society and its problems. This episode of "crisis" came to a close with the design of a new secondary school program in Flanders in 1990. History was then recognized as a compulsory subject, which implied that standards should be developed and approved by Parliament. The authors of the standards, a committee consisting of three academic historians involved in university history teacher training programs and secondary school history teachers, felt pressure to include and ensure the societal relevance of history as a school subject in a document that had to be approved in Parliament. They themselves were also genuinely convinced of the civic role of history education—the main argument they had used again and again in their defence of history as a school subject during the past two decades. Inspired by the "New Social History" movement—the linguistic turn and constructivism would only make a full entry in Flemish universities in the course of the 1990s—they approached history education as a critical introduction into contemporary society and its problems. The standards they drew up, and which are still in use today, consist of specific attainment targets per stage, and an explanatory text, called "basic principles", which are more or less the same for all stages.[2] They define the development of historical consciousness as the principal goal of history education. In reading and analyzing the standards, three aspects related to the core of what historical consciousness is and how it should be achieved, according to the standards, struck me.

The first aspect concerns the position of the present in the standards. On the one hand, the explanatory text approaches the school subject of history as an introduction to history as a scientific discipline, in which the past can be discerned after an extensive learning process of analyzing sources. On the other hand, much attention is paid to the functions and goals of history with regard to "students as members of society."[3] These goals are defined as: (1) the development of "historical consciousness" (whereby students have to relate past, present, and future to each other), (2) cultural education (with a view to understanding past societies), (3) individual and social identity-building, and (4) training in social "resilience" (in order to have students take up responsibility in today's society). Three out of these four goals hold a direct link with contemporary society. While I had expected these texts to include a combination of scientific and civic ambitions, and hence also a tension between a classical historicist and a more present-oriented approach to the past, I had not expected "the presence of the present" to be so pervasive in texts on *history* education. In the standards' approach to the concept of historical consciousness, the present is ascribed a prominent role:

> History education becomes functional when students succeed in bringing the past in relationship with the present and the future. In doing so, students learn to understand which solutions were formulated, which means were used, where they led to, what realizations have been achieved, and what still needs to be done. History thus works on relating past and present, and on revealing lines of thinking in the direction of the future.[4]

The standards seem to implicitly equate historical consciousness with the awareness that the past is useful for the present, and with an instrumental understanding of the relationship between past and present. They hold onto an ambitious ontological stance of *historia* being *magistra vitae*. At the same time, the standards testify to a rather naïve epistemological idea of history and of the presumed direct and univocal connections between past and present. Little attention is given to a critical, epistemological reflection on the influence each contemporary present exerts on historical representations, and hence on the connections between past and present.

A second core characteristic of the Flemish history standards is their strong focus on critical thinking skills and attitudes, meant to make students proficient in the use of subject-specific methods. An important, even fundamental part of that is the critical examination of sources. In general, the standards especially address the issue of reasoning *with* sources, and note that students should be able to select information from various sources in an effective manner in order to answer an historical research question. The guidelines regarding the strategic use of sources are rather vague and do not go beyond some general terms. The standards only state that students must be capable of approaching this information in a critical and multi-perspectival manner. Being "critical" is mainly understood as the ability to discern "reliable" from "unreliable" sources, an activity which is presented as a skill per se, independent from the questions we ask about the past. In line with this rather naïve approach of historical methodology, the texts hardly touch upon the constructed and interpretative nature of historical knowledge. Nor do they provide strategies to reason *about* sources. It seems as if critical thinking skills and attitudes are meant to support the abovementioned instrumental and ontologically ambitious understanding of the relationship between past and present. Skills and attitudes are specifically mentioned in terms of active and student-centered teaching methods rather than in terms of epistemological reflection about the nature of historical knowledge.

A third characteristic is that the history standards do not present an extensive enumeration of knowledge that has to be acquired. They offer criteria to select subject matter, hence leaving individual teachers a lot of freedom of choice. The standards do require the gradual building of a historical frame of reference, of which the main focus is on Western (and especially Western European) history. National (Belgian) or subnational (Flemish) perspectives are only marginally present. Historical consciousness is therefore not limited to national history. On the contrary, students are explicitly encouraged to try to frame historical phenomena in a broader, worldwide context. This almost complete absence of the national past and a national perspective in the standards is striking, both from a diachronic and an international comparative perspective.

These observations inspired me to initiate historical research into the origins and the development over time of these characteristics.[5] At the same time, these characteristics informed the direction of my first steps into history education research, for which I sought support from colleagues from the Education Department and on which, from 2010 onwards, I could fortunately collaborate with Karel Van Nieuwenhuyse on the Teacher Training Program in History at the University of Leuven.

A first research strand we set out concerned the position of the present in history education in Flanders. Previous German research had suggested that "presentism" is part of actual teaching practices, as judgments based on overtly contemporary perspectives are frequently and easily made in classrooms by students and teachers alike.[6] As for our own research, we were initially interested in prospective teachers' opinions about the connection between past and present.[7] In a quantitative study on their beliefs, we found that they strongly valued the involvement of the present in history education and in their history lessons, rejecting a purely "historicist" approach to the past. The prospective teachers we surveyed valued the present to stir interest among students, to explain the past from the present as well as to come to an understanding of the present via the past, and to draw lessons from the past for a better present and future. At the same time, we found the prospective teachers displayed a certain openness towards more complicated understandings of the interrelatedness of past and present in terms of representation and memory, although only in a modest way.

From these findings, our curiosity rose regarding how these opinions would translate into concrete classroom practice. To this end, we analyzed how the relationship between past and present is dealt with by teachers, using a collection of 190 written history exams given by 70 teachers working in grades 11 and 12 as our data set.[8] We only asked for exams, and did not ask for teachers' answer keys, as those risked being produced solely in response to our request. As the research was not about students' performances or assessment practices, we did not collect students' answers or the teachers' assessment of students' responses. Even though exams represent only one element of teaching practices, they nevertheless provide a rather unique and valid insight into what individual teachers consider important and feasible to realize in their history classes. More specifically, they give a clear picture of what teachers expect from their students as a result of their history lessons throughout the school year. In Flanders, there are no central or national exams. Every teacher designs his or her own exams, sometimes in consultation with colleagues of the same grade and/or track, and in accordance with the prevailing standards. The way in which the relationship between past and present is addressed in these exams can thus be considered a good indication of how it is dealt with in class. Our conclusion from this research was that teachers' actual classroom practices are mainly past-oriented. Nevertheless, a majority of the participating teachers also referred to history as an interpretation and/or representation, by asking at least one question raising this issue.

On a more theoretical level, we investigated the epistemological bases of the phenomenon of "remembrance education," an educational approach that was officially introduced into Flemish secondary education in 2010.[9] Remembrance education expects students to learn from the "dark chapters" of the past, in order to build a better present and future society. Remembrance education is hence even far more present-oriented than history education. In general, we can conclude from our various studies that teacher beliefs and curricular standards are predominantly present-oriented. Classroom practices on the other hand tend to be more past-oriented and also include, to a certain extent, a perspectivist approach, meaning that they include some attention to history as requiring interpretation. An explanation for this divergence between beliefs and practices may be that Flemish teachers' beliefs about the need to orient history education towards the present might be more informed by a wish to legitimize the existence of history as a school subject and by the wish to conform to the prevailing norms of the standards, than by deeply rooted personal beliefs. However, as all Flemish history teachers in the grades 11 and 12 are academically schooled historians, a historicist approach inspired by a genuine, straightforward interest in and even passion for the past possibly prevails over the standards' demands to refer to the present. Furthermore, linking past and present sometimes makes history lessons more complicated, especially when students' knowledge of topical affairs is limited. Teachers might therefore tend to concentrate on the past. A third and last explanation might be found in the intention of many Flemish history teachers to pursue a "complete" overview of history. Although the standards do not prescribe this, Flemish history teachers tend to give priority to providing a "complete" historical overview as it is presented in most textbooks, thus lacking time to make many sidesteps to the present, or to make connections between past and present.

Given our observation that the history standards strongly focus on critical thinking skills and attitudes, yet almost neglect epistemological questions on the nature of historical knowledge, we developed a second research strand on the application of skills in history education. We were interested in the extent to which history teachers mobilize skills to foster substantive (content related) knowledge or strategic knowledge (related to an understanding of how history is constructed).[10] We performed a secondary analysis on the abovementioned set of written history exams through this lens and found that a majority of the participating teachers, notwithstanding the standards, did pay at least some attention to epistemological issues. At the same time, we also wanted to get a view on actual classroom practice. Therefore, we observed and analyzed eighty-eight secondary classroom history lessons.[11] Partly in line with previous research from, among others, Sam Wineburg and Jeffery Nokes, our main focus was on how primary sources are dealt with in the classroom: to provoke reasoning *with* and/or *about* sources, and hence to foster substantive or strategic knowledge.[12] Our analysis showed that history teachers mainly used primary sources to build substantive knowledge rather than to foster strategic knowledge.

A third research strand was inspired by our amazement about the marginal position of the national past in Flemish history education, and by international research on the role of the national past in history education (in the UK, Spain, Argentina, the Netherlands, Canada, and the US, among others). By using student essays and questionnaires, we examined which historical narratives about the national past 107 young people have in mind at the end of secondary school history education, whether they reflect on the fact that the national past can be narrated in different ways, and to what extent they share a common reference knowledge.[13] Reference knowledge is understood here as the factual knowledge of names, dates and places that spontaneously comes into students' minds when asked to narrate the nation's history. Students' reference knowledge reflected male, political, and military approaches to the national past, and mostly drew from the past two centuries. This is not surprising: previous internationally comparative research has already shown that wars and recent history play a prominent role in students' representations of the past.[14] A second conclusion from this research was that no ingrained, nationally-oriented master narrative was found in the students' essays; epistemological reflection was found to some extent, for instance in critical remarks on how episodes from the national past are used in patriotic or nationalist discourses. In a second study, partly following the methodology of Carla Peck,[15] we analyzed the historical narratives that twelve young adults constructed about their national past, including the extent to which (if any) those narratives were underpinned by existing narrative templates, and whether the narratives were connected to the students' sense of belonging.[16] Here, we found that students' supranational identities seem to parallel their embrace of European and Western-oriented historical narratives based on an

Enlightenment discourse of progress. Their historical identification hence goes beyond national borders and the strict national past.

Interdisciplinary and Mixed Method Approaches: Possibilities and Limitations

Since we are both trained as historians, it was quite a challenge to launch educational research that is methodologically different from classical historical research. To this end, we set up an ongoing, interdisciplinary collaboration with the Leuven Centre for Instructional Psychology and Technology. Together with researchers from this Centre, such as Geraldine Clarebout, Fien Depaepe, and Lieven Verschaffel, we discussed the appropriate methodologies in the light of the specific research questions we drew up for each of our research strands and projects.

From the start, we preferred qualitative to quantitative research, since we were first and foremost interested in gaining an in-depth understanding of (underlying reasons and motivations for) the phenomena we examined, including teachers' ontological and epistemological beliefs and the extent to which they are reflected in practice, rather than in generalizing results from a sample of the population of interest. This does not, however, mean that we avoided all quantitative approaches; we often used a mixed methods approach.

When analyzing educational practices via classroom observations and the examination of written history exams, our focus was on teacher behavior. Based on existing literature, we built analytical research tools in which all of the important elements under examination were framed. In the research regarding the use of primary sources for instance, the type of sources as well the kinds of contextual information provided, and the educational use of the sources were framed as categories, and codes per category were designed.[17] In our research into the position of the present in written history exams, we built four main categories. A question such as "Give an example of a present-day totalitarian state. Explain on what grounds you characterize its regime as totalitarian," was categorized as a question only dealing with the present and making no references to the past. The category of questions relating past and present to each other consisted of questions such as, "Why is the French Revolution the foundation of our modern western society?" or "Each year, the Japanese prime minister pays a visit to the Yasakuni shrine. Explain in a sufficient manner why this is so touchy in the 'neighboring countries' China and Korea (North and South). Explain in your answer what the Yasakuni shrine precisely is."[18] The analytical research tools were always tested on a small sample of our data set and refined. Subsequently, the validity of the tool was tested by two independent raters, in order to ensure inter-rater reliability. In applying the tools, we used a mixed methods approach. The categorization helped to measure the quantity of certain aspects (such as the uses of sources, or the presence of questions related to the present) and to distinguish different subcategories. Afterwards, categories were further analyzed in a qualitative way, allowing for a more detailed analysis and a deeper understanding of the issue. At the same time, the qualitative analysis provided us with concrete cases that we could use in disseminating our research results to the professional field of history teachers and in discussing concrete strategies with teachers to provoke change in classroom practice.

In trying to get a view on (prospective) teachers' and students' opinions, beliefs and/or narratives, we always faced the challenge of finding appropriate methods and accompanying instruments that would allow us to get to the core of the participants' actual thinking. In examining prospective teachers' opinions about the position of the present, we made use of a questionnaire and a set of performance tasks (with accompanying semi-structured interviews). Again, a mixed methods approach was used. A factor analysis was performed to explore the results of the questionnaire, while the outcome of the performance tasks and the interviews were qualitatively analyzed. In investigating students' historical narratives about the national past, and in a second study that focused on the connection between their narratives and their sense of belonging, we used methods such as a questionnaire combined with the writing of a paragraph, an open essay assignment, a performance task, and individual and group interviews.

Application of these mainly qualitative research methodologies always yielded a rich harvest of data, allowing an in-depth understanding of the phenomena under study. This should, however, not make us blind to some limitations or challenges we encountered during our research. One concerns the time-consuming character of qualitative research. In combination with the limited duration of some research projects, this too often compelled us to choose between research into educational practices and into (prospective) teachers' or students' beliefs and opinions. Ideally, these are of course combined, especially since we found discrepancies between beliefs and practices. Throughout our research, we tried to solve this problem by triangulating data of different research projects.

A second challenge we encountered concerns the influence that the method of data gathering exerts on the outcome of the research. This became clear throughout our research into the historical narratives young people construct about the national past at the end of secondary education. Asking 107 students to write an essay about the national past the way they know and see it led to different results when compared to a method of data gathering via a performance task, in which we provided twelve participants with a set of thirty important events from the national past. We asked them to select ten events, and afterwards to explain a possible connecting thread between the events. The analysis of the performance tasks and accompanying interviews showed that no ingrained, nationally-oriented master narrative dominated the students' thinking. They narrated the Belgian past as a story of progress towards freedom, equality, and democracy, and hence developed a progressive, human rights narrative which is a European rather than a Belgian narrative. In the essays on the other hand, this European approach was far less present; the students constructed a much more specifically Belgian story here. It is not easy to account for this difference. Did the provision of certain historical events as building blocks of a narrative trigger students' European-oriented frame of reference as learned in school? Or does the fact that the 107 students were beginning history students while the twelve students participating in the other study were not history students, explain the difference? This finding shows the necessity and the importance of reflection on the methods used.

Unsolved, Yet Vivid Issues: History Education for Whom, for What Purposes, and How?

The abovementioned analysis of three core characteristics of Flemish history education revealed the possibilities and pitfalls they carry with them to foster students' historical consciousness as the Flemish history standards construct this notion. At the same time, the analysis also revealed remaining, important questions and unresolved issues.

It became clear, first of all, that the position of the present creates an inevitable, and moreover insoluble field of tension in secondary school history education, connected to its main goals and the diversity of expectations. For on the one hand, history education is expected to contribute to the intellectual development of young people by introducing them to the academic discipline of history. Young people should understand the interpretative nature of historical knowledge, always constructed in a contemporary context, which influences the representation of the past. On the other hand, history education is also expected to contribute to the personal and social development of young people, in order to come to a "private understanding" of history, so that they can position themselves in the present and towards the future.[19] This means that a presentist approach does not meet with the disciplinary expectations, while a purely historicist approach is not in line with the societal, civic expectations of history education. This tension prompted our thinking about how to combine both, and also to introduce a more perspectivist approach in history education. In an ongoing reform of the

Flemish history standards, we recently proposed a revision to the concept of historical consciousness, which we defined as follows:

> Historical consciousness is first and foremost about understanding and organizing information about the past, with the aim of describing, comparing and explaining historical phenomena (people, groups, events and developments from the past). It is important, in this respect, to understand that the past and the present are fundamentally different. Therefore, historical consciousness is also about an understanding of and a reflection on the complex relationship between past, present and future. This can, among others, be done by drawing analogies between the past and the present, in search for similarities and differences. Historical consciousness hence requires an understanding of both the past and historical practice, which are inextricably bound up with each other. For one needs to know how knowledge of the past is constructed, and one needs to understand the tentative character of historical knowledge.[20]

In this definition, we aim to temper the ontologically very ambitious yet epistemologically somewhat naïve (instrumental) idea of *historia* as *magistra vitae*; on the other hand, we plead for a more sophisticated, epistemologically grounded perspectivist conceptualization of historical consciousness. The extent to which it is feasible to bring students to such a historical consciousness, and how to do it, needs further examination via empirical research. At the same time, the belief of many history educational scholars that fostering students' historical consciousness automatically contributes to good civic behavior and more open-minded civic attitudes should be empirically examined as well, because robust evidence does not yet exist.

A second pressing question is related to what history and whose history should be addressed in history education? While for a long time, many history classrooms were mainly homogeneously composed of autochthonous students, processes of globalization and migration, especially in postcolonial times since the 1960s, have brought along drastic changes, insofar that ethnoculturally and nationally diverse classrooms have become the rule rather than the exception. In such a context, a history education that wants to meet this diversity cannot be especially oriented towards the national past. Such an orientation has little historical significance to offer for many students, and since little attention is paid to "the other," many students will not recognize themselves in such history education; by contrast, they will feel ignored. Taking the socio-constructivist paradigm into account, which implies that it is important to connect private understandings of history and school history, as well as the historiographical principle of including multiple perspectives in building historical narratives, it is advisable and even essential to pay attention to non-Western history in the classroom. At first glimpse, it seems the Flemish history standards have met this concern, by implementing a broad geographical basic frame of reference, including references to world history. Various research points out, however, that Flemish history education is at the same time very Eurocentric, suggesting that the most important part of history is to be found in the historical trajectory of Europe and the Western World. In that sense, the curriculum constitutes a new articulation of the old division between the West and "The Rest."[21] This bears the risk that students from non-European origins do not feel part of this history education either, as they feel that their history (still) is ignored. The question arises about how to deal with this concern. A world history approach has been suggested as an answer, as well as a bigger emphasis on migration history and on intercultural contacts throughout history via the interaction and communication model including perspectives of both the West and "the other," and mutual representations.[22] Research measuring effects of such approaches, however, is for the most part absent. As a result, it is unclear if efforts to break through Eurocentrism can give solace and a feeling of historical connectedness to students from non-European origins with the history taught at school.

While the two previous issues dealt especially with the final goal of history education and for whom it is meant, questions also occur about how history education *in concreto* should look. Since the 1970s, the focus in Flemish history education shifted from a teacher-centered to a student-centered approach, and emphasis was put on activating students and fostering their historical skills. Our own research and that of others revealed that activating students and the use of skills in practice applies particularly to teaching methods and to fostering students' substantive knowledge rather than fostering their strategic knowledge, and hence their historical consciousness (the way we defined it). An important question here is which teaching methods and skills can expressly contribute to the development of historical consciousness? Further research in this respect needs to be done and should take into consideration the idea that history education researchers agree that historical thinking constitutes an "unnatural act," meaning that students do not automatically develop historical consciousness when engaging with the past. Here, the key role of the teacher comes to the fore. It is the teacher first and foremost who has to guide the development of historical consciousness. This challenges the dogma of activating student-centered teaching methods, which some educationalists advocate, and asks for reflection on its effectiveness. Not every form of independent or "active" work of students in the history classroom fosters historical thinking—it can just as well foster ahistorical thinking. And, inversely, a skilled history teacher may have the capacity to prompt students' historical thinking skills by using methods—storytelling, for instance—which are easily dismissed because they are associated with the reduction of students to "passive" recipients of knowledge. It therefore seems important to develop and test the effectiveness of active and student-centered teaching methods that contribute to the development of their historical consciousness. At the same time, the role of storytelling in history education should be re-examined and reflected upon as well.

The three abovementioned unsolved, yet pressing issues relating to the core of history education all point to the need to provide high-quality subject-specific and educational training to prospective teachers to enable them to deal with the complexity of teaching history. Student teachers need to be aware of the importance of epistemology in understanding and teaching history. This not only requires an understanding of the (evolving) epistemological underpinnings of the discipline of history, but also assumes that students' own epistemological beliefs are made explicit and are critically examined and challenged. Secondly, if we expect prospective teachers to break through Eurocentrism in their teaching practice, their training needs to provide them with a solid knowledge basis of non-Western cultures. Because if one does not build an in-depth understanding of non-Western societies, one risks getting stuck in superficial and stereotypical representations, hence reinforcing rather than deconstructing existing prejudices about "the other." Finally, teacher training programs in history should offer student teachers tools which enable them to assess current educational practices, pedagogical theories and normative educational frameworks (such as standards and curricula). Students should not be trained to passively and uncritically adopt what is proposed to them. By contrast, we should stimulate them to reflect critically, based on the examination of relevant research, on the feasibility and desirability of educational expectations.

Karel Van Nieuwenhuyse is Associate Professor of History Didactics, in the Faculty of Arts, University of Leuven, Belgium. His main research interests related to history education are: the position of the present, the use of historical sources and historical film, students' historical narratives about the national past and the connection with their identification, historical representations of the colonial past, and the teaching of intercultural contacts. In 2014, he was Visiting Professor at the UCL (Université Catholique de Louvain-la-Neuve, Belgium), and in 2015 Visiting Researcher at the Georg Eckert Institute for International Textbook Research in Braunschweig (Germany).

Kaat Wils is Professor of European Cultural History and head of the research group "Cultural History since 1750" at the University of Leuven, Belgium. Between 2001 and 2013, she coordinated the Academic Teacher Training Program in History. Her research fields include contemporary historical culture, the history of history education and the history of 19th and 20th century scientific and intellectual culture. She co-directed a five-volume secondary school history textbook, *Passages* (2009–2012), which aims to connect school history to contemporary historical research themes and perspectives.

Notes

1. Since both authors did not start as history educational researchers at the same time, and hence did not conduct all of their research together, the use of "we" and "I" will be alternated. In order to be clear, we will put the exact name between brackets, when using the pronoun "I."
2. Flemish Ministry of Education and Training, *Secundair onderwijs, derde graad ASO: uitgangspunten*; Flemish Ministry of Education and Training, *Secundair onderwijs, derde graad ASO: vakgebonden* [Secondary education, third stage of general education: history standards].
3. Flemish Ministry of Education and Training, *Secundair onderwijs, derde graad ASO: uitgangspunten*.
4. Flemish Ministry of Education and Training, *Secundair onderwijs, derde graad ASO: uitgangspunten*. Authors' translation.
5. See for instance Wils, "The evaporated canon"; Wils, ed., "Longing for the Present." See also three PhD dissertations that have been written under my supervision: Meirlaen, "Vlijt, voorzienigheid en vooruitgang"; Albicher, "Heimwee naar het heden"; Lobbes, "Verleden zonder stof."
6. Von Borries, "(Re-)constructing history."
7. Wils et al., "Past and present."
8. Van Nieuwenhuyse et al., "The present in Flemish secondary history education."
9. Van Nieuwenhuyse and Wils, "Remembrance education."
10. Van Nieuwenhuyse et al., "Making the constructed nature of history visible."
11. Van Nieuwenhuyse et al., "Reasoning with and/or about sources?"
12. Wineburg, *Historical Thinking*; Nokes, *Building students' historical literacies*. Similar research was done for the use of primary sources in English and French upper secondary history textbooks: Van Nieuwenhuyse, "Reasoning with and/or about sources on the Cold War."
13. Van Havere et al., "Flemish students."
14. Liu et al., "Social representations."
15. Peck, "Ethnicity and Students' conceptions."
16. Van Nieuwenhuyse and Wils, "Historical narratives."
17. Van Nieuwenhuyse et al., "The present in Flemish secondary history education." Husbands, *What is History Teaching?*
18. Karel Van Nieuwenhuyse et al., "The present in Flemish secondary history education."
19. Husbands, *What is History Teaching?*
20. Van Nieuwenhuyse, "Knowing & doing history?"
21. Van Nieuwenhuyse and Wils, "Historical narratives."
22. Standaert, *Methodology*.

Bibliography

Albicher, Alexander. "Heimwee naar het heden. Betrokkenheid en distantie in het Nederlandse geschiedenisonderwijs (1945–1985)." PhD diss., University of Leuven, 2012.
Flemish Ministry of Education and Training. *Secundair onderwijs, derde graad ASO: uitgangspunten bij de vakgebonden eindtermen geschiedenis* [Secondary education, third stage of

general education: basic principles of the history standards]. Brussels, 2000. Retrieved 26 August 2016 from http://www.ond.vlaanderen.be/curriculum/secundair-onderwijs/derde-graad/aso/vakgebonden/geschiedenis/algemeen.htm.

———. *Secundair onderwijs, derde graad ASO: vakgebonden eindtermen geschiedenis* [Secondary education, third stage of general education: history standards]. Brussels, 2000. Retrieved 26 August 2016 from http://www.ond.vlaanderen.be/curriculum/secundair-onderwijs/derde-graad/aso/vakgebonden/geschiedenis/algemeen.htm.

Husbands, Chris. *What is History Teaching? Language, Ideas and Meaning in Learning about the Past.* Buckingham: Open University Press, 1996.

Liu, James, Rebekah Goldstein-Hawes, Denis Hilton, Li-Li Huang, Cecilia Gastardo-Conaco, Emma Dresler-Hawke, Florence Pittolo, Ying-Yi Hong, Colleen Ward, Sheela Abraham, Yoshihisa Kashima, Emiko Kashima, Megumi Ohashi, Masaki Yuki, and Yukaku Hidaka. "Social representations of events and people in world history across 12 cultures." *Journal of Cross-Cultural Psychology* 36, no. 2 (2005): 171–91.

Lobbes, Tessa. "Verleden zonder stof. De gedaanten van het heden in het Belgische geschiedenisonderwijs (1945–1989)." PhD diss., University of Leuven, 2012.

Meirlaen, Matthias. "Vlijt, voorzienigheid en vooruitgang. Geschiedenis in het secundair onderwijs in de Zuidelijke Nederlanden, 1750–1850." PhD diss., University of Leuven, 2011.

Nokes, Jeffery D. *Building students' historical literacies. Learning to Read and Reason with Historical Texts and Evidence.* New York: Routledge, 2013.

Peck, Carla. "'It's Not Like [I'm] Chinese and Canadian. I am in between': Ethnicity and Students' conceptions of Historical Significance." *Theory and Research in Social Education* 38, no. 4 (2010): 574–617.

Standaert, Nicolas. *Methodology in View of Contact Between Cultures: The China Case in the 17th Century.* CSRCS Occasional Paper nr. 11. Hong Kong: Centre for the Study of Religion and Chinese Society, Chung Chi College, Chinese University of Hong Kong, 2002.

Van Havere, Timo, Fien Depaepe, Lieven Verschaffel, and Karel Van Nieuwenhuyse. "Flemish students' historical reference knowledge and narratives of the Belgian national past at the end of secondary education." *London Review of Education* 15, no. 2 (2017): 272–85.

Van Nieuwenhuyse, Karel. "Reasoning with and/or about sources on the Cold War? The use of primary sources in English and French history textbooks for upper secondary education." *International Journal for History and Social Sciences Education* 1, no. 1 (2016): 19–52.

———. "Knowing & doing history? De spanning in aandacht voor historische kennis 'versus' kennisconstructie door historici." *Tijdschrift voor Geschiedenis* 130, no. 2 (2017): 265–68.

Van Nieuwenhuyse, Karel, and Kaat Wils. "Remembrance education between history teaching and citizenship education." *Citizenship Teaching and Learning* 7, no. 2 (2012): 157–71.

———. "Historical narratives and national identities. A Qualitative Study of Young Adults in Flanders." *Belgisch Tijdschrift voor Nieuwste Geschiedenis. Journal of Belgian History* 45, no. 4 (2015): 40–72.

Van Nieuwenhuyse, Karel, Hanne Roose, Fien Depaepe, Lieven Verschaffel, and Kaat Wils. "Reasoning with and/or about sources? The use of primary sources in Flemish secondary school history education." *Historical Encounters, A journal of historical consciousness, historical cultures, and history education* 4, no. 2 (2017): 48–70.

Van Nieuwenhuyse, Karel, Kaat Wils, Geraldine Clarebout, and Lieven Verschaffel. "The present in Flemish secondary history education, through the lens of written history exams." *McGill Journal of Education* 50, no. 2/3 (2015): 433–52.

Van Nieuwenhuyse, Karel, Kaat Wils, Geraldine Clarebout, Greet Draye and Lieven Verschaffel. "Making the constructed nature of history visible. Flemish secondary history education through the lens of written exams." In *Joined-up history. New directions in history education research,* edited by Arthur Chapman and Arie Wilschut, 231–53. Charlotte, NC: Information Age Publishing Inc., 2015.

Von Borries, Bodo. "(Re-)constructing history and moral judgment: On relationships between interpretations of the past and perceptions of the present." In *Cognitive and Instructional Processes in History and Social Sciences,* edited by Mario Carretero and James F. Voss, 339–355. Mahwah, NJ: Lawrence Erlbaum Associates, 1994.

Wils, Kaat. "The evaporated canon and the overvalued source: history education in Belgium. An historical perspective." In *National History Standards. The Problem of the Canon and the Future of Teaching History,* edited by Linda Symcox and Arie Wilschut, 15–31. Charlotte, NC: Information Age Publishing Inc., 2009.

Wils, Kaat, ed. "Longing for the Present in the History of History Education." Special issue, *Paedagogica Historica: International Journal of the History of Education* 48, no. 6 (2012).

Wils, Kaat, Andrea Schampaert, Geraldine Clarebout, Hans Cools, Alexander Albicher, and Lieven Verschaffel. "Past and present in contemporary history education. An exploratory empirical research on prospective history teachers." *Yearbook—Jahrbuch—Annales. International Society for History Didactics* 32 (2011): 217–36.

Wineburg, Sam. *Historical Thinking and Other Unnatural Acts: Charting the Future of Teaching the Past.* Philadelphia: Temple University Press, 2001.

CHAPTER 4

Historical Consciousness

A Learning and Teaching Perspective from the Netherlands

CARLA VAN BOXTEL

Introduction

Historical consciousness is a much debated and researched concept. In this chapter, I do not approach historical consciousness as a cultural or historical phenomenon, but as an individual's understanding of the past which helps to orientate him/her in time, I approach historical consciousness from a learning and teaching perspective. From this perspective, key questions are: What actually develops when we speak of the development of historical consciousness? And how can history teaching in and outside school contribute to the development of historical consciousness? My sense of historical consciousness is shaped by the context of history education in the Netherlands, Anglo-Saxon and German conceptualizations of historical consciousness and thinking, and my own work on historical reasoning and heritage as a resource for learning about history and (historical) culture. I depart from the idea that historical consciousness is manifested in the way individuals think and reason about the past both in and outside school. I deliberately use the term *historical thinking and reasoning,* because most of my research focuses on students' historical reasoning. Elsewhere, Jannet van Drie and I extensively discussed our conceptualization of historical reasoning, which we define as a coherent set of historical thinking activities that aim at reaching justifiable conclusions about historical phenomena.[1]

Notes for this section begin on page 72.

Ultimately, I approach historical consciousness as an integrative construct in which historical interest, historical knowledge, understanding of the nature of history, and the ways people in the present relate to the past when a person thinks or reasons about the past. More than that, historical consciousness also explores the ways people use the past to think about themselves in the present and imagine themselves in the future. In this chapter, I reflect on research that is a joint endeavor of mine and several colleagues at the University of Amsterdam and other universities in the Netherlands. I first discuss the context, aims, and methods of the research into historical reasoning that I am involved in. Secondly, I discuss the relationship between collective memory and historical thinking and reasoning. Finally, I reflect on how the insights that I have developed on the basis of my research contribute to my understanding of historical consciousness.

Researching Historical Reasoning in the Classroom: Context, Aims, and Methods

My research into the learning and teaching of historical thinking and reasoning is situated in the Netherlands. Here, the formal attainment targets for school history are based upon the 2001 advice of a committee installed by the Minister of Education.[2] Historical consciousness is the main construct underlying these targets. The advice refers to publications of Jörn Rüsen and Karl-Ernst Jeismann and operationalizes historical consciousness as the ability to apply—in a coherent way—historical thinking and reasoning skills and a chronological frame of reference. The historical thinking and reasoning skills that are mentioned, for example, include the ability to critically examine historical sources or to identify aspects of continuity and change, and are strongly related to the metahistorical concepts of the discipline of history, such as causation, continuity and change, and historical evidence. In 2001, these skills were not new in the Dutch history curriculum; the ability to understand how historians develop historical interpretations and the ability to construct one's own interpretations became part of the history examination program as early as the 1990s.

A new component in the Dutch history curriculum proposed in 2001 and implemented soon after, is a chronological frame of reference. That emphasis was a response to the request of the Ministry to pay more attention to the development of historical overview knowledge. This request resulted from a public debate about the "shortcomings" of a history curriculum that was very much thematically organized and emphasized historical skills, and a central examination that focused on only two historical topics (e.g., the Vietnam War and the Dutch Republic) instead of overview (broad) knowledge. The chronological frame of reference that was implemented consists of a ten-eras framework with "round" dates and easy to remember labels (e.g., 500–1000: The era of monks and knights) and includes characteristic historical developments and phenomena (e.g., the rise of Islam, Christianization of Western Europe) for each era. The committee used only part of Rüsen's idea of "historical orientation." Key to the new curriculum was the ability to situate historical persons, events, objects, and developments in time, or more specifically, in the ten-eras framework. Despite the title of the advice, "Past, present and future," the new curriculum did not do much justice to Rüsen's ideas about the practical function of historical interpretations; how historical knowledge and understanding is used to understand the present and to orientate to the future. Only recently, the Dutch formal history curriculum has been extended with two targets related to "significance nowadays."

To summarize, although German conceptualizations of historical consciousness were a source of inspiration for the designers of the new Dutch history curriculum, the actual targets that focus on historical overview knowledge and historical thinking and reasoning skills are not clearly related to these conceptualizations. Since the teaching of historical thinking and reasoning skills has become an important aspect of Dutch history education, Dutch history teachers and teacher educators try to develop teaching strategies and activities that are effective in improving these skills. Teaching interpretational history is, however, still quite a challenge for Dutch history teachers.[3]

My own interest in historical thinking and reasoning also has its origin in the way I was taught history when I was in secondary school: I was taught history for six consecutive years by the same history teacher, who very much challenged his students to critically analyze historical representations and to construct a historical reasoning themselves. Only later did I realize how special this way of teaching was. Biesta (2007) argues that educational research has both a cultural and an instrumental function. The instrumental function I aim for is to provide practitioners with insights about how students learn history, and how students' historical thinking and reasoning can be enhanced. The research I am involved in results in design principles, teaching strategies, and observation and assessment instruments that can be used by history teachers and teacher educators.

Meanwhile, the cultural function I aim for is to provide history education researchers and practitioners with ideas, concepts and models that help to see aspects of history teaching and learning differently, to see new problems, and to think of new solutions. Theoretical and empirically grounded concepts such as historical reasoning can be used to reflect on aims, content, and approaches in history education. Together with my colleagues I conceptualized the idea of dialogic history education[4] and dynamic heritage education,[5] which are both meant to inspire practitioners in and outside schools.

While historical consciousness is not the most prominent construct in my research, it is connected to my research into historical reasoning in the classroom, which I started with Jannet van Drie in the 1990s. Our first studies focused on students' historical reasoning in the context of historical inquiry tasks. We built upon conceptualizations that were related to "historical literacy" and "historical understanding." We defined historical reasoning in terms of several components and types of reasoning.[6] This conceptualization helped us analyze the quality of students' reasoning and investigate the effects of different teaching approaches and learning tasks. We distinguished three types of reasoning: (1) about processes of continuity and change, (2) about causes and effects, and (3) about differences and similarities between historical phenomena or periods. Furthermore, we stated that the construction or analysis of reasoning consists of the asking of historical questions, the construction of temporal and causal relationships utilizing substantive and metahistorical concepts, historical contextualization, and the construction of a historical argument based upon a critical examination of historical sources. This conceptualization of historical reasoning was meant as an analytic framework that can be used to study historical reasoning as one of the key activities in the history classroom.

Our first studies focused on tasks in which students had to reason about aspects of continuity and change. Subsequently, we focused on other types and components of historical reasoning. We tried to define what it means to ask historical questions,[7] to contextualize,[8] to reason about causes and consequences,[9] and to reason about the historical significance of historical events and persons.[10] Recently, we extended our conceptualization of historical reasoning by adding the resources that students use to construct or analyze their reasoning: historical interest, knowledge of historical facts, concepts and chronology, knowledge of metahistorical concepts and beliefs about the nature of history, and the construction of historical knowledge. Below, I will show that these resources are not completely situated in an individual and are not only shaped by disciplinary history but also by collective memory.[11]

Part of our research on historical reasoning consists of process studies. We analyze, for example, think-aloud protocols, transcripts of students' interaction during collaborative learning, or interviews with students during and after performance of a particular task.[12] These process studies enable a more precise description of what it means to think or reason historically. In the studies of Albert Logtenberg, for example, students were asked to think aloud during the reading of an introductory text on the Industrial Revolution. We analyzed questions students spontaneously asked during reading and the context in which these questions developed. We consider historical questions as a kind of engine for historical reasoning: one engages in the construction of reasoning or the critical analysis of a provided reasoning when trying to answer a historical question. During and as a result of this reasoning, new questions arise.

In the German FUER model of historical thinking, the ability to ask historical questions is related to Rüsen's idea of "the need for orientation" as part of historical consciousness.[13] Historical questions are asked in the present, when experiencing uncertainty or interest. Analysis of the think-aloud protocols in Logtenberg's study confirmed that an important part of the questions asked was embedded in a historical reasoning process, for example, historical questions were formulated when attempting to contextualize the acts of people in the past. That is, historical questions were not only grounded in cognitive processes, such as an experienced deficit of knowledge or a cognitive conflict. An important part of the questions were the emotions that were displayed during the reading of the text, such as indignation or astonishment. In particular, when students, after displaying these emotions, tried to contextualize the behavior of the historical actor that they did not completely understand, they asked a historical question. However, many instances of indignation or astonishment did not give rise to the asking of questions. We concluded that it is important that teachers support students in formulating questions out of affective experiences and stimulate historical contextualization.

With intervention studies we try to gain more insight into the effects of tasks and teaching strategies on the quality of students' historical reasoning. We focused on historical inquiry tasks, particularly collaborative learning tasks, teacher-guided whole class discussions, and explicit instruction. Experimental studies provide opportunities to gain a better understanding of how historical interest, substantive knowledge, knowledge of metahistorical concepts, epistemological beliefs, and the quality of historical reasoning are interrelated. Although many scholars assume these relations to be there (for example, that students with more nuanced epistemological beliefs demonstrate a higher level of historical thinking), evidence from empirical studies is still scarce.

Recently, we conducted two experimental studies on the effects of explicit teaching of historical causation.[14] In the experimental group, students received explicit instruction about concepts and strategies related to historical causation (e.g., to look for multiple causes) during a unit on World War I in which students investigated the causes of the war. Students in the control group did not receive this explicit instruction. Students in the group with explicit teaching scored significantly higher on historical interest, knowledge of causal-reasoning strategies, and second-order concepts, and attributed a higher value to epistemological beliefs than students in the control group. No effects were found on topic knowledge and the quality of students' causal reasoning in a post-measurement writing task. In this and other experimental studies, we had to develop valid and reliable instruments in order to measure students' knowledge of second order concepts, strategies, and their epistemological beliefs. Unfortunately, such instruments are still hardly available.

The Interplay between Collective Memory and Historical Thinking and Reasoning

The question of how to conceptualize historical consciousness as an intellectual ability can be approached by conceiving historical thinking and reasoning as an individual and cognitive process and using insights into disciplinary practices of inquiry and writing. A large part of my research takes this approach and connects to general educational theories on concept development, development of domain-specific expertise, reasoning, argumentation, writing, critical thinking, interest, and epistemological beliefs. However, both teaching and learning are social and situated activities. Students develop their understanding and thinking about the past through history education, but also as a result of participation in the historical culture of the communities of which they are a part. Furthermore, the "tools" provided to students to learn history in schools are very much shaped by collective memory.[15]

Sociocultural theory on learning states that learning and development are socially and culturally situated. This theory is based upon the Vygotskyian idea that development begins with interactions between people which—through a process of internalization—results in the development of higher mental abilities.[16] For research on the development of historical consciousness, or its manifestation in historical thinking and reasoning, this means that we need to explore the historical, cultural, and social contexts in which students learn about the past and use their historical understanding. That's why collective memory research is relevant for research on history education.

Kansteiner conceptualizes collective memory as the result of an interaction between the intellectual and cultural traditions that frame our representations of the past, the memory makers who manipulate these traditions, and the consumers who use, transform, or ignore such artifacts.[17] When we position students within this triadic interaction, collective memory is significant in the following ways. First, collective memory is "present" in the classroom, because it manifests itself in the ideas that both teachers and students bring to the classroom, as well as in educational resources, such as history textbooks and museum exhibitions. Textbooks, for example, often make sense of national history by presenting a "grand narrative" excluding the experiences of, for example, minorities. In the Netherlands there is still not much research on the presence of narrative templates in students' thinking, textbooks, or stories told by the history teacher. A recent study of the narratives constructed by prospective Dutch history teachers who had just completed their secondary education revealed that the ten-eras framework did not function as a scaffold to construct a narrative of Dutch history, and that students did not tell a nationalistic story, but did emphasize positive episodes in Dutch history (e.g., the cultural and economic prosperity in the seventeenth century, and resistance to German occupation).[18]

Second, history teachers and professionals working in museums or heritage organizations can aim at improving students' understanding of collective memory (e.g., of how people relate to a particular past) developing the ability to critically examine historical representations in the media, museums, or the communities in which they participate.[19] In this way students learn to conceive of themselves as active agents in the continuous transformation of collective memory and can become reflective practitioners in heritage and memory practices. An example of how this learning can take place can be found in a case study conducted by Geerte Savenije.[20] Savenije interviewed and observed students of a Dutch secondary school visiting a slavery museum and the National Slavery Monument in Amsterdam. The visit contributed to students' understanding of the ways significance is attributed to the history of slavery. For example, one of the students—having seen roses that were left at the monument—realized that people commemorate the victims of slavery. The results also showed that each student attributed meaning in her or his own way. Sometimes, students held false presumptions of other students' perspectives. For example, not all students who were descendants of enslaved people attributed significance to this part of history, because it had occurred so many generations before them.

Many scholars investigate the learning and teaching of historical thinking and reasoning in contexts in which students are engaged in "source work": primary historical documents and images and accounts of historians. This also holds for my own research. More research is needed on students' thinking and reasoning in the context of tasks in which students investigate historical representations that are produced outside the discipline of history. When we conceive of historical consciousness as the ability to orientate in time, it is even more urgent to do research on *how* people use their understanding of the past to orientate in the present and think about the future. In the field of history education research these studies are still scarce.

Reflections on the Construct of Historical Consciousness

Above, I concluded that although Rüsen's conceptualization of historical consciousness was a source of inspiration for the history curriculum in the Netherlands, the actual attainment targets are difficult to trace back to his conceptualization. Rüsen's conceptualization might have been too abstract to inform curriculum designers about what exactly should be taught when we aim at development of historical consciousness. This is not so surprising. Conceptualizations of historical consciousness are not very explicit in terms of the activities or abilities involved in the process of historical meaning-making, nor on what, exactly, it means to connect "interpretations of the past, an understanding of the present and expectations for the future."

When I am asked about the relationship between our conceptualization of historical reasoning and the construct of historical consciousness, I mostly refer to Hans Jürgen Pandel's multidimensional model of historical consciousness.[21] Although I agree with Körber about some flaws in this model,[22] the model itself is interesting because Pandel is one of the first scholars who formulated the dimensions of historical consciousness in terms of concrete abilities and understanding. I believe that researchers investigating students' historical thinking and reasoning can contribute to a more elaborated description of Pandel's types of consciousness. The first three dimensions in Pandel's model form the foundation of historical consciousness. "Time consciousness" is described as the ability to discern past, present, and future and to situate historical events in a chronology of events and developments. In order to do this, one needs knowledge of the vocabulary that is used to describe historical time, such as "century," "before and after Christ," and names of periods, and knowledge of historical phenomena that are considered characteristic for the periods discerned.[23] This type of knowledge enables historical contextualization: situating phenomena and acts of people in the context of time, historical location, long-term developments, or particular events, in order to be able to give meaning to these phenomena and acts.[24]

With Jannet van Drie, I investigated how students approached tasks in which they had to relate a given historical document or image to a broader historical phenomenon or development and decide upon the time in which it was constructed. We found that a rich associative network of historical knowledge organized around colligatory historical concepts (e.g., the Cold War or the Golden Age) and knowledge of so-called landmarks or turning points (e.g., the Fall of the Berlin Wall or the abolition of slavery) is crucial for successful contextualization. The selection of key concepts and boundary points is of course an issue of debate. Students should not be taught a historical framework that represents an essentialist, national narrative, but one that also supports transnational and global perspectives.

A second dimension in Pandel's definition of historical consciousness is "consciousness of reality," which refers to the ability to discern fact and fiction and the understanding that historical facts have to be based upon historical evidence. Because history is about a reality that is no longer present, and traces of the past are incomplete and can provide conflicting accounts, statements about historical developments, causes, and consequences must be considered interpretations that can be criticized using disciplinary criteria, but also enriched by using other sources, perspectives, or questions. A critical attitude towards historical sources and historical representations is important not only to learn about the nature of history (to advance students' epistemological beliefs), but also to facilitate the understanding that historical representations in newspapers, on television and the internet, in museums, or movies, are biased, sometimes unsupported by historical evidence or excluding counter narratives. Although our own definition of historical reasoning includes both the *construction* and *evaluation* of a reasoning, until now most of our research has focused on students' construction of reasoning. The German FUER model of historical thinking makes a similar kind of distinction and emphasizes the importance of what is called the "de-construction of historical narratives."[25]

The third basic dimension mentioned by Pandel is "consciousness of historicity." This is the understanding that things can change, but that at the same time other things can stay the same, and that the world we live in is the "product" of history. The identification of aspects of continuity and change is considered a key component in all conceptualizations of historical thinking and reasoning. It requires knowledge of the sequence of events over a longer period, but also the understanding that there are different types of change (e.g., political or cultural), which can differ in tempo and impact (e.g., a revolution), and that changes can be the unintended consequence of actions of historical actors. Understanding historical changes also requires reasoning about causes and consequences and attributing significance. In our current research on historical reasoning we focus on causal historical reasoning, but in the near future we would like to do more research on students' reasoning about continuity and change. I think consciousness of historicity, which can manifest itself in thinking and reasoning about continuity and change, is the core of historical consciousness.

When we investigate historical consciousness as an individual competency, we have to take into account that we can look only at manifestations or expressions of historical consciousness. When we want to draw conclusions about the presence of a particular type or about the development of historical consciousness, we need to look for (changes in) patterns of expressions in a variety of situations in which students think or reason about the past in relation to the present and future. Since longitudinal studies are lacking, we don't know much about how students' historical thinking and reasoning develops and to what extent it is stable across a variety of situations. It is difficult to measure historical consciousness apart from students' thinking or reasoning in concrete situations.

Recently Catherine Duquette reported on a study that aimed to investigate the relationship between students' historical thinking and their historical consciousness.[26] To identify levels of historical consciousness, Duquette looked at how students identified historical causes of a contemporary problem, which I would also consider historical thinking activities. This raises the question whether historical consciousness is only demonstrated when a person is asked to reflect on an issue in the present or to give a perspective on the future, and, when that is the case, this thinking or reasoning activity or ability differs from thinking and reasoning about *past* events. Duquette's research is important, because in the research literature there is not much attention on students' historical thinking about contemporary problems or situations.

Several scholars have made major contributions to our understanding of historical thinking by defining key historical thinking concepts and related strategies,[27] however, most don't say much about how these concepts and strategies are interrelated. The German FUER model of historical thinking provides a more coherent framework. I think it is also one of the strengths of our own conceptualization of historical reasoning—as a particular form of historical thinking—that reasoning can be described as a coherent set of activities. Taken together, activities such as the asking of historical questions, historical contextualization and argumentation contribute to the construction or analysis of a historical reasoning. In our recent conceptualization of historical reasoning, we also included interest, (first order and second order) knowledge, and beliefs that can be considered resources of historical reasoning. There is still not much attention given to the question of how first order historical knowledge, shapes the quality of historical thinking. When we take Pandels' operationalization of historical consciousness, and also include other dimensions he notes (e.g., political and social consciousness), we can infer different types of knowledge such as knowledge of the vocabulary used to discern past, present, and future; knowledge of chronology and periodization; and knowledge of concepts with which we analyze the political, social, economic and cultural aspects of society.

Conclusion

I described historical consciousness as an understanding that manifests itself in students' thinking and reasoning about the past, present, and future. The concept of historical consciousness might be easier to use in history teaching and research on the learning and teaching of history when it is approached as an integrative concept bringing together historical thinking activities, resources for historical thinking, and students' personal meaning making (e.g., understanding of present society, oneself, and others, and expectations for the future). Students' historical thinking is shaped by their interest in history, knowledge of historical facts, concepts and chronology, knowledge of the metaconcepts of the discipline of history, understanding of how people relate to the past, and beliefs about the nature and construction of historical knowledge. The use of these resources produces—in interaction with a particular context in or outside school—a certain level of historical thinking. Historical thinking consists of several activities, such as, asking historical questions or identifying aspects of change, and can take the form of constructing or analyzing a historical narrative, or a more specific type of historical narrative: a historical reasoning.[28]

There are several questions that remain to be studied. I would like to gain more insight into the way students progress in their historical thinking and reasoning, the role of content knowledge in historical reasoning, the role of emotions, and how students use their understanding of the past to reflect on the present and future. In the above I didn't pay much attention to the moral dimension, although this is also prominent in Rüsen's conceptualization of historical consciousness. Moral values might be added as one of the resources of historical consciousness, next to interest, knowledge, and epistemological beliefs. However, I am not yet sure whether we must consider moral judgment as an activity or ability that is different from the ability to reason historically (but may precede or follow on this reasoning process), or as a defining part of it.

What are the implications of my reflections on historical consciousness and historical thinking and reasoning for the teaching for history? I think history education can contribute to the development of students' historical consciousness by enhancing and enriching students' historical interest, historical knowledge, and understanding of the nature of history. To do this, it must actively engage them in historical thinking and reasoning activities through historical inquiry and dialogic teaching, and connecting past, present, and future, while acknowledging the dynamic and situated character of how people relate to the past.

Carla van Boxtel is Professor of History Education at the Research Institute of Child Development and Education and the Amsterdam School for History of the University of Amsterdam. She is also Director of the Dutch Center for Social Studies Education and member of the management of the teacher training programs of the University of Amsterdam. She is trained as historian and educational scientist. Her main research interests are the learning and teaching of history in schools and museums, and particularly how to improve students' historical thinking and reasoning. Recent publications are

Sensitive Pasts: Questioning Heritage in Education (2016) and articles in peer-reviewed, international journals.

Notes

1. For a recent conceptualization of the construct of historical reasoning, see van Boxtel and van Drie, "Historical Reasoning." This conceptualization is an extension of the framework that we published in 2008: van Drie and van Boxtel, "Historical Reasoning."
2. *Verleden, Heden en Toekomst*.
3. Wansink et al., "The Certainty Paradox."
4. Gert Biesta, "Bridging the gap between educational research and educational practice: The need for critical distance," *Educational Research and Evaluation* 13, no. 3 (2007): 295–301. Dialogic history teaching is a teaching approach in which teachers try to create collective and supportive classroom talk and promote higher order contributions of students (e.g., explanations, justifications, and hypothesis-generation) and thinking in a context of multiple perspectives and uncertainty. See van Boxtel and van Drie, "Engaging Students."
5. I developed the idea of "dynamic heritage education" in the context of the Research program, Heritage Education, Plurality of Narratives and Shared Historical Knowledge, funded by the Netherlands Organization of Scientific Research, conducted by Maria Grever and Carla van Boxtel (2009–2014). Researchers in this program were Pieter de Bruijn, Stephan Klein and Geerte Savenije. See van Boxtel et al., eds., *Sensitive Pasts*; van Boxtel et al., "Heritage as a Resource"; Grever and van Boxtel, *Verlangen naar Tastbaar Verleden*.
6. Van Boxtel and van Drie, "Historical reasoning," 87–110.
7. Logtenberg, "Questioning the past."
8. Van Boxtel and van Drie, "'That's in the Time of the Romans!'"; Huijgen et al., "Toward Historical Perspective Taking."
9. Stoel et al., "The Effects of Explicit Teaching of Strategies"; Stoel et al., "Teaching towards Historical Expertise."
10. Van Drie et al., "Writing in History."
11. Van Boxtel and van Drie, "Historical Reasoning."
12. For an example of peer interaction analysis see van Drie et al., "Effects of Representational Guidance." For an example of a think-aloud study see Logtenberg, "Questioning the Past"; Huijgen et al., "Toward Historical Perspective Taking"; van Boxtel and van Drie, "'That's in the Time of the Romans!'" For an example of a task-based interview see de Leur et al., "'Just Imagine . . .'"
13. FUER refers to the project group Förderung und Entwicklung reflektierten Geschichtsbewusstseins (Promotion and development of reflected and self-reflexive historical consciousness); Schreiber et al., *Historisches Denken*.
14. Stoel et al., "The Effects of Explicit Teaching"; Stoel et al., "Teaching for Historical Expertise."
15. See, for example, Barton and Levstik, *Teaching History*; VanSledright, "Narratives."
16. Vygotsky, "Interaction."
17. Kansteiner, "Finding Meaning in Memory."
18. Kropman et al., "Small Country."
19. Van Boxtel et al., "Heritage as a resource."
20. Savenije et al., "Learning About Sensitive History"; Savenije et al., "Sensitive 'Heritage' of Slavery."
21. Pandel, "Dimensionen des Geschichtsbewusstseins."
22. Körber, "Historical consciousness"; Körber, "Historical Thinking."
23. De Groot-Reuvekamp et al., "The understanding of historical time."

24. Van Boxtel and van Drie, "'That's in the Time of the Romans!'", 113–145.
25. Van Boxtel and van Drie, "'That's in the Time of the Romans!'"
26. Duquette, "Relating Historical Consciousness."
27. Second-order concepts were defined by Lee, "Putting Principles into Practice"; Lévesque, *Thinking Historically*; Seixas and Morton, *The Big Six Historical Thinking Concepts*; VanSledright and Limón, "Learning and Teaching Social Studies." Historical strategies are described in Nokes et al., "Teaching High School Students"; Reisman, "Reading Like a Historian"; Wineburg, "Historical Problem Solving."
28. According to the historian Peter Gay historical narration without analysis is trivial, and historical analysis without narration is incomplete; Gay, *Style in History*, 189.

Bibliography

Barton, Keith, and Linda Levstik. *Teaching History for the Common Good*. Mahwah, New Jersey: Routledge, 2004.

Biesta, Gert. "Bridging the gap between educational research and educational practice: The need for critical distance." *Educational Research and Evaluation* 13, no. 3 (2007): 295–301.

De Groot-Reuvekamp, M.J., Carla van Boxtel, Anje Ros, and Penelope Harnett. "The understanding of historical time in the primary history curriculum in England and the Netherlands." *Journal of Curriculum Studies* 46, no. 4 (2014): 487–514.

De Leur, Tesse, Carla van Boxtel, and Arie Wilschut. "'Just Imagine . . .' Students' Perspectives on Empathy Tasks in Secondary History Education." *International Journal of Historical Learning, Teaching and Research* 13, no. 1 (2015): 69–84.

De Rooy, Piet. *Verleden, Heden en Toekomst. Advies van de Commissie Historische en Maatschappelijke Vorming* [Past, Present, and Future: Advice of the Committee on Historical and Social Education]. Enschede: SLO, 2001.

Duquette, Catherine. "Relating Historical Consciousness to Historical Thinking Through Assessment." In *New Directions in Assessing Historical Thinking*, edited by K. Ercikan and P. Seixas, 51–63. New York: Routledge, 2015.

Gay, Peter. *Style in History*. New York: W. W. Norton & Company, 1974.

Grever, Maria, and Carla van Boxtel. *Verlangen naar Tastbaar Verleden. Erfgoed, Onderwijs en Historisch Besef* [Longing for a Tangible Past. Heritage, Education and Historical Consciousness]. Hilversum: Verloren, 2014.

Huijgen, Tim, Carla van Boxtel, Wim van de Grift, and Paul Holthuis. "Toward Historical Perspective Taking: Students' Reasoning When Contextualizing the Actions of People in the Past." *Theory & Research in Social Education* 45 (2017): 110–44. Retrieved 26 April 2017 from DOI:10.1080/00933104.2016.1208597.

Kansteiner, Wulf. "Finding Meaning in Memory: A Methodological Critique of Collective Memory Studies." *History and Theory* 41, no. 2 (2002): 179–97.

Körber, Andreas. "Historical Thinking and Historical Competencies as Didactic Core Concepts." In *Teaching Historical Memories in an Intercultural Perspective*, edited by H. Bjerg, A. Körber, C. Lenz, O. von Wrochem, and E. Thorstensen, 69–93. Bielefeld: Metropol, 2014.

———. "Historical consciousness, historical competencies—and beyond? Some conceptual development within German history didactics." 2015, 56 S. Retrieved 26 April 2017 from URN: urn:nbn:de:0111-pedocs-108118.

Kropman, Marc, Carla van Boxtel, and Jannet van Drie. "Small Country, Great Ambitions. Prospective Teachers' Narratives and Knowledge About Dutch History." In *Joined-Up History. New Directions in History Education Research*, edited by A. Chapman and A. Wilschut, 57–84. Charlotte, NC: Information Age Publishers, 2015.

Lee, Peter. "Putting Principles into Practice: Understanding History." In *How Students Learn: History, Mathematics, and Science in the Classroom,* edited by M.S. Donovan and J.D. Bransford, 31–77. Washington, DC: National Academies Press, 2005.

Lévesque, Stéphane. *Thinking Historically. Educating Students for the Twenty-first Century.* Toronto: University of Toronto Press, 2008.

Logtenberg, Albert. "Questioning the past. Student Questioning and Historical Reasoning." PhD diss., University of Amsterdam, 2012.

Nokes, J.D., J.A. Dole, and D.J. Hacker. "Teaching High School Students to Use Heuristics while Reading Historical Texts." *Journal of Educational Psychology* 99, no. 3 (2007): 492–504.

Pandel, Hans-Jürgen. "Dimensionen des Geschichtsbewusstseins—Ein Versuch, seine Struktur für Empirie und Pragmatik Diskutierbar zu Machen." *Geschichtsdidaktik* 12, no. 2 (1987): 130–42.

Reisman, Avishag. "Reading Like a Historian: A Document-based History Curriculum Intervention in Urban High Schools." *Cognition and Instruction* 30, no. 1 (2012): 86–112.

Savenije, Geerte, Carla van Boxtel, and Maria Grever. "Learning About Sensitive History: 'Heritage' of Slavery as a Resource." *Theory & Research in Social Education* 42, no. 4 (2014): 516–47.

———. "Sensitive 'Heritage' of Slavery in a Multicultural Classroom: Pupils' Ideas Regarding Significance." *British Journal of Educational Studies* 62, no. 2 (2014): 127–48.

Schreiber, Waltraud, Andreas Körber, Bodo von Borries, Reinhard Krammer, Sibylla Leutner-Ramme, Sylvia Mebus, Alexander Schöner, and Béatrice Ziegler. *Historisches Denken. Ein Kompetenz-Strukturmodell.* Neuried: Ars una, 2006.

Seixas, Peter, and Tom Morton. *The Big Six Historical Thinking Concepts.* Toronto: Nelson Education, 2012.

Stoel, Gerhard, Jannet van Drie, and Carla van Boxtel. "Teaching towards Historical Expertise: Developing a Pedagogy for Fostering Causal Reasoning in History." *Journal of Curriculum Studies* 47 (2015): 49–76.

———. "The Effects of Explicit Teaching of Strategies, Second-Order Concepts, and Epistemological Underpinnings on Students' Ability to Reason Causally in History." *Journal of Educational Psychology* 109, no. 3 (2017): 321–37. Retrieved 26 April 2017 from http://dx.doi.org/10.1037/edu0000143.

Van Boxtel, Carla, and Jannet van Drie. "'That's in the Time of the Romans!' Knowledge and Strategies Students Use to Contextualize Historical Images and Documents." *Cognition and Instruction* 30, no. 2 (2012): 113–145.

———. "Historical Reasoning: Conceptualizations and Educational Applications." In *International Handbook of History Teaching and Learning,* edited by S.A. Metzger and L. McArthur Harris, 149–176. Hoboken: John Wiley & Sons, 2018.

———. "Engaging Students in Historical Reasoning: The Need for Dialogic History Education." In *International Handbook of Research in Historical Culture and Education. Hybrid Ways of Learning History,* edited by M. Carretero, S. Berger and M. Grever, 573–589. London: Palgrave McMillan, 2017.

Van Boxtel, Carla, Maria Grever, and Stephan Klein. "Heritage as a Resource for Enhancing and Assessing Historical Thinking: Reflections from the Netherlands." In *New Directions in Assessing Historical Thinking,* edited by K. Ercikan and Peter Seixas, 40–50. New York: Routledge, 2015.

Van Boxtel, Carla, Maria Grever, and Stephan Klein, eds. *Sensitive Pasts. Questioning Heritage in Education.* New York: Berghahn Books, 2016.

Van Drie, Jannet, and Carla van Boxtel. "Historical Reasoning: Towards a Framework for Analyzing Students' Reasoning about the Past." *Educational Psychology Review* 20 (2008): 87–110.

Van Drie, Jannet, Carla van Boxtel, J. Jaspers, and Gellof Kanselaar. "Effects of Representational Guidance on Domain-specific Reasoning in CSCL." *Computers in Human Behavior* 21 (2005): 575–602. Retrieved 26 April 2017 from http://dx.doi.org/10.1016/j.chb.2004.10.024.

Van Drie, Jannet, Martine Braaksma, and Carla van Boxtel. "Writing in History. Effects of Writing Instruction on Historical Reasoning and Text Quality." *Journal of Writing Research* 7, no. 1 (2015): 123–56.

VanSledright, Bruce. "Narratives of Nation-State, Historical Knowledge, and School History." *Review of Research in Education* 32 (2008): 109–146.

VanSledright, Bruce, and Margarita Limón. "Learning and Teaching Social Studies: A Review of Cognitive Research in History and Geography." In *Handbook of Educational Psychology,* edited by P.A. Alexander and P.H. Winne, 545–70. Hillsdale, NJ: Erlbaum, 2006.

Vygotsky, Lev. "Interaction between learning and development." *Readings on the development of children* 23, no. 3 (1978): 34–41.

Wansink, Bjorn, Sanne Akkerman, and Theo Wubbels. "The Certainty Paradox of Student History Teachers: Balancing between Historical Facts and Interpretation." *Teaching and Teacher Education* 56 (2016): 94–105.

Wineburg, Sam. "Historical Problem Solving: A Study of the Cognitive Processes Used in the Evaluation of Documentary and Pictorial Evidence." *Journal of Educational Psychology* 83 (1991): 73–87.

CHAPTER 5

Historical Consciousness and Representations of National Territories

What the Trump and Berlin Walls Have in Common

Mario Carretero

Historical Consciousness and the Importance of Territories' Representations

History education research has experienced an important development in the last three decades. Since the seminal work of British history educators,[1] the development of a number of cognitive educational studies at the beginning of the 1990s,[2] the influence of authors like Piaget and Bruner, and the comparison of experts and novices in different disciplines, diverse research approaches have been developed in different contexts. Most of these contributions were motivated by a well-established fact: that history as a school subject was having rather poor results in numerous school systems.[3] The proposals to improve this situation were based on two new objectives: to make history school content closer to both the discipline itself and its methods, and to teach not only historical facts and data but how to think historically.[4] These initiatives have been developed also in both Spain and Latin America since the 1990s.[5]

There is no doubt that history education research has made enormous progress. For example, Thünemann, Zülsdorf-Kersting, and Köster present a comprehensive overview of different innovative theoretical approaches around the world and their applied developments in the last decades.[6] Most

---

Notes for this section begin on page 86.

of these approaches are making efforts to better understand how to make historical content meaningful for both students and citizens. In this context, the idea of developing the historical consciousness of students has been an outstanding one and it has received increasing attention since the publication of the seminal work by Seixas, which was influenced by both British and German thinkers.[7]

As mentioned above, there is no doubt that in the last three decades important progress has been achieved not only in research on history education in formal settings but also in terms of research focused on how human beings represent and make sense of the past. Disciplines such as social psychology, memory and museum studies, and cognitive psychology, among others, have made important contributions.[8] But more research is needed, particularly from an interdisciplinary approach.[9]

In this chapter I will reflect on a question of historical consciousness. I will not present empirical data as this project is only just beginning for my research team. It focuses on a specific issue not much considered in history education research: *where* past events have taken place—in other words, how national territories as represented by historical maps could favor a lack of differentiation between past and present if students do not understand that previous national territories have experienced very often dramatic changes across times. This confusion of the past and the present is not only important for understanding the past but also the present—hence its importance for the development of historical consciousness. As the title of this paper indicates, a specific example of present-day politics will be used. I think US President Trump's ideas about the construction of a wall between the US and Mexico, and immigration in general, provide particularly apt cues for understanding why historical consciousness is so necessary and relevant in our societies. Also, from an interdisciplinary point of view, historical consciousness research could benefit very much from present contributions on borders.[10]

Borders, Nations, and Walls in the Minds of the Students

Let me start with a personal anecdote. By 1992, conflict in the former Yugoslavia was at a peak of violence between Serbs and Bosnians. Along with my daughter Soledad, who was eleven years old, I was watching the television news and seeing how that violence had terrible consequences. At one moment, my daughter started this dialogue:

Hey Dad, why is this war not being stopped? It is terrible what is happening to these people. They are killing each other.
Well it is complicated. Sad but very complex.
I do not think it is complicated. It is very simple. I have the solution!

What would you do?

Well I would build a wall for preventing these massacres. So the Bosnians will live in one part and the Serbians in the other part. And it will be forbidden to cross that wall![11]

But it is not easy to do this.

Why?

Because you have both Serbians and Bosnians living in both parts. So if they should be moved from their land to a new place there will be unhappy people in many places. Also, neither all the Serbians nor all the Bosnians probably will agree with this solution. For example, some families have both Bosnians and Serbians among their members.

So, what to do then, Dad?

This conversation continued for a while. In the verbal and conceptual exchange, I had to explain to my daughter that Serbians and Bosnians were living together in the same nation-state (Yugoslavia) as a result of the consequences of World War II. One of these consequences was the division of Europe into two blocs: one communist, the other democratic. Of course, I also had to introduce the notion that Yugoslavia was a very "recent" nation. It did not exist before World War II. Interestingly enough, this surprised my daughter the most. Anyway, the final result was a modest but successful one from an educational point of view.[12] We were unable to find a solution for this very complicated problem, but at least I was able to teach my daughter that physical, concrete, and very simple solutions such as building walls along borders are not real solutions.

In other words, to teach a student the reasons for a present-day political problem and to contribute to the advancement of her historical consciousness three issues are really necessary: (1) to improve her understanding of social and political concepts in the sense of making them more abstract and complex,[13] (2) to introduce a historical perspective showing a meaningful relation between past events and present issues, and (3) to make sense of an historical explanation in the form of a narrative. That is, to historicize the situation considering its origins, causes, and consequences.

The above-mentioned ideas of my daughter can easily be found among many children and even teenagers because they correspond to the ways students usually understand social, political, and historical issues.[14] It is important to remember that historical concepts and problems require a considerable amount of abstract thinking and cannot just be based on a direct perception of social events. This is an essential challenge for history education because many of the labels of historical concepts are the same as the ones used by everyday language like "nation," "border, "and "immigration." This could produce very misleading conclusions when naïve historical arguments are being developed as happened in the dialogue with my daughter. For example, if a child uses the word "nation" it could be inferred that she is understanding such a notion but perhaps the child has a very simplified and concrete idea about what a nation is.[15] While historical content is developed by both educators and historians through a narrative format, it is also essential to take into account that those narratives themselves incorporate concepts, and it is very important to consider what kind of concepts are being used. The interaction of narratives and concepts in the process of any history education process is an extremely important issue from both theoretical and applied points of view.[16]

Trump's Wall and the Development of Historical Consciousness

The previous example about the former Yugoslavia illustrates how complex historical understanding is essential to understanding present issues and problems. It is also important to emphasize the territorial dimension of the above example, which has not been analyzed in detail. The description of the previous example, the Balkans War (1992–94), has been described in terms of *what* happened. But in my opinion, it is also necessary to consider *where* it happened because usually this "where" implies a specific territory that is under dispute. Of course, when I use the term "territory" I do not just mean a specific part of the planet with a number of geographical features; I mean how that territory has been politically organized and how political and military battles have been carried out precisely because of that territory. In other words, the historical analysis of territories, and their teaching, should include attention to historical developments related to the disputes of different social groups about different parts of the planet. This attention is important because otherwise students could conceive of present territories as unchanged political units across times. Historical maps usually describe this process of change, but unfortunately, they have not been studied much by contemporary history education researchers nor particularly in relation to the development of historical consciousness and history education in general.[17] There are few studies about the importance of geographical maps for national identity construction.[18]

Present-day political events provide good examples of both the importance of being able to understand territorial issues in history education and how this could contribute to the development of historical consciousness among students. Therefore, let us continue this part of the chapter with a concrete case. As it is very well known, US President Donald Trump is trying to accomplish one of the most controversial goals announced in his presidential campaign: the construction of a 5000-kilometer wall spanning the entire US border with Mexico. This decision also includes a demand that the Mexican state pay the cost of the wall. The stated reason for such a goal is to defend the US territory from illegal Mexican immigrants and to prevent them from entering the US. The announcement of this project was accompanied by very negative and xenophobic characterizations of Mexican citizens as dangerous, violent criminals and also by a very controversial decision preventing the arrival of citizens from several predominantly Muslim countries to the US as refugees. Most of these actions are rejected by an important part of the public, the academic community, NGOs, and politicians across the world. But the fact of the matter is that Trump has been elected President of the United States by about fifty million people, who we can assume consider these ideas and decisions not only feasible, but also even desirable.

In what follows, I will try to show that these ideas about the construction of such a wall contain both social and historical dimensions, which certainly have a historical origin. By this term I mean both their own historical origin as such and their historical origin as part of citizens' representations. This is to say that the building of a physical wall will serve to replace a symbolic and imaginary one. In other words, national borders usually are not actual physical barriers between countries. While there is an agreement among nations that recognizes the existence of an imaginary line separating two or more nations, this line is not necessarily physical. It has no real existence.[19]

There are no walls separating nations across the world, except in some specific and also very controversial cases, such as Israel. What are real and physical are the checkpoints where passports and other documents are controlled. But most countries do not try to install physical control of the whole border. This lack of separation of the physical and the symbolic dimension of the border is certainly essential for our analysis: international analysts such as J. Carlin have found a strong similarity between President Trump's idea about the wall and the typical childish misconception of dividing whole national territories through physical borders. In both cases, there is both a concrete meaning of national borders as well as a lack of separation between their physical and symbolic dimensions. Interestingly enough this lack of differentiation is not only important for the development of historical consciousness but also for both civic education and behavior. If civic issues are understood just in concrete terms without the contribution of their symbolic and abstract dimensions there is a high risk of not being able to understand and to respect the other's perspective.[20]

In any case, let us continue with the analysis of the historical origin of national borders. I think that for the purpose of this chapter it is of great help to discuss when and how the present US–Mexico border was created. Why and how was this border established? Were there other borders before this one? How have the borders of the United States of America changed across time? It is clear that these questions have to do with changes of the national US territory across time and answers should be based on the historical under-

Map 5.1. Territories lost by Mexico and obtained by the US after their war (1846–1848). Map by the author.

standing of those transformations. As I mentioned earlier this understanding should be considered as an essential component of citizens' historical consciousness because without both diachronic and synchronic representations it is almost impossible to establish a meaningful relationship between past and present. In this sense, Trump's famous phrase of "America first" no doubt has a meaning which is very much related to historical changes of the territory.

Let us consider the relations between Mexico and the US from a historical point of view. As can be seen in Map 5.1, these two nations had a vastly different territory in 1846 when the Mexican–American War started. The war started when the US invaded Mexico and its army arrived in Mexico-DF, the capital of the country. The US won this war and obtained an enormous amount of new territory, which obviously required a modification of their borders as can be seen in Map 5.1. Mexico lost about half of its territory and the US gained significantly, including access to the Pacific through California. It is important to consider how this war was a consequence of an imperialist and expansionist trend among US politicians, which also found resistance among a number of its influential intellectuals. For example, Thoreau (1817–1862), an emblematic figure of US culture, decided not to pay the taxes the government was charging to finance the war and he was punished because of this. It is also important to consider that this war was a clear prologue of the American Civil War (1870) because the new territories were in favor of slavery.

After the war both countries continued their process of national construction. The annexation of the former Mexican territory was one of the last dramatic transformations of the US, which by 1786 was experiencing a very expansionist period since its origins after the American Revolution, as it can be seen in Map 5.2. For example, most of the present territory of several states used to belong to the Native Americans who were expelled, very badly treated, and even relocated to other places. Interestingly enough, most of both present and past US history textbooks do not mention this violence against Native Americans in a detailed way.[21] Rather, the violent annexation of their territories appears only superficially and is justified as a need for the progress of the nation.[22] The standard historical map shown in Map 5.2 does not mention the Native Americans either. It is clear that without examining this historical representation of how the territory was changing across time, it is very difficult to really understand, historically, the relation between the nation and the state as well as how the two nations have been constructed.

It is important to say that by historical maps we mean not just the representation of the territory but its changes across time, the representation of the physical and geographical territories where past events took place. If this is not correctly understood a number of misconceptions could easily appear. For example, when either a Mexican or an American student learns that "The US won the Mexican–American War of 1850," it is essential that she understands what was, exactly, the territory of each nation before and after the war. Otherwise the student could imagine the US and Mexico going to war with more or less the same territory as they have now. This is precisely what my research team has found among Spanish students when asked to discuss their representations of the so-called Spanish Reconquest, which covers the presence of the Arabs in the Iberian Peninsula for eight-hundred years (711–1492).[23] Also, we have found related assumptions in the case of Greek citizens.[24] Probably the main reason for this common misconception about the changes to the national territory comes from history textbooks and other formal and informal educational resources, which very often misrepresent historical maps.[25]

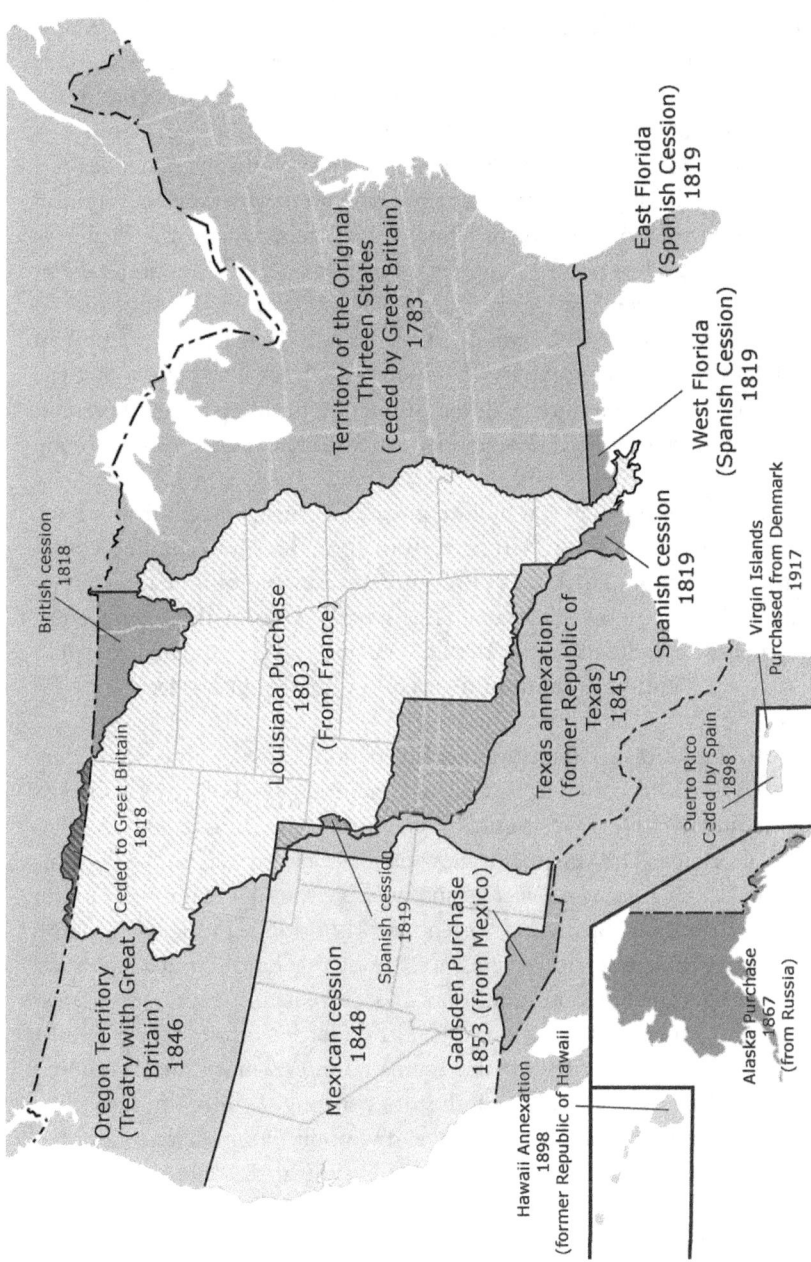

Map 5.2. Territorial development of the US. Map by the author.

Berlin's Wall and Some other Thoughts as Conclusion

As a conclusion to this chapter, it is important to note that previous initiatives of building walls along borders were strongly criticized by both US politicians and society, and also by numerous democratic leaders of the world.[26] Probably the most famous case was the Berlin Wall, which was considered a symbol of the communist lack of freedom and political oppression. It is extremely paradoxical then that President Trump supports the same idea of a physical wall, but supposedly from a democratic point of view. Does it mean that his ideas are also close to the limitation of freedom and the establishment of some kind of political oppression? What does his thinking have in common with former East German and Soviet authorities? It is not easy to answer these questions. But certainly, they could be used as an example of a historical consciousness activity for students.[27] What is certain is that the solution to this paradox requires a clear distinction between past and present, and this is important for the development of historical consciousness among citizens.

While the Berlin Wall was built to prevent German citizens from escaping from the GDR to West Germany, from communism to the free world, "Trump's wall" would be built to prevent Mexican and other Latin American citizens' entrance into that same "free world." Despite the apparent politically opposite contexts of the Berlin Wall and the proposed Mexico-US wall, they are identical in terms of their conception about borders:

1. An intention of transforming the national border into something physical and concrete instead of something symbolic. This view is definitely close to an essentialist view about the nation and its historical origins. This essentialist view has been clearly categorized by Billig (1995) as *banal nationalism* and we have found it extensively in our work in both Spain and Argentina.[28] No doubt President Trump's ideas about historical events are full of this banal approach, which is important for both educators and citizens as it represents a clear lack of historical consciousness. No doubt historical cases of similar attempts, the borders of the Roman Empire and China, could be excellent examples to use in history teaching. I think understanding the difference between physical and symbolic components of borders across historical times could foster historical consciousness among students.

2. An intention of completely preventing circulation of people across the border, which is also very close to an idea of criminalizing immigrants' actions. In general terms, national borders are porous in the majority of nations of the world because immigration has been

a common behavior of any society. In other words, immigration is a permanent historical trend of any society whereas national borders are changing, symbolic, and artificial. From a historical consciousness point of view this is what makes sense to teach even though it is the opposite of what President Trump apparently thinks about it.

It is clear that if history education imagines achieving an understanding of present relations among different nations of the world—for example the relationship between the US and Mexico—based on past events, a serious introduction to a number of political and historical concepts and narratives is sorely needed. Let us just name them as part of this conclusion:

1. The present borders are the consequence of both political and military actions across history. Borders are the not the causes of divisions among nations. On the contrary, they are consequences of historical fights for territories. Territories do not belong to national groups because of "God's plan" or "national destiny" but because of the processes of domination and oppression (see Maps 5.1 and 5.2).
2. Borders do not have an essential meaning. This is to say they are neither eternal nor unchangeable. On the contrary, they are symbolic resources that require conventions and negotiations among societies and governments.
3. Therefore, to transform borders into strict physical limits certainly has the risk of fostering a concrete and childish representation among citizens.
4. The porosity of borders represents human rights, which should not be violated because they represent possibilities of a better life for other human beings.

Such suggestions reveal the potential of historical consciousness—as a theoretical and pedagogical tool. It also demonstrates how in my own interdisciplinary research, across history education, educational psychology, and historical geography, this contemplation of historical consciousness has increasingly taken on contemporary relevance and consideration.

Mario Carretero is Professor at Autonoma University of Madrid, Spain, and Researcher at FLACSO, Argentina. He has carried out an extensive research on history education. His latest books are *History Education and the Construction of National Identities* (2012, co-ed.), *Constructing Patriotism* (2011, funded by the Guggenheim Foundation), and *Palgrave Handbook of Research on Historical Culture and Education* (2017). He has been Santander Visiting Scholar at the D. Rockefeller Center on Latin American Studies at Harvard

University and Bliss Carnochan Visiting Professor at the Humanities Center of Stanford University.

Notes

This chapter's elaboration has been posible due to the support of Projects EDU-2015-65088P from MINECO-FEDER Funds (Spain) and PICT2016-2341 from ANPCYT (Argentina), coordinated by the author. Also I would like to acknowledge valuable comments from M. Grever, S. Berger, and two anonymous reviewers.

1. Dickinson et al., eds., *Learning History*; Shemilt, *History 13-16 Evaluation Study*. See also further work by Seixas (2016 and 2017) where both the intellectual origins of this idea and its relation to other approaches such as historical thinking are explored.
2. Carretero and Voss, eds., *Cognitive and Instructional Processes*; Leinhardt et al., *Teaching and Learning*.
3. Ravitch and Finn, *What do our 17-year olds know?*
4. Wineburg, *Historical Thinking*; see also Freedman, "What Happened Needs to Be 'Told,'" for a view on critical thinking in history education.
5. Carretero, "History Learning in Spain and Latin America."
6. Köster et al., eds., *Researching History Education*.
7. Seixas, *Theorizing Historical Consciousness*; Dickinson et al., *Learning History*; Rüsen, "Historical consciousness"; Clark and Grever, "Historical Consciousness."
8. Gonzalez de Oleaga, "Democracy and History Museums"; Paez et al., "Social Representations."
9. Carretero et al., eds., *Palgrave Handbook*.
10. Morrissey et al., *Key concepts in historical geography*.
11. J. Carlin recently compared Trump's ideas with childish thoughts in the sense of being very concrete and simplified.
12. It is also true that both parents and educators are always very optimistic about the result of our educational actions.
13. Carretero and Lee, "Learning historical concepts."
14. Carretero and Lee, "Learning historical concepts."
15. See López et al., "Conquest or reconquest?" for an empirical study on the notion of nation.
16. Carretero et al., "Conceptual change."
17. Kamusella, "School History Atlases."
18. Morrissey et al., *Key concepts in historical geography*.
19. For example there is a city in North America where the border is part of a library, which includes both a US part and a Canadian part (see Faus, "When the border").
20. Carretero et al., "Civic Learning."
21. Stoskopf and Bermudez, "The sounds of silence."
22. For example, there is almost no indication of it at the National Museum of American Indians in Washington.
23. López et al., "Conquest or reconquest?"
24. Kadaniaki et al., "Using National History."
25. Herzog, "Historical Rights to Land."
26. Ahrens, "Trump: 'Immigration.'" As the journalist writes in this note, "The President of the United States has the dream of building walls. The German Chancellor (Angela Merkel) suffered in the flesh the dictatorship of a wall."
27. Also, Trump's conception about immigration as a "privilege but not a right" also deserves a discussion in terms of historical consciousness development (ibid.).

28. Carretero and van Alphen, "History, Collective Memories or National Memories?"; Carretero and van Alphen, "Do master narratives change among high school students?"

Bibliography

Ahrens, Jan Martínez. "Trump: 'La inmigración es un privilegio, no un derecho'" [Trump: "Immigration is a privilege, not a right."] *El País*. Retrieved 20 March 2017 from https://elpais.com/internacional/2017/03/17/estados_unidos/1489780254_496094.html.

Billig, Michael. *Banal Nationalism*. London: Sage, 1995.

Carlin, John. "A Man Baby in the White House." *El País*. Retrieved 14 March 2017 from https://elpais.com/elpais/2017/01/20/inenglish/1484911522_528712.html.

Carretero, Mario. *Constructing patriotism. Teaching of history and historical memory in globalized world*. Charlotte, NC: Information Age Publishing, 2011.

———. "History Learning in Spain and Latin America." In *Researching History Education. International Perspectives and Disciplinary Tradition*, edited by M. Köster, H. Thunemann, and M. Züelsdorf-Kersting, 52–70. Schwalbach, Germany: Wochenschau Verlag, 2014.

———. "Teaching History Master Narratives: Fostering Imagi-Nations." In *Palgrave Handbook of Research in Historical Culture and Education*, edited by Mario Carretero, Stefan Berger, and Maria Grever, 511–28. London: Palgrave, 2017.

Carretero, Mario, Stefan Berger, and Maria Grever, eds. *Palgrave Handbook of Research in Historical Culture and Education*. Basingstoke: Palgrave, 2017.

Carretero, Mario, Jose A. Castorina, and Leonardo Levinas. "Conceptual change and historical narratives about the nation: A theoretical and empirical approach." In *International Handbook of Research on Conceptual Change*, 2nd ed., edited by Stella Vosniadou, 269–87. New York: Routledge, 2013.

Carretero, Mario, Helen Haste, and Angela Bermudez. "Civic Education." In *Handbook of Educational Psychology*, 3rd ed., edited by Lyn Corno, and Eric M. Anderman, 295–308. London: Routledge, 2016.

Carretero, Mario, and Peter Lee. "Learning historical concepts." In *Handbook of Learning Sciences*, 2nd ed., edited by R. Keith Sawyer, Cambridge: Cambridge University Press, 2014.

Carretero, Mario, and Floor van Alphen. "Do master narratives change among high school students? A characterization of how national history is represented." *Cognition and Instruction* 32, no. 3 (2014): 290–312.

———. "History, Collective Memories or National Memories? How the representation of the past is framed by master narratives." In *Oxford Handbook of Culture and Memory*, edited by Brady Wagoner, 283–304. Oxford: Oxford University Press, 2017.

Carretero, Mario, and James F. Voss, eds. *Cognitive and Instructional Processes in History and Social Sciences*. Hillsdale: Erlbaum, 1994.

Clark, Anna. *Teaching the Nation*. Melbourne: Melbourne University Press, 2004.

Clark, Anna, and Maria Grever. "Historical Consciousness: Conceptualizations and Educational Applications." In *The Wiley International Handbook of History Teaching and Learning*, edited by Scott A. Metzger and Lauren McArther Harris, 177–201. New York: Wiley Blackwell, 2018.

Dickinson, Alaric K., Peter J. Lee, and P. J. Rogers, eds. *Learning History*. London: Heinemann, 1984.

Faus, Joan. "Cuando la frontera entre Canadá y Estados Unidos es una biblioteca y no un muro" [When the border between Canada and the United States is a library and not a wall]. *El País*. Retrieved 14 March 2017 from https://elpais.com/internacional/2017/02/07/estados_unidos/1486491766_660614.html.

Freedman, Eric B. "What Happened Needs to Be Told: Fostering Critical Historical Reasoning in the Classroom." *Cognition and Instruction* 33, no. 4 (2015): 357–98.

Gellner, Ernest. *Thought and Change*. Chicago: University of Chicago Press, 1978.

Gonzalez de Oleaga, Marisa. "Democracy and History Museums. Museo de América." In *Palgrave Handbook of Research in Historical Culture and Education*, edited by Mario Carretero, Stefan Berger, and Maria Grever, 133–151. Basingstoke: Palgrave, 2017.

Herzog, Tamar. "Historical Rights to Land: How Latin American States Made the Past Normative and What Happened to History and Historical Education as a Result." In *Palgrave Handbook of Research in Historical Culture and Education*, edited by Mario Carretero, Stefan Berger, and Maria Grever, 91–107. Basingstoke: Palgrave, 2017.

Kadaniaki, Irini, Eleni Andreouli, and Mario Carretero. "Using National History to Construct the Boundaries of Citizenship: An Analysis of Greek Citizens' Discourse About Immigrants' Rights." *Qualitative Psychology* 5, no. 2 (2018): 172–87.

Kamusella, Tomasz. "School History Atlases as Instruments of Nation-State Making And Maintenance: A Remark on the Invisibility of Ideology in Popular Education." *Journal of Educational Media, Memory, and Society* 2, no. 1 (2010): 113–38.

Körster, Manuel, Holger Thünemann, and Meik Zülsdorf-Kersting, eds. *Researching History Education: International Perspectives and Disciplinary Traditions*. Schwalbach, Germany: Wochenschau Verlag, 2014.

Leinhardt, Gaea, Isabel L. Beck, and Catherine Stainton. *Teaching and Learning in History*. New York: Routledge, 1994.

López, Cesar, and Mario Carretero. "Commentary: Identity Construction and the Goals of history Education." In *History education and the construction of national identity*, edited by Mario Carretero, Mikel Asensio, and Mario Rodríguez-Moneo, 139–52. Charlotte, NC: Information Age Publishing, 2012.

López, Cesar, Mario Carretero, and Maria Rodríguez-Moneo. "Conquest or reconquest? Students' conceptions of nation embedded in a historical narrative." *Journal of the Learning Sciences* 24, no. 2 (2015): 252–85. Retrieved 27 April 2017 from doi: 10.1080/10508406.2014.919863.

Morrissey, John, David Nally, Ulf Strohmayer, and Yvonne Whelan. *Key concepts in historical geography*. Los Angeles: Sage, 2014.

Paez, Dario, Magdalena Bobowik, and James Liu. "Social Representations of Past and Competences in History Education." In *Palgrave Handbook of Research in Historical Culture and Education*, edited by Mario Carretero, Stefan Berger, and Maria Grever. Basingstoke: Palgrave, 2017.

Ravitch, Diane, and Chester E. Finn, Jr. *What do our 17-year olds know? A Report on the First National Assessment of History and Literature*. New York: Harper & Row, 1987.

Rüsen, Jörn. "Historical Consciousness: Narrative Structure, Moral Function, and Ontogenetic Development." In *Theorizing Historical Consciousness*, edited by Peter Seixas, 63–85. Toronto: University of Toronto Press, 2004.

Seixas, Peter. *Theorizing Historical Consciousness*. Toronto: University of Toronto Press, 2004.

———. "Translation and its discontents: key concepts in English and German history education." *Journal of Curriculum Studies* 48, no. 4 (2016): 427–39.

———. "A model of historical thinking." *Educational Philosophy and Theory* 49, no. 6 (2017): 593–605.

Shemilt, Denis. *History 13-16 Evaluation Study*. Edinburgh, UK: Holmes McDougall, 1980.

Stoskopf, Alan, and Angela Bermudez. "The sounds of silence: American history textbook representations of non-violence and the Abolition Movement." *Journal of Peace Education* 14, no. 1 (2017): 92–113.

Wineburg, Sam. *Historical Thinking and Other Unnatural Acts*. Philadelphia: Temple University Press, 2001.

Part II

HISTORICAL CONSCIOUSNESS WITHIN AND BEYOND BORDERS

CHAPTER 6

Mothers' Darlings of the South Pacific

ANGELA WANHALLA

Between 1942 and 1945, over two million servicemen occupied the southern Pacific theatre, the majority of them Americans in service with the Marines, Army, Navy, and Air Force. Numerous studies of the American occupation of the South Pacific, however, rarely acknowledge that the US forces left behind thousands of children born to Indigenous women. In 2010, a three-year interdisciplinary collaborative research project funded by a Royal Society of New Zealand Marsden Grant, led by historian Judith A. Bennett and myself, and involving a large group of researchers, set out to trace the histories and lived experiences of these women and their children, covering numerous small island societies in the South Pacific Command Area.[1] Known as the Mothers' Darlings Project, the research team was interested in uncovering the various intimate relationships forged during wartime between Indigenous women and US servicemen stationed in the South Pacific, as well as the legacies of global war in shaping and forming the parent-child-family relationship for a group popularly known as "GI Babies."

Mothers' Darlings focuses on the narratives and experiences of Indigenous women and their children, two groups who barely register in the abundant scholarship on war in the Pacific, including studies of war and memory in that region. While there is a flourishing scholarship concerned with the intersections between gender, war, and militarization, as well as a growing literature concerned with the impact of war on children in the past and present (particularly important in the European theatre are the autobiographies

---

Notes for this section begin on page 101.

of Holocaust survivors), the examination of children's lives during wartime mobilization in the Pacific is a largely untouched subject. Indigenous servicemen from the South Pacific region who served during World War I and World War II are a recent addition to a significant body of scholarship concerned with military history, but Indigenous women's experiences are far less visible. In part, the absence of women and children is partly attributable to the nature of the available source material, which is fragmentary at best, but also to the dominance of particular methodologies that have favored battle histories over approaches concerned with social issues, including the family. Social anthropologist and historian Jacqueline Leckie, who was also an Associate Investigator on the Mothers' Darlings Project, describes wartime intimate encounters as "uncelebrated war memories" that do not neatly fit official narratives inscribed in public monuments, war memorials, or the rituals of remembrance enacted on national days of commemoration.[2] While these intimacies exist on the very margins of public consciousness, Leckie reminds us "they are never forgotten" by those involved.[3]

Studies of memory and war in the Pacific have been undertaken using a range of methodologies, including material culture, such as studies of war artifacts and cultures of display, as well as examinations of the cultural politics of memory work in the Pacific, inclusive of participant observation, and interviews. Until Mothers' Darlings, there had been no in-depth research on Indigenous women's wartime experiences. As such, the project represents the first major examination of wartime intimacies in the Pacific and their legacies, embodied by the children left behind, sometimes knowingly, by their servicemen fathers. These relationships and the children are not mere footnotes to war history, or an inevitable outcome of the mobilization of large numbers of young men to overseas territories for months or years at a time. Rather, as Mothers' Darlings found, intimate relations were of major significance during the war—to the young Americans and Indigenous women, to extended families, and to the colonial administrations and governments and to the military who turned a blind eye to the social consequences of intimate relationships because it made tolerable the monotony of rear bases. With an estimated four-thousand children fathered by US servicemen in the South Pacific Command, war was life-creating and life-changing for thousands.

Our approach to uncovering the experiences of women and children was to undertake traditional archival research, notably the records created by colonial administrations in the South Pacific and the US military, as well as newspaper reports, but of most importance to the project's success was gathering numerous oral histories from now adult children, any surviving mothers, and sometimes American fathers, as these were crucial to our goal of illuminating the social impacts of American occupation in the South Pacific theatre. Although the experiences of women and children can be found in the edges and shadows of US military and government records, it was the approximately 120 oral histories the research team collected that were essential to illuminating the emotional and affective legacies of war, particularly because state, colonial, and military archives rarely gave space to Indigenous women's voices and experiences or took much interest in the social consequences of global war. While not specifically framed in the field of historical consciousness, this research explored issues critical to that growing body of theoretical work: studying the voices, stories, and legacies of these historical narratives gives vital context and meaning to issues of inheritance, silence, motherhood and Indigenous experience, as well as to histories of war in the Pacific.

Before discussing the oral history strand of the project in depth, it is important to set the historical context in which Indigenous women encountered American servicemen. Wartime relationships took place against the backdrop of large-scale imperialist expansion and ambition, advanced by military forces during and after World War II. Although a reluctant participant, American involvement in the Pacific and European campaigns saw American global military presence grow from 14 overseas bases in 1938, to 30,000 installations (large and small) by the end of 1945, which retracted to 2,000 installations across 100 countries by the end of the decade.[4]

Prior to World War II, the United States sought to protect the territories it had acquired in the Pacific, Southeast Asia, and Latin America, where it had established coaling and provisioning bases for its navy.[5] These bases, notably in the Philippines, American Samoa, and Midway, would prove to be critical when the US entered the Pacific campaign on 7 December 1941. As the Japanese advanced, American bases were quickly established across the Pacific, one of the first being a fuelling station at Bora Bora in February 1942. The US naval base at American Samoa was reinforced in January 1942, with bases across the South Pacific Command Area established at New Caledonia, New Hebrides (now Vanuatu), and Western Samoa in March. Tongatapu and Wallis Island were occupied in May. A month later, bases at Fiji and New Zealand were in operation. In August, US forces were stationed at the Solomon Islands, followed by Tuvalu in October, and the Cook Islands and Kiribati in November. This "tsunami" of men, camps, and military technology occupied South Pacific bases for a short, but intense, period, beginning in 1942, with the majority of personnel back in the United States by the end of 1945, although a few stayed on into 1946 and 1947 as the bases were slowly closed. The role of these bases ebbed and flowed with the course of the war, with some used for training, or supported hospitals, while many became refuelling stations, and provided facilities for the repair of ships.[6]

Defending the largest ocean on earth required negotiation with a range of imperial and colonial governments to gain territorial access to build airfields, equip bases, and establish hospitals so as to enable a mobilization that has been described as "undoubtedly the fastest and most widespread dispersal of a country's citizens in the history of the human race."[7] On arriving in the South Pacific, American forces encountered a highly culturally diverse region, about which they knew little except for what they had gleaned from Hollywood representations, and they entered worlds where island peoples were governed by a mixture of competing imperial and colonial authorities. When US forces arrived, the Cook Islands and Western Samoa were under New Zealand control; Fiji was a British Crown Colony; Tonga, a monarchy and British protectorate; while the French had interests in Vanuatu and New Caledonia. Competing interests and objectives often led to tensions between local administrators and the US military command, usually centred on the misconduct of troops, which in turn was underpinned by growing anxiety from imperial and colonial administrations about expanding American interests in the Pacific.[8]

In a region where "one of the biggest events of human history was being enacted on some of the world's smallest islands in its largest ocean," war also initiated social impacts that affected the lives of Indigenous inhabitants, but particularly those of women.[9] For those living on small Pacific Islands situated within what became the US South Pacific Command Area (including the islands of Tonga, Fiji, Samoa, the Cook Islands, Kiribati, Vanuatu, and New Zealand) the mass arrival of American troops brought about new opportunities. Located away from the battle zones, much of the South Pacific Command Area operated as locales for rest, relaxation, training, and recovery. Military personnel were stationed in the region ranging from a matter of days, if their ship called in for provisioning, to months or years, giving men plenty of opportunity to develop relationships with local women. Intimate encounters ranged the full spectrum from romantic, and enduring, through to the commercial, and the opportunistic. These relationships were negotiated within the context of American laws and social practices applied on bases, including assumptions about race, sexuality, and gender, which were mapped onto Pacific peoples and societies. American troops' treatment of local women was, as Sean Brawley and Chris Dixon have demonstrated, influenced by Hollywood depictions of the South Pacific where Indigenous women were cast as sexually permissive, scantily clad, and exotic.[10]

Legal marriage was an option for couples, but access was heavily monitored by military authorities, who were willing to accept socializing across the "color line" for the purposes of maintaining morale but discouraged men from making the relationship more permanent. Commanding officers controlled the marriage opportunities of their troops, for their permission was required before a marriage could proceed. In 1942, military commanders could refer to the US War Department's marriage regulation, which limited the right of American servicemen to marry by imposing US legal codes extra-territorially, overriding too the social and cultural traditions and practices of local peoples, to oppose any application from a couple to marry where it threatened the "colour line."[11] Any couple wanting to marry faced the difficulties imposed by the marriage policy adopted by the US Army and Navy in 1942, which was formulated in response to the mobilization of US forces to British colonies in the Caribbean where mainly white troops were stationed amongst predominately African host communities.[12]

The US military's marriage regulation was developed in the context of racial segregation, and at a time when twenty-nine states operated laws prohibiting interracial marriage, in addition to a federal immigration policy that denied entry to those who could not meet the race-based requirements set out under the law. If a couple was unable to prove suitability for entry to the United States under immigration law, military commanders were empowered to deny the right of marriage to the couple, which they based on an investigation into the woman's background, employment, and family life. Controlling servicemen's right to marriage was underpinned by a determination to retain American racial hierarchies overseas, with African American applicants least likely to succeed. US troops came from diverse cultural and ethnic backgrounds, though, and while the limits placed upon African American troops' marital opportunities are well-known, historians know little about the success rates of Mexican-Americans, Filipino-Americans, and Indigenous Americans serving with US forces in the European and Pacific campaigns.[13]

Using records of the US consulates in New Zealand and Fiji, the project team was able to track the specific ways in which US military authorities governed marriage and used race as a determining factor in their decisions. Some commanders were sympathetic, and supported marriage, but that was unusual. Some couples negotiated the restrictions by finding sympathetic clergy or marrying according to local custom. Marriage, whether legal or by custom was, rare. Few couples had the opportunity to marry, and so most women were left behind by their American lover. That is not to say that these men did not want to be fathers, but that their opportunities were constrained by regulations and the contingencies of wartime operations. During wartime and after demobilisation some men tried to reunite with their family, but immigration restrictions were complex and difficult to negotiate, especially in cases of financial constraint. Nevertheless, there were numerous servicemen who refused to acknowledge their child, and the military command were unwilling to enforce fatherly responsibilities, often transferring a serviceman to a new station "somewhere in the Pacific," making him difficult to trace for the purpose of serving a paternity claim upon him.

Mothers' Darlings is part of a scholarly conversation detailing the reach and impact of war on the host communities who live with the legacies of militarization. To uncover those impacts the research team turned to oral history. Although we recognized in our research approach that the archival record and oral histories offer very different sets of "truths," each equally valid, oral histories were a priority because it gave us access to the less tangible impacts of wartime relationships. As it is an emotional subject we took a flexible approach to conducting interviews, preferring to regard them as conversations, in keeping with the protocols and practices of the local culture and being sensitive to cultural inflections and differences. We took into account that self-censorship is enacted in interviews, that memories can be selective, events can be retold in different ways over time and that memory is mobile and selective. Despite these issues, we considered that together, interviews and the archives could provide a richer account of intimate relations in wartime and their consequences.

We advertised our project widely across New Zealand and the South Pacific, and also in Australia. Interviews with print media and appearances on radio stations helped spread the word about the project within relevant communities. Researchers spoke to community groups to publicize the project, too, and to also build relationships. In 2011, *Sunday,* a Television New Zealand investigative program, aired a twenty-minute segment about Arthur Beren's search for his American father. Combined, these efforts saw the project leaders inundated with emails and phone calls from individuals interested in the project. Of these hundreds, around 120 were willing to participate formally.

Our archival work, which illuminated policy and practice, meant that the project team was in a position to help our participants to contextualize the decision-making of their parents, who had to navigate difficult emotional terrain. But in pursuing our oral history project, a number of unanticipated consequences arose. First, we did not consider the possibility that many people would contact us seeking assistance to locate their US serviceman father, if he was still alive, or any family they might have in the United States. Most who made contact had researched for decades without luck and saw the project as an opportunity to obtain assistance in their quest to find family, and to answer questions they had long had about their identity. A very small number, such as New Zealander Michael Gaeng, had already successfully located their US family, and saw the project as an opportunity to share that story in order to give hope and encouragement to others. Many oral histories I undertook for the project naturally ended up focusing on the search for a father, which many had been pursuing for decades. Our participants had their own agenda, which was different from that of the researchers. We listened, though. Overwhelmed by the numerous requests for help, and our desire to practice reciprocity, we set up a website (US Fathers of Pacific Children) to both advertise the project, but also provide guidance to those seeking to locate family, providing references to useful secondary sources as well as websites. On the US Fathers of Pacific Children website, we also post details about any American serviceman father who is being sought in the hope that information might be provided by a third party.

Such was the sensitivity of the subject matter that most people who made contact wanted advice but were unwilling to take part in the project; others wrote secretly on behalf of a parent requesting help but also anonymity and privacy; while a number withdrew from the project from fear of family discovering their quest, or for sharing private information with a third party. The many email exchanges, phone conversations, and formal interviews we conducted with individuals illustrated starkly how secrecy and shame were significant components of the wartime experience of women, which had a lasting legacy and impact for their children, who grew up in the shadows of the past and its burdens.

Reasons for undertaking the search varied. Take this example from New Zealand of a woman who was adopted as a child by a non-Indigenous couple, and raised with no knowledge of her Māori mother, or her American father. She began her search for her birth parents as an adult, but focused solely on locating her biological mother, because she did not have a close connection or an emotional bond with the woman who raised her. Having succeeded and been welcomed into her birth mother's family after some initial suspicion about her motivations, she has only recently sought to find her biological father. Having had a close relationship with the man she regards as her father prevented her from searching, out of respect for his feelings. As she noted, she had little need to look for her US serviceman father because she felt no urgency nor a feeling of emptiness.[14] Others did not grow up with kind and caring fathers or stepfathers, and so sought to locate their US father in the hope of a real and meaningful connection. In a few cases we have been able to provide people with information to help them locate their family, and some have had positive and warm responses from US relatives. But there are just as many who have received only silence, or rejection, from potential relatives suspicious of their motivations.

It is important to note that our project was not the catalyst for people to search for their absent father: everyone who contacted us had been trying to locate him for decades, often from young adulthood, drawing on evidence from overheard conversations or from letters, documents or objects hidden away that were accidentally discovered, teasing from other children, differential treatment by family (being either placed on a pedestal, ignored, or mistreated), or partial truths blurted out by family members in angry moments. Some posed questions, but often these went unanswered, with aunts, uncles, and mothers having "forgotten" a name or "lost" documents that may reveal clues to a father's identity. In other cases, worried they may anger their parents, they did not ask any questions, or they kept silent feeling their quest for birth parents represented a rejection of those who raised them. To do least harm to others has been a principle that has driven those I have spoken to for the project.

Secrecy was related to the nature of the parental relationship and the circumstances under which a child was born: illegitimacy and adoption, whether through the courts or by custom, generated need for a level of secrecy, silence, or half-truths, as did the shame of divorce, an extra-marital affair, a casual relationship, and single motherhood. Because individuals self-identified and selected to participate in the project, our oral histories do tend towards romantic interpretations of relationships, even when evidence shows they were casual, fleeting encounters. Few oral histories collected touched upon prostitution or coercive encounters, both of which are known to have existed across the South Pacific Command.

Oral histories revealed just how secrecy was practiced, and revelations were made, demonstrating that there is no linear and progressive overcoming of secrecy, shame, and guilt over time.[15] Historian Deborah Cohen has noted that secrecy has psychological and emotional costs, which is measured only once those secrets come to light. Indigenous women faced a range of legal barriers when it came to formalizing their wartime relationship, gaining entry to the United States, and establishing the citizenship status of their children under American law. Most Indigenous women were unable to marry their American serviceman partner due to race-based US marriage and nationality laws. Instead, the more common outcome of wartime relationships was non-marital pregnancy and fatherless children. Without a husband or father, women and children became socially marginalized. Abandoned, pregnant, and afraid of how family might respond to their situation, some women broke down emotionally and psychologically. Mothers' Darlings signals how women's emotional and mental states were shaped by wider social attitudes to their wartime experience, which could involve limited choices: single motherhood or putting the child up for adoption. Indigenous family structures (which had been placed under pressure to conform to western models by a range of outside groups) were certainly flexible enough to accommodate these children, with grandparents often taking on the role of caregivers, but this does not mean these children felt they were well-treated. Oral accounts, which illuminate the practice and meaning of intimacy and bring to life the specific and ongoing legacies of global war, reveal unhappy childhoods, and for some people this included experiencing interpersonal violence, resulting in low self-esteem and depression. Mental illness is one of the least understood aspects of war and its legacies, and for some mothers the shame of institutionalization would shape their lives and their children's into the postwar decades.

Mothers' Darlings has been unravelling secrets, but what are the costs and benefits of this research? At its outset we did not appreciate the implications of our project: embarrassment and shame, for example, is still keenly felt by some mothers who resolutely refuse to speak about the past with their adult children. While we have provided resolution for a small number of people, finding a father may in fact bring forth new and complicated questions. We certainly did not consider the impact our research might have on family in the United States.

Nor did we think about the legal repercussions, particularly around claims to citizenship. One opportunist American lawyer made contact with the project leaders via email seeking access to personal information about our participants so he could represent them in claims against the US Government. Protecting the privacy of our participants was vital, and a major consideration throughout the entire project. Added to this are the material consequences of uncovering paternity, because in some societies one's parentage is linked to land rights, which the revelation of an American father threatens. We have also faced barriers to conducting research from influential individuals suspicious of the project and who fear the revelations are designed to shame people; that in scrutinizing the past actions of community and chiefly leaders, we may reveal a less than acceptable history. In small-island societies it is hard to lose your past. These are societies where private matters are common knowledge, but they are not discussed openly. If you are an insider to that society and culture, you are privy to this private information, but if private information officially becomes public knowledge, people get hurt, and reputations are damaged. Such experiences raise the important question of how research projects like ours impact on participants' historical consciousness.

Shame is an individual matter, but it is also shaped by cultural concerns, and so the Mothers' Darlings researchers had to navigate fraught emotional terrain but also balance out our project objectives with the competing needs and desires of those who shared their stories with us. These needs and desires have brought immense nuance and complexity to the project, but also registered the ongoing impacts of global war. Our project points to the dramatic impacts and costs of militarization upon families: the shame attached to having a child out of wedlock, resulting in the societal rejection of the mother and child; the physical, emotional and psychological trauma of living with that past; as well as the legal complexities. Tracing the particular circumstances of cases draws attention to how policy and law was interpreted and imposed at different administrative levels (military, consular, and immigration officials), helping to illuminate how border control worked in practice.

An area for future research is the limits and constraints placed on US servicemen who may have wanted to settle in places like Australia and New Zealand, which had in place their own racially restrictive immigration laws. There is also much to be done on the stationing of Australian and New Zealand troops in overseas territories during war, and their impacts on local populations that goes beyond the war bride narrative. This is an untold story, and such a project would do much, I think, to offer nuance and complexity to the official rhetoric on heroic military masculinity in New Zealand and Australia.

Mothers' Darlings is engaged in a different kind of "memory work" that has dominated recent approaches to the Pacific war: it looks beyond memorials, artifacts and material culture, and beyond official narratives sponsored by nation states keen to shape public consciousness of the importance and significance of war sacrifice and heroism. The project disrupts military patriotism and national celebration around soldier masculinity by reconnecting the personal and intimate legacies of war in the Pacific with the structural circumstances that produced it. By their very existence, the South Pacific war children, born out of conflict, reveal deep ties and connections to the American military presence in the Pacific. We have done this by doing traditional archival research and oral history, combined with family history research and approaches, which has enabled us to stitch together the impact and legacies of the American military presence in new ways and in places and through people (Indigenous women and children) whose experiences often exist on the very margins of social and cultural histories of global war.

Our project explored patterns of sexual commerce but also relationships of affiliation, kinship, and family, inclusive of the many and various ways families formed during and after the war. In privileging intimate worlds, we gain access to the human mosaic of the past, adding complexity to histories of intimacy that document the sexual, but also encompass emotional bonds as well as ties of affiliation in a part of the world often located on the very margins of social and cultural histories of global war. Nevertheless, Mothers' Darlings also demonstrates that each case is complex, and serves as a reminder that these stories and experiences are not easy to relate and not all are ready to tell them.

Angela Wanhalla is an associate professor in the Department of History and Art History, University of Otago, New Zealand. Angela researches the intersection between race, gender, and histories of intimacy within colonial societies. She is the author of *Matters of the Heart: A History of Interracial Marriage in New Zealand* (2013), and a co-editor, with Judith A. Bennett, of *Mothers' Darlings of the South Pacific: The Children of Indigenous Women and US Servicemen, World War II* (2016).

Notes

1. Mothers' darlings: children of Indigenous women and World War II American servicemen in New Zealand and South Pacific societies, Royal Society of New Zealand Marsden Grant, UOO-023. Principle Investigator, Judith A. Bennett; Co-Principle Investigator, Angela Wanhalla; Associate Ivestigators: Jacqueline Leckie and Phyllis Herda. Also attached to the project were Rosemary Anderson, Kate Stevens, Alumita Durutalo (all University of Otago), Louise Mataia (Victoria University of Wellington), and Kathryn Creely (University of California, San Diego). Numerous publications have resulted from the project, most notably, Bennett and Wanhalla, eds., *Mothers' Darlings of the South Pacific*. In 2013, three participants in the Mothers' Darlings project contributed to a documentary, co-funded by the University of Otago and the Marsden Fund, called *Born of Conflict*. It is available for viewing on YouTube.
2. Leckie, "Islands, Intimate and Public Memories," 19.
3. Leckie, "Islands, Intimate and Public Memories," 19.
4. Lutz, "Introduction," 10. Also see Höhn and Moon, eds., *Over There*.
5. Lutz, "Introduction," 11.
6. See Bennett, "Prologue."
7. Coates and Morrison, "The American Rampant," 206.
8. Henningham, "The French Administration."
9. Bennett, *Natives and Exotics*, 7.
10. Brawley and Dixon, *Hollywood's South Seas*, xv and 69–71.
11. See Bennett et al., "Mothers' darlings."
12. Neptune, *Caliban and the Yankees*, 172.
13. Ota, "Flying Buttresses," 700.
14. Interview with Jill, conducted by the author, 6 February 2012.
15. Cohen, *Family Secrets*, xiii.

Bibliography

Bennett, Judith A. *Natives and Exotics: World War II and Environment in the Southern Pacific*. Honolulu: University of Hawaii Press, 2009.

Bennett, Judith A. "Prologue: War comes to the Pacific." In *Mothers' Darlings of the South Pacific: The Children of Indigenous Women and US Servicemen, World War II*, edited by Judith A. Bennett and Angela Wanhalla. Hawaii/Dunedin: University of Hawaii Press/Otago University Press, 2016.

Bennett, Judith A., and Angela Wanhalla, eds. *Mothers' Darlings of the South Pacific: The Children of Indigenous Women and US Servicemen, World War II*. Hawaii/Dunedin: University of Hawaii Press/Otago University Press, 2016.

Bennett, Judith A., Jacqueline Leckie, and Angela Wanhalla. "Mothers' darlings: secrets and silences in the wake of the Pacific War." In *The Pacific War: Aftermaths, remembrance and culture*, edited by Christina Twomey and Ernest Koh. New York: Routledge, 2014.

Brawley, Sean, and Chris Dixon. *Hollywood's South Seas and the Pacific War: Searching for Dorothy Lamour*. New York: Palgrave Macmillan, 2012.

Coates, Ken, and W. R. Morrison. "The American Rampant: Reflections on the Impact of United States Troops in Allied Countries during World War II." *Journal of World History* 2, no. 2 (1991): 201–21.

Cohen, Deborah. *Family Secrets: Shame and Privacy in Modern Britain*. Oxford: Oxford University Press, 2013.

Henningham, Stephen. "The French Administration, the local population, and the American presence in New Caledonia, 1943–44." *Journal de la Société des Océanistes* 98 (1994): 21–41.

Höhn, Maria, and Seungsook Moon, eds. *Over There: Living with the U.S. Military Empire from World War Two to the Present.* Durham: Duke University Press, 2010.

Leckie, Jacqueline. "Islands, Intimate and Public Memories of the Pacific War." In *Heritage and Memory of War: Responses from Small Islands,* edited by Gilly Carr and Keir Reeves, 19–35. London: Routledge, 2015.

Lutz, Catherine. "Introduction: Bases, Empire, and Global Response." In *The Bases of Empire: The Global Struggle against U.S. Military Posts,* edited by C. Lutz, 1–44. New York: New York University Press, 2009.

Neptune, Harvey R. *Caliban and the Yankees: Trinidad and the United States Occupation.* Chapel Hill: University of North Carolina Press, 2007.

Ota, Nancy K. "Flying Buttresses." *DePaul Law Review* 49, no. 3 (2000): 693–728.

CHAPTER 7

Looking Back at *Canadians and Their Pasts*

PETER SEIXAS

Half way into the first decade of the new century, despite healthy growth in almost every aspect of public history, vibrant recent debates about history curriculum in schools, and a new budget-cutting prime minister nevertheless willing to invest in (and politicize) commemoration, Canadians had no comprehensive picture of their collective interest, involvement, or understanding of the past. Of course, Canada was not alone in this. One of the first attempts to articulate the questions whose answers would provide such a picture on a national scale—Rosenzweig and Thelen's *The Presence of the Past* in the United States—was still new.[1] The debates their study generated, even between its two co-authors, made clear what a complex and multifaceted challenge they had taken on. A second, smaller study in Australia using a similar methodology provided another precedent for the work that would unfold in the next few years in Canada.[2]

The six Canadian academics who came together in 2006 to investigate Canadians and their pasts were a diverse team in terms of region, language, and disciplinary background. They came from history departments, public history, and schools of education. Yet, each had collaborated with at least one other of the group on previous projects and several knew each other well. Early on, following in the Americans' footsteps, the group committed to base the core of its work on a large survey and formed a partnership with York University's Institute for Social Research, which had the expertise and infrastructure to carry out telephone interviews with large samples ef-

---

Notes for this section begin on page 111.

ficiently, and with reliability checks, in Canada's two official languages. Its principal became the seventh—crucial—partner in the team.

Each of the investigators brought particular expertise, background, and interests. The group worked well: no deep, ongoing schisms developed. And what emerged in the end was very much a collective project, reflecting the contributions of all. In the writing of the final report, *Canadians and Their Pasts,* one or two of us took the lead on each of the chapters, received input and critique from others, and the whole took shape.[3] Nevertheless, there were differences in positions and I am taking this chapter as an opportunity to discuss the project, retrospectively, through my own position, not as a spokesperson for the group.

Historical Consciousness as a Lens for the Project

I came to the study of historical consciousness via an earlier career as a high school history teacher. So, my questions about historical thinking were, from the outset, normative: what does "better" or more competent historical thinking look like, and how could I help my students become more competent? I saw models of competence, or rather expertise, in historical thinking in the work of historians, who displayed respect for evidence, a critical attitude towards received knowledge, and acknowledgement of the interpretive nature of their own narratives.[4] How, I wondered, could teachers help their students develop some of these qualities, which Jon Levisohn has called "interpretive virtues"? The respect for academia as a model of expertise was reinforced early in my tenure as an assistant professor in the influential expert-novice studies in the educational literature, specifically Sam Wineburg's "On the reading of historical texts," which demonstrated how poorly school history taught historians' virtues.[5]

Also key in my early development as a history education scholar was the writing that came out of the British Schools History Project. For someone with a PhD in history, their research methodologies were a revelation: they aimed to understand children's thinking through the analysis of interviews, discussions among students in groups of three, and more traditional paper-and-pencil exercises. Equally important was their conceptual framing of the analysis, now a foundation in the field, through students' progression in their ability to handle second-order history concepts such as evidence, cause, and accounts. At the top of each progression were understandings and practices that looked more like those of historians.

A third formative influence in my early years as an academic was Jörn Rüsen's concept of "historical consciousness" in English translation. Of the many aspects of Rüsen's theories, the most accessible are his four types of historical consciousness: traditional, exemplary, critical, and genetic. These are ranked from the most simple and basic to the most complex and sophisticated. They are reflected, potentially, both in the development of human cultures over time and in the development of children as they get older.

All of these influences have a common substratum: the notion of potential progress in understanding history. It necessitated a judgment of "levels" of competence against a standard that students and teachers might not even have understood. But it also assumed that expert teachers with a well-developed curriculum, using well-crafted texts and materials, would be able to foster improvement in historical understanding of their students.

This idea ran up against a counter-current among the historians and public historians in the team. Who are we to judge, they asked, how people understand and use the past; such assessments should not be part of our investigation. Their careers, in Prairie and Aboriginal history, women's history, labor history, and public history, involved a commitment to understanding how ordinary people lived and worked, using the stories of those lives to expand the depth and richness of Canadian historiography beyond the narrower political histories that had dominated earlier writing. How ordinary Canadians make sense of the past and use it in shaping their lives thus has a certain populist ring which sits uneasily with assessments, levels, ranking, and judgments of competence, sophistication, or lack thereof. Again, who are we to judge?

Reinforcing the populist approach was our immediate precursor, *The Presence of the Past*. Rosenzweig and Thelen used interviews with about eight hundred American adults, plus three special samples of two hundred African Americans, Sioux Indians, and Mexican Americans, as a basis for exploring Americans' interests and involvements in the past. They systematically avoided the term "history," assuming that it would be associated with the school subject and alienate their respondents with the ghosts of memorized dates, boring teachers, musty professors, and dusty archives. In their effort to demonstrate what they called Americans' "connection" to the past, they avoided "history's" connotations of distance, personal irrelevance, and academic expertise.

In adopting this trajectory, as pointed out by Michael Kammen, they largely sidestepped the epistemological problem posed by "history" and "the past."[6] The broad sweep of "the past" to which they sought Americans' "connection" made no distinctions among myth, legend, heritage, and history. As Kammen put it, "they substituted a seemingly innocuous phrase, 'the past,' and then permitted a very wide array of warm and fuzzy past-oriented activities to qualify as history . . ."[7] Kammen's critique was on my mind as we embarked on our study.

The American tension demonstrated in Kammen's critique is also a problem for European theorists of historical consciousness. Rüsen's first and most basic type of historical consciousness is "traditional," characterized by connections to the past. It is consistent with a cyclical notion of time, and a premodern consciousness, where it is both possible and desirable to hand down community values and norms without the need to accommodate or acknowledge new conditions, changed circumstances or other peoples. This is contrasted, at the top of the hierarchy, with "genetic" historical consciousness, which acknowledges the past, but understands the need to adapt to the new and to accommodate the other. While traditional historical consciousness is suitable to the small, insular, homogeneous premodern community, genetic historical consciousness is the best for contemporary cosmopolitan societies, embodying the values of Enlightenment liberalism. The whole scheme has thus been subject to the accusation that it is a restatement of a West-is-best ideology. Some of Rüsen's followers have taken that vulnerability as an opportunity to focus on consciousness of diversity and social inequality.[8]

In large scale, empirical studies of historical consciousness, normative assumptions are unavoidable. Making these explicit, as we did among our team, opens more possibility for discussion. In the culminating publication, there were aspects of both approaches expressed in different chapters.

Methods, Sample, Questions, Findings

Canadians and Their Pasts began with the ambitious idea, reflected in the title, that we wanted to be able to paint the largest and most comprehensive picture possible, reflecting Canadian diversity in a statistically robust way. Two of our team members had extensive backgrounds and expertise in quantitative methods and statistical analysis. Canadian politics, historically and in the present, is largely defined by regions. We designed a sample that would be large enough to make statistically significant comparisons among five regions: British Columbia, the Prairies, Ontario, Québec, and Atlantic Canada, with four hundred interviews each. We also recognized the potentially distinctive ideas of people in Canada's largest cities, so we had an additional sample of nine hundred in Montreal, Toronto, Edmonton, Calgary, and Vancouver. Finally, following Rosenzweig and Thelen, we had special samples of marginalized groups: one hundred each of Aboriginals, Francophone Acadians in New Brunswick, and recent immigrants. We targeted adults, eighteen and over. The response rate to the telephone invitations was an impressive 53 percent. We achieved this rate through persistence: the average refusal to participate received fourteen additional telephone invitations before they were dismissed as non-participants. The interviews, with seventy-five to eighty items, including eleven open ended-questions, averaged twenty-two minutes to complete. In the end, we conducted interviews with 3,419 people.

Six large categories framed the questions, followed by a section on demographic information. In the first section, we asked about general interest in history and the past. For these questions, in order to test Rosenzweig and Thelen's assumption, we divided the entire sample randomly, using "the past" for one third, "history" for one third, and "history and the past" for the final third, to ask about general interest in the past. There were no statistically significant differences in the response rates. Canadians' interest in their families' histories, like the Americans in Rosenzweig and Thelen, trumped interest in national history.

The second section asked a series of questions about activities related to history and the past. Here, we opened the doors as wide as we knew how, to both family and public history, and not only to engagement with representations of history (from books to gaming to visiting an old family house) but also with preservation (such as taking pictures and making scrapbooks). The third section of the interview was introduced by this preamble:

> We would now like to ask how the activities you do that are related to the past help you to understand the past, understand yourself, and feel connected to the past. By "the past" we mean everything from the very recent past to the very distant past, from your personal and family history to the history of Canada and other countries.

Our shorthand for this section was "understanding and connection."

A fourth section asked about what the respondents felt was a trustworthy source of information about the past. Here museums outstripped any other generic category. Towards the end of the section, an open-ended question asked why they believed the source that they had called the most trustworthy was so. The final question in this section read, "When people disagree about something that happened in the past, how do you think they can find out what is most likely to have really happened?" The analysis of the answers to these questions yielded glimpses of the respondents' beliefs about historical epistemology. More than half of the respondents gave answers that we categorized as recognizing the role of the interrogation of sources and a community of inquiry to validate historical interpretations.

We called the final section (before the demographic questions), "the sense of the past." The first were about progress over time: have things improved or gotten worse and what things? And finally, "what is it about history [or 'the past'] that you think should be handed down to the next generation?"

The demographic questions asked about birthplace, ethnic or cultural group, religion if any, language, family status, education, occupation, income, postal code, and access to the internet. These enabled analysis of variance across multiple factors. Across many of the interview questions, education and income, not surprisingly, made a difference: those with more income and education were more likely to visit museums, read books, and engage with other forms of history. Yet, there was no association between income level and expressions of interest in or importance of various levels of the past.[9]

Women were more likely than men to express interest and participate in history-related activities, and even more so with family-related activities. Interest in history increased with older age categories. Across all demographic categories, there was a clear interest in the personal past set within a family context. For many, the researchers found, family history "serves as a foundation for a broader historical consciousness and is a fundamental building block of people's citizenship in their communities, in their country, and in the world."[10]

Family stories and museums occupied two ends of a continuum in inspiring trust, which varied consistently across education, income, and expressions of interest in the past. Those with higher levels of education, income, and interest in the past tended to trust museums more. Those with lower levels tended to trust family stories more. The study concluded that these differences stemmed from trust rooted in personal, relatively unmediated relationships, as opposed to trust rooted in public institutions with standards of professionalism and expertise.[11] The members of the Aboriginal sample expressed less trust in museums and more in stories handed down within families.

Immigrants differed from Canadian-born respondents in some predictable ways: they expressed interest in the pasts of their countries of origins, and interest in passing on this heritage to their children. But their activities in relation to the past were remarkably similar to other Canadians. Moreover, those who had been in Canada more than ten years were even more similar than recent immigrants.

The marginal differences between immigrants and native-born Canadians were responsible for small differences between the responses of populations of the large cities (where more immigrants were concentrated) and the rest of Canada. Those who live in small cities and rural Canada were more likely to be interested in the past close to home than "the past in general."

The investigation concluded,

> [W]e would be wrong to dwell on the differences among Canadians in their relationship to history. A vast majority of people everywhere in the country have turned to the past to help them situate themselves in a rapidly changing present, to connect themselves to others, and to fill their leisure hours.[12]

We also compared the Canadian survey to its recent precursors in the United States and Australia. In a field of considerable similarity, a few differences stood out: the importance of national history was lower for Canadians than in the other two countries; education was more significant in determining engagement with the past for Canadians, compared to Americans; and Americans were more likely than Canadians and Australians to trust personal and family stories. Yet, the study concluded, "the consistency among the three countries in patterns of engagement with the past is what is most striking",[13] reflecting broad similarities in their historical development and contemporary social make-up.

Possibilities and Limitations of this Research

We were well aware of the limitations of survey research from the outset of the project. A twenty-minute phone interview could not plumb the intricacies of an individual's ideas about or understandings of the past. We wrote about twice as many questions as we included in the final survey, recognizing the trade-off between the length of the survey and the number of participants who would be willing to continue to the end of the session. The interview's open-ended questions at least opened a door to those respondents who were interested and able to speak at more length, and many did. *Canadians and Their Pasts* made use of statistical analysis of the quantifiable answers as well as verbatim quotations drawn from the recorded open-ended responses. On the questions of trust in sources, we used qualitative data analysis to code open-ended responses and make some broad generalizations. The research team was aware that, even with the diverse methods of a seven-member team with different disciplinary expertise, there were many paths not taken to explore the mountain of data that we had collected. And so we welcomed compliance with the main funder's rule that the data should be made openly available to the broader research community at the completion of the study.

None of these analytical approaches fully overcame the limitations of the snapshot. We developed some tentative hypotheses about change over time based on variation by the age of respondents, but these were limited. The snapshot based on a single randomized telephone survey was largely unable to provide the basis for claims about trends over time or robust explanations for the differences we found. Despite the fact that we started the study with questions about community and collective memory, the survey methodology is founded on an assumption of atomistic individuals, in the way the data are gathered, in the way they are analyzed, and the way they are reported.

This weakness is the flip side of a strength, however. The dominant tradition in writing about collective memory, at the time when we undertook the study, was the analysis of monuments, memorials, textbooks, other cultural artifacts and even ideas, an approach that reached its apogee in Pierre Nora's *Lieux de Mémoire*. This body of writing depended upon the writer's analysis of the meanings of cultural artifacts. The interview-based survey was, in some sense, an attempt to understand cultural meaning more directly, by hearing people's ideas straight from them. Of course, there is no way to present an unmediated version of Canadians' picture of the past: as noted above, the survey itself involved choices and mediation at every step of the way, from the formulation of the questions, to the analysis of the responses, to the writing of the reports.

A clear example of these choices lies in the positive valuation of "connection" to the past, akin to "understanding." This valuation drew from Rosenzweig and Thelen's writing, as a response to widespread public assertions of alienation from history and loss of the past. We, like they, successfully demonstrated most people's connection to the past, very broadly defined. On the other hand, it could be argued that recognition of *distance* from the past is just as important as a *connection* to the past in understanding our own historicity. The complex dyad of connection and distance is an important stance for understanding and using the past in the present, but difficult to assess in the context of a twenty-minute interview.

What are the possibilities for a robust, dynamic large-scale assessment of historical consciousness that goes beyond the limitations of the survey methodology? The concept of "historical culture," developed most fully by Europeans, notably at Erasmus University's Centre for Historical Culture, points in a very promising direction in that it incorporates both the public expressions of memory in museums, school textbooks, commemorations and the like, and the personal expressions of individuals that we explored in *Canadians and Their Pasts*. Grever and Adriaansen define the conceptual problem succinctly:

> The problem with memory studies is that is has become a discourse that focuses too much on the mnemonic *representations* of specific events within specific social groups, thereby disregarding the production, performance and dissemination of memories in communicative interaction between people, groups and institutions.[14]

The mnemonic infrastructures that enable the creation, transmission, and preservation of cultural memory require study in relation to the ideas, interests, and narratives articulated by individuals. Although *Canadians and Their Pasts* touched on these with a chapter on the institutions of public history in Canada, the survey study itself left these largely in the background, by definition.

The next development in large-scale studies of historical consciousness might attempt to integrate the achievements of the broad survey with a targeted sample of case studies of the institutions and circulation of cultural memory. Creating a theoretical framework for the selection of those cases would be the first task. It might include considerations of scale: from local, community institutions to national and even international. Other considerations might be publicly accountable vs. private initiatives; traditional and long term vs. transient and mobile institutions; and various populations who participate in, contribute to, transform, or simply accept the cultural memories expressed through larger institutions. Coordinating these case studies with survey research will be a daunting task. Interestingly, these ideas were actually part of the initial conception of *Canadians and Their Pasts*, which the job of doing the survey in large part eclipsed. Needless to say, such a project would demand major commitment of teams of researchers as well as funding agencies.

Peter Seixas is Professor Emeritus in the Department of Curriculum and Pedagogy at the University of British Columbia. He was the Founding Director of the Centre for the Study of Historical Consciousness and of The Historical Thinking Project. His writing on teaching and learning history has been recognized with, among other honors, the Canada Research Chair in Historical Consciousness (2001–2014), a fellowship in the Royal Society of Canada, the American Studies Association's Constance Rourke Award, the American Historical Association's William Gilbert Award, and the 2015 Grambs Distinguished Research Career Award from the National Council for Social Studies.

Notes

1. Rosenzweig and Thelen, *Presence of the Past*.
2. Ashton and Hamilton, "At Home with the Past."
3. Conrad et al., *Canadians and Their Pasts*.
4. Seixas, "The Community of Inquiry."
5. Levisohn, *The Interpretive Virtues*; Wineburg, "On the Reading of Historical Texts."
6. Kammen, "Review of Rosenzweig and Thelen."
7. Kammen, "Review of Rosenzweig and Thelen," 233.
8. For an overview, see Kölbl and Konrad, "Historical Consciousness."
9. Conrad et al., *Canadians and Their Pasts*, 41.
10. Conrad et al., *Canadians and Their Pasts*, 83.
11. Conrad et al., *Canadians and Their Pasts*, 55.
12. Conrad et al., *Canadians and Their Pasts*, 47.
13. Conrad et al., *Canadians and Their Pasts*, 150.
14. Grever and Adriaansen, "Historical Culture," 7.

Bibliography

Ashton, Paul, and Paula Hamilton. "At Home with the Past: Background and Initial Findings from the National Survey." *Australian Cultural History* 23 (2003): 5–30.

Conrad, Margaret, Kadriye Ercikan, Gerald Friesen, Jocelyn Létourneau, Delphin Muise, David Northrup, and Peter Seixas. *Canadians and Their Pasts*. Toronto: University of Toronto Press, 2013.

Grever, Maria, and Robbert-Jan Adriaansen. "Historical Culture: A Concept Revisited." In *Palgrave Handbook of Research in Historical Culture and History Education,* edited by Mario Carretero, Stefan Berger, and Maria Grever, 73–89. London: Palgrave Macmillan, 2017.

Kammen, Michael. "Review of Rosenzweig and Thelen, the *Presence of the Past: Popular Uses of History in American Life.*" *History and Theory: Studies in the Philosophy of History* 39, no. 2 (2000): 230–42.

Kölbl, Carlos, and Lisa Konrad. "Historical Consciousness in Germany: Concept, Implementation, Assessment." In *New Directions in Assessing Historical Thinking,* edited by Kadriye Ercikan and Peter Seixas, 17–28. New York: Routledge, 2015.

Levisohn, Jon A. *The Interpretive Virtues: A Philosophical Inquiry into the Teaching and Learning of Historical Narratives*. New York: Wiley-Blackwell, forthcoming.

Rosenzweig, Roy, and David Thelen. *Presence of the Past: Popular Uses of History in American Life*. New York: Columbia University Press, 1998.

Seixas, Peter. "The Community of Inquiry as a Basis for Knowledge and Learning: The Case of History." *American Educational Research Journal* 30, no. 2 (1993): 305–24.

Wineburg, Samuel S. "On the Reading of Historical Texts: Notes on the Breach between School and Academy." *American Educational Research Journal* 28, no. 3 (1991): 495–519.

CHAPTER 8

Private Lives, Public History
Navigating Australian Historical Consciousness

Anna Clark

[History] can be constructed at the dinner table, over the back fence, in parliament, in the streets, and not just in the tutorial room, or at the scholar's desk.
—Tom Griffiths, *Hunters and Collectors*

Australian history has generated intense political and historiographical interest in recent years, as historians, politicians, and public commentators weighed into captivating and divisive contests over the nation's past. Commemorations, museums, and school syllabuses became sites of great public interest and contestation, powerful reminders of the politics of collective memory. While such discussions continue to stimulate argument and analysis in scholarly articles, opinion pieces, and public commentary, little is known of their impact on the wider community. What do so-called "ordinary Australians" think about the nation's past? Are the historical questions raised also debated in our sports clubs, living rooms, and community center kitchenettes? Does that historical concern reach *beyond* opinion pages or academic journals, and across the garden fences that Tom Griffiths wrote about in relation to historical practice?

Private Lives, Public History was to be an answer of sorts. I had been studying Australian historiography, particularly public debates over Australian history, for many years. Yet, I increasingly came to wonder whether anyone outside its often-heated historical perimeters felt similarly engaged

---

Notes for this section begin on page 123.

(or disengaged, I suspected). I wanted to research how everyday people think about history: to ponder how Australians contemplate the national past in the context of their own local and intimate narratives; and, conversely, to try and understand people's own private histories in the context of those powerful historical discourses that dominate public debate.

In devising the project, I drew heavily on Jörn Rüsen's idea of historical consciousness as an aggregation of public historical culture, family/community historical narratives and formal history education. Historical consciousness, Rüsen insists, covers "every form" of thinking about the past, from "historical studies" to the "use and function of history in private and public life." Historical consciousness, as American historian David Glassberg elaborated, asks, "how ideas about history are created, institutionalized, disseminated, understood, and change over time." Taken together, these processes describe humanity's interest in its past—the ways we remember and why, as well as how we learn and engage with historical knowledge and practice.[1]

In particular, I was drawn to Rüsen's inference that historical consciousness explains how individuals make sense of the past as a way of understanding the present and anticipating the future—for historical consciousness is uniquely and ubiquitously human. "We all make histories endlessly," the ethnographic historian Greg Dening once mused. "It is our human condition to make histories." But what do people themselves make of their own "historicity," to use Ricoeur's term? And what do they make of the history around them?[2]

★ ★ ★

That historical condition certainly seems to be booming at a community level. There are tens of thousands of local history groups and museums around Australia, as well as genealogical societies and family history groups. The past is consumed widely, via heritage tours, reading groups, as well as historical fiction, and film and television programs, such as *Who Do You Think You Are?* The growing digitization of archives has also enabled unprecedented access for people to research and write their own family histories. All this has amounted to a great democratization of popular and personal historical practice in recent decades. But to what extent do those intimate pasts intersect with broader historical questions and debates? How do people navigate the *range* of history across those public and private spheres that historical consciousness implies?[3]

Several significant attempts have already been made to explore the historical consciousness of particular nations and communities—like them, I'm interested in navigating history and historiography as social and cultural, as well as professional and political. Studies conducted in the US, Australia, and Canada (which Peter Seixas explores in some detail in his chapter), fundamentally challenged professional understandings about who practices history and what constitutes historical knowledge. They revealed a distinct lack of community engagement with more formal national narratives, which people sense are too prescribed and disconnected from their everyday lives; and they noted a simultaneous popular contemplation of history that Australian researchers Paul Ashton and Paula Hamilton neatly called "past-mindedness."[4]

Although participants in those studies often found it difficult to engage directly with the national history they learned at school, for example, their own stories and experiences generated very strong connections with the past. Respondents kept objects to pass on to their own children or grandchildren, participated in family reunions, compiled genealogies, and visited museums, heritage trails, and historical societies. They talked about the past with their friends and families, and they avidly consumed history—in the form of historical fiction, documentaries, and popular history books.

In other words, as Ashton and Hamilton noted, such research sensed an uneasiness, a "[d]isjuncture between professional historical practice and 'people's History' or history in the 'everyday world.'" One is official and knowledge-based—taught in schools, tested in surveys, and promoted by public institutions. The other is familiar, experiential, and tactile, and is deeply connected to people's families and communities. Yet in thinking through my own research, I wondered whether we could see that space not simply as a disjuncture but also as a possible *intersection*: do these distinct types of history ever come together? And if so, how? How do people think about their own histories in the context of a pervasive national past? And, just as critically, how do they negotiate Australian history in light of their own family and community pasts? These are the questions that framed my work and provided the rationale for its method and approach.[5]

★ ★ ★

The *Private Lives, Public History* project was significantly influenced by those larger mixed-methods studies that preceded it, but it wasn't modelled on them. Instead, I wanted to "listen in" on historical conversations in an attempt to glean the ways Australians negotiate their own individual and collective historical consciousness. And for that, I needed conversations to listen to: small affinity group interviews in distinct communities. I was prepared to sacrifice the bigger quantitative data in order to capture historical dialogue that was as genuine as possible. Using what Adele Clarke calls a "situational analysis," the project mapped the voices of "ordinary people" alongside public debates and discourses, contemplating themes of historical engagement and inheritance, as well as commemoration, historical contestation, and place.[6]

Although it's well to remember that distinguishing the emblematic words of ordinariness from the public discourse they inhabit is both tricky and problematic: politicians and public commentators notoriously draw on the imagery of "ordinary" people for political traction, and as a way of enhancing their political legitimacy. Paradoxically, while "ordinary people" are constantly co-opted into public discourse, little is actually known about how they engage with the nation and how they articulate their own historical consciousness in the context of powerful public historical narratives. Significant scholarship has examined how history is produced and publicly debated around the world, yet the ways ordinary people respond to those public narratives is much harder to gauge, as David Glassberg has intimated. Consequently, there have been "few attempts to track how the processes of historical memory play out in the lives of ordinary people," as history educationist Sam Wineburg notes. How is it "that the proverbial person-on-the-street embodies (or doesn't) the broad social processes posited by theorists of collective memory"?[7]

Despite the obvious problem—using such terms has the tendency to brush over their political potency—I persisted with the image of "ordinary Australians" because it is a well-worn term in the community itself, many of my own respondents self-identified as ordinary people, and I also see the term as fundamental to understanding everyday historical engagement. The participants in this study aren't professional historians, politicians, or public commentators, but they do have opinions about Australian history that warrant acknowledgement and examination.

In the end, I chose five communities that broadly reflect Australia's geographical, cultural, and socioeconomic diversity: Marrickville (a suburb of inner-city Sydney), Chatswood (a community in Sydney's affluent North Shore), Brimbank (a multicultural and working-class community in Melbourne's outer-west), Rockhampton (a large country town and regional hub in Central Queensland), and Derby (a remote town with a large Indigenous population in far northwestern Australia). This wasn't a random or demographically representative snapshot of the Australian population, but a purposive sample of participants who came from different generations, schooling, ethnic background, and class. I was keen to include a range of voices and experiences in these conversations, which would be critical to my exploration of historical consciousness.

Across the five communities, I interviewed twenty-three such groups, which included sporting clubs, historical or heritage societies, bush-regeneration groups, and art groups, as well as seniors' centers, migrant resource centers, and youth groups. The groups averaged four to five participants, which tended to generate fluent, engaged discussion, and lasted for about an hour. In total, I spoke with one hundred people. The average age of the participants was forty-nine, twelve years above the Australian average. This can probably be explained by two factors. First, according to the Australian Bureau of Statistics, Australians are more involved in community groups and volunteering in middle age and following retirement, so that demographic was likely to be over-represented in the community groups I visited. Second, people tend to become more interested in history as they get older, and this was certainly confirmed in my research. In order to minimise that anticipated generational skew, I organized interviews with two youth groups from Chatswood and Brimbank, as well as students from two university classes in Rockhampton and Brimbank.[8]

There was also a significant gender bias among my participants. Only thirty-three men took part in this project. While significant numbers of both men and women participate in volunteering and community engagement in Australia, women tend to be more active in the production of family and community histories.[9] As a result, women were more likely to self-select in response to my interview requests to talk about historical connectedness. To counteract the gender discrepancy that was increasingly apparent as the interviews progressed, I arranged to speak with a group from a men's shed in Chatswood and made sure I conducted one-on-one male interviews in each of the five communities.

Indigenous people were over-represented in these interviews, making up 10 percent of all participants (they comprise 3 percent of the national population). Partly, this was because I was keen to explore their responses to public debates that so prominently hinge on Indigenous history—such as arguments over use of the word "invasion" to describe the European colonization of Australia, or the apology to the "Stolen Generations" (children forcibly removed from their families by successive governments during the twentieth century). Despite their historical prominence, Indigenous voices have been notably absent from the history wars themselves. Meanwhile, migrants made up about 25 percent of the participants, reflecting the migration ratios of the broader community, and they contributed fascinating discussions about the complexity of history and identity, for example, in relation to ideas of home, inheritance, and nation.

This purposive approach to qualitative interviews—what I termed "oral historiography"—enabled me to hone in on particular groups and demographics to explore questions about historical practice that were playing out in my mind as I devised the project. I was particularly interested in whether there were distinct differences between urban and rural respondents in relation to histories of place, for example, as well as the difference in attitudes to Australian history between older white Anglo-Saxon respondents and Indigenous people, as well as people from migrant backgrounds, who have generated important vernacular counter-narratives to the "Australian story."

Yet, I soon came to realize that this more targeted approach also had its own problems. For one thing, I couldn't possibly explore all the different cultural allegiances and identities with such a small sample. So, the question of historical consciousness among the groups and identities I didn't key into increasingly played on my mind. I had hoped that intersections between queer sexuality and history would emerge in the wide-ranging discussions that the interviews prompted (naively, I can see now). And I now regret not speaking with any LGBTI (Lesbian, Gay, Bisexual, Transgender, or Intersex) groups, given the counter-histories—to family, inheritance, and place—they may have generated. I also didn't visit any religious institutions in the five communities. I already had enough community groups taking part without including those from organized religions, and my interviewees included Christians, Muslims, and Hindus, as well as a member of a Chatswood synagogue. Yet, given the influence of religion on historical consciousness, which Roy Rosenzweig and David Thelen explored in depth in their US study, I wonder now whether including a deeply religious group would have offered another perspective.[10] Having said that, it is also clear that even with those demographic limitations mentioned above, the community-based conversations generated by this research were still wide-ranging, and they challenged assumptions that ordinary people don't have much to say about Australian history.

In their interviews, participants were asked to discuss their attitudes and engagement with the histories around them—intimate and personal, as well as national and public. Broadly, the characteristics of historical consciousness highlighted in earlier studies played out. Participants in this project confirm that intriguing historical paradox noted by others: collectively, they maintain deep historical connections day-to-day; they also express a distinct lack of engagement with more formal national narratives, which they consider to be much more prescribed and remote.

For example, these university students from Brimbank in Melbourne were very interested in questions of personal historical inheritance:

> Katy: I have a pendant that my mother received from Ireland when she was a baby. And because it was so expensive to send things over, my aunt sewed it into the gown of one of her baby outfits. She's passed it onto me, and I've passed it onto my daughter now.
> Sylvie: That's nice.
> Sandra: When I got married, my Oma gave me her wedding ring. That's pretty special.[11]

And yet, while history figures in these participants' lives, they don't particularly sense any collective inheritance of Australian history as a national narrative:

Do any of you feel connected to Australia's past?

All: No

Sylvie: Personally, no.

Why is that?

Sandra: I think, I don't know, for me, like, we never even really learnt much Australian history in school. I can't even remember learning about explorers, I mean, let alone Indigenous Australia, or anything.

A group of youth workers in Brimbank also expressed an explicit lack of interest in an official national history:

Do any of you feel at all connected to Australia's past?

Adam: I don't feel particularly connected. Because I see myself as an Aussie and stuff, but like, my family tree and stuff just cut into Australia's history. So we weren't there from the beginning and we don't really have any Australian ancestors or anything like that. So I don't feel particularly connected, but it's interesting. It's not really a part of me so much.

Mike: The thing is, we all pretty much know the Australian history. The Hume and Hovell monument is over there [pointing], we know about the goldrush and all that stuff. But all that stuff happened however long ago, and all that stuff changes so quickly, it's just not us. We're us for us, not for what they were.

I tended to visit these communities, like Brimbank, over the course of about a week in order to contextualize the groups with the place itself. In between interviews I walked around taking notes, I read local history books, I visited community and historic sites, and I listened to the ways people talk about local history around their monuments, memorials, and museums. The Hume and Hovell monument that the youth workers referred to commemorates the journey of the two famous explorers who walked from Sydney to Port Phillip (present-day Melbourne) in the 1820s, and after whom the present national highway between the two cities is named. Although, the large stone cairn they referred to is located, rather perfunctorily I thought, next to a busy suburban road.

Clearly, while participants were aware of its existence, they didn't feel any strong literal connection to that history of colonial exploration. Those young Australians feel as if they have been exposed to an official national narrative, but that narrative doesn't properly speak to their own experiences—"it's just not us," as Mike admitted. It was a clear illustration of the paradox of historical consciousness that Rosenzweig and Thelen tried to unravel. But in these conversations, it seemed that many respondents were working through it themselves. A few even sought to explain why family history elicits such strong personal meaning when official histories seem to fall flat. *Do these family stories make you feel more connected to the past than, say, history that you learn in class?* I asked Manisha, a university student from Brimbank. "I think it's different," she said, "because you're connected to that history or that part of history, rather than history as a whole, you know what I mean? That's my personal view anyway." Douglas from Marrickville said that he felt connected to Australian history "in an intimate unofficial way." But in "an official sense," he continued, "I feel totally alienated from what it means to be an Australian."

For some, comments like these verify the disjuncture between professional historical practice and popular history-making noted by several historians. In a review of Rosenzweig and Thelen's *Presence of the Past,* the late Michael Kammen argued that despite the pressure to democratize the discipline of history, everyday historical understandings are not equivalent to scholarly expertise: "family and pastness are clearly not the same as history and should not be casually conflated with it." John Tosh made a similar claim when he insisted that "thinking *about* history" and "thinking *with* history" are not the same thing. "Increasingly, the popular embrace of history is an emotional embrace," Australian historian Mark McKenna more recently added, "one that runs counter to the more critical understanding brought to the past by historians."[12]

The *Private Lives, Public History* project certainly confirmed that gap between national and intimate, public and private. Yet it also found several vital points of intersection, which confound such interpretations of a booming popular interest in the past, as public and official narratives languish beside them. In fact, it suggests historical consciousness is composed of *constant* intersections between public and private encounters with the past, such that it's sometimes hard to distinguish between the official and the intimate. *How do you feel on a historic day such as Australia Day?* I asked the Bushcare Group in Chatswood. *Do you feel connected to the past?*

> Daniel: Absolutely. I think it's a great celebration. [The Bicentenary in] '88 was fantastic—you could almost walk across the harbour! It was a sensational day. One big party, I suppose, that's why it appealed.
>
> *For its history or its celebration?*
>
> Daniel: Um, well the history was when Australia was discovered—that's what they were celebrating.
>
> Nick: Or invaded, if you want a different perspective, I do sympathize with the Aboriginal point, that this is not an appropriate day to celebrate, and that maybe we should have a different day.

National, public narratives constantly overlap with our own historical views, as this group at the Chatswood men's shed reveal in a conversation about how they felt about the apology to the Stolen Generations:

> Nigel: What gets me with the Stolen Generation is that it was going on when I was alive and I didn't know anything about it, and I'm embarrassed by the fact that my parents didn't do anything about it, in a political way.
>
> Robert: They wouldn't have thought that it was wrong. They thought that they were doing what was right at the time.

Taken together, both comments reveal the tension of historical empathy and judgment across time: Nigel is dismayed that he could have been ignorant of the Stolen Generation, and that his parents "didn't do anything" about it; Robert empathises with the historical protagonists, sensing they acted in the belief that what they were doing "was right at the time." Their conversation also reveals a significant moment of historical consciousness—between the history of Australia, and people's personal experience of that history: I see in these interviews that Australians *do* grapple with the tensions between past and present. Given the high-stakes of the history wars, that everyday capacity to understand not only history's subjectivity, but also the difficulty of historical judgment was surprising. I also never anticipated the groups would be so gently accommodating of each other's historical differences.

Clearly, these vernacular historical attachments don't uphold the sort of historical complexity and sophistication of scholarly historians. But that doesn't mean their histories are parochial or simplistic, either: participants' interests in the past are broad and complex, they're aware of history's subjectivity, and they understand its elusiveness—that it can be remembered *and* forgotten. What's more, it's in their conversations that we are able to discern the intersections of public and private that coalesce in forming historical consciousness.

Over the last thirty or forty years there has been a great *peopling* of history—a historical "enfranchisement," as Jerome de Groot calls it. History has become more and more inclusive, both in its content and its practice: "ordinary people" are more visible in historical narratives, and are also increasingly equipped to produce their own. This radical democratization of the discipline has challenged professional assumptions about what history is, who does it, and how. Eighty years after American historian Carl Becker famously called for the recognition of "Mr. Everyman" as a historian, we might just about be there.[13]

And yet many academic historians are wary of this impressive expansion, balking at the very connectedness so many Australians feel in relation to the histories they consume: from collective commemorations such as Anzac Day, historical re-enactments and pilgrimages, to popular histories written outside the academy. "In popular memory, the *distance* from the past prized by professional historians takes second place to being *present* in the past, to the language of immediacy, spectacle and recreation," writes McKenna. "The boundaries that once separated history from fiction and myth appear more blurred."[14]

Yet the *Private Lives, Public History* project also reveals that these historical domains overlap continuously in everyday life. The impact of the history we learn at school, view in museums, and commemorate collectively is simultaneously shaped by our family and community histories. Contests over the past between historians, politicians, and public commentators echo our own historical subjectivities.

What I wasn't able to show was why.

While the research provides an important account of historical consciousness in Australia, in particular, the ways individual and collective historical narratives intersect, it raises several historical questions that demand attention. For example, the interviews reveal a profound historical pluralism across the Australian community, indicating that simplistic and divisive historical debates such as the history wars simply don't match up with people's own historical experiences. Take this quote from Deborah in Sydney's Chatswood: "Well, I think the line between history and politics is often very thin," she observed. In Brimbank, Silvie was similarly suspicious: "I tend to think that if it's a politician, that they've got a hidden agenda," she explained. "So I'm always sceptical if there is a public debate with politicians or with governments involved—that there is something behind it, that they're trying to convey another message, an alternative message." And yet, if so-called "ordinary Australians" don't buy into politicized debates over the past, why does Australian history continue to generate such political traction? Despite conducting a pilot focus group interview before the project, that question of why only became apparent towards the end of writing up the research. And I think answering it requires a different sort of analysis from historical consciousness.

Further unanswered questions also quickly became apparent after the interviews. If people connect to the past through personal experience, is it possible to have historical critique and interrogation that doesn't offend or silence other people's "pasts" and "stories"? And if they are drawn to histories that connect them, how should citizens learn about more removed, or "boring" histories that are also deemed important?

What I see now as a gap in my research is at least in part a result of the research design itself: because I wanted to populate public historical discourse with the voices of everyday Australians, the sort of critical interrogation of their transcripts required for such analysis never seemed quite right. Building on de Groot, I wanted to enfranchise my participants with this research, and produce a piece of work they would be interested to see themselves represented in, rather than deconstruct their every utterance. But in taking that approach, I can now see moments in the interviews and data analysis where edgier critique might have produced some meatier answers—although would have simultaneously run the risk of offending the participants. That is surely one of the conundrums of work in historical consciousness: to what extent do we (as researchers) need to understand it as a social process, or as a way of discerning hierarchies of historical understanding?

Even now, I'm not certain I have the answer to that one. Ultimately, I'm proud of this project, but I can't pretend those analytical gaps don't niggle. Hopefully, I can revisit them with a punchier set of research questions next time.

Anna Clark holds an Australian Research Council Future Fellowship at the Australian Centre for Public History, University of Technology Sydney. She has written extensively on history education, historiography and historical consciousness, including: *Private Lives, Public History* (2016), *History's Children: History Wars in the Classroom* (2008), *Teaching the Nation: Politics and Pedagogy in Australian History* (2006), and the *History Wars* (2003) with Stuart Macintyre, as well as two history books for children, *Convicted!* and *Explored!* Reflecting her love of fish and fishing, she has also recently finished a history of fishing in Australia.

Notes

1. Rüsen, "The Didactics of History," 281; Glassberg, *Sense of History*, 18.
2. Seixas, "Introduction"; Rüsen, "Tradition," 45; Dening, *Performances*, 35; Ricoeur, *Hermenuetics*, 274.
3. Arrow, "'I Just Feel it's Important'"; Sear, "A Thousand Different Hands."
4. Ashton and Hamilton, *History at the Crossroads*; Conrad et al., "Canadians and Their Pasts"; Conrad et al., *Canadians and Their Pasts*; Rosenzweig and Thelen, *The Presence of the Past*.
5. Ashton and Hamilton, *History at the Crossroads*, 8.
6. Clarke, *Situational Analysis*.
7. Glassberg, *Sense of History*, 16; Wineburg, *Historical Thinking*, 249.
8. Ashton and Hamilton, *History at the Crossroads*; Conrad et al., *Canadians and Their Pasts*; Rosenzweig and Thelen, *The Presence of the Past*.
9. Ashton and Hamilton, *History at the Crossroads*; Conrad et al., *Canadians and Their Pasts*; Rosenzweig and Thelen, *The Presence of the Past*.
10. Rosenzweig and Thelen, *The Presence of the Past*.
11. Names of participants have been changed.
12. Kammen, "Carl Becker Redivivus," 234; Tosh, *Why History Matters*, 6–7; McKenna, "The History Anxiety," 580.
13. de Groot, "Empathy and Enfranchisement"; Becker, "Everyman his Own Historian," 235.
14. McKenna, "The History Anxiety," 580.

Bibliography

Arrow, Michelle. "'I Just Feel it's Important to Know Exactly What He Went Through': In Their Footsteps and Australian Television History." *Historical Journal of Film, Radio and Television* 33, no. 4 (2013): 594–611.

Ashton, Paul, and Paula Hamilton. *History at the Crossroads: Australians and the Past.* Sydney: Halstead Press, 2010.

Becker, Carl. "Everyman his Own Historian." In *Everyman his Own Historian,* edited by Carl Becker. Chicago: Quadrangle Books, 1966.

Clarke, Adele. *Situational Analysis: Grounded Theory After the Postmodern Turn.* Thousand Oaks, CA: Sage Publications, 2006.

Conrad, Margaret, Jocelyn Létourneau, and David Northrup. "Canadians and Their Pasts: An Exploration in Historical Consciousness." *The Public Historian* 31, no. 1 (2009): 15–34.

Conrad, Margaret, Kadriye Ercikan, Gerald Friesen, Jocelyn Létourneau, Delphin Muise, David Northrup, and Peter Seixas. *Canadians and Their Pasts.* Toronto: University of Toronto Press, 2013.

de Groot, Jerome. "Empathy and Enfranchisement: Popular histories." *Rethinking History* 10, no. 3 (2006): 391–413.

Dening, Greg. *Performances.* Melbourne: Melbourne University Press, 1996.

Glassberg, David. *Sense of History: The Place of the Past in American Life.* Amherst: University of Massachusetts Press, 2001.

Griffiths, Tom. *Hunters and Collectors: The Antiquarian Imagination in Australia.* Melbourne: Cambridge University Press, 1996.

Kammen, Michael. "Carl Becker Redivivus: Or, Is Everyone Really a Historian?" *History and Theory* 32, no. 2 (2000): 230–42.

McKenna, Mark. "The History Anxiety." In *The Cambridge History of Australia,* vol. 2, edited by Alison Bashford and Stuart Macintyre, 561–80. Port Melbourne: Cambridge University Press, 2013.

Ricoeur, Paul. *Hermenuetics and the Human Sciences.* Cambridge: Cambridge University Press, 1981.

Rosenzweig, Roy, and David Thelen. *The Presence of the Past: popular uses of history in American life.* New York: Columbia University Press, 1998.

Rüsen, Jörn. "The Didactics of History in West Germany: Towards a New Self-Awareness of Historical Studies." *History and Theory* 26, no. 3 (1987): 275–86.

Rüsen, Jörn. "Tradition: A Principle of Historical Sense-Generation and its Logic and Effect in Historical Culture." *History and Theory* 51, no. 4 (2012): 45–59.

Sear, Martha. "A Thousand Different Hands: History in Communities." In *Australian History Now,* edited by Anna Clark and Paul Ashton, 198–214. Sydney: New South, 2013.

Seixas, Peter. "Introduction." In *Theorizing Historical Consciousness,* edited by Peter Seixas, 3–24. Toronto: University of Toronto Press, 2006.

Tosh, John. *Why History Matters.* Bassingstoke: Palgrave Macmillan, 2008.

Wineburg, Sam. *Historical Thinking and Other Unnatural Acts: Charting the Future of Teaching the Past.* Philadelphia: Temple University Press, 2001.

CHAPTER 9

"Chinese and Their Pasts"

Exploring Historical Consciousness of Ordinary Chinese—Initial Findings from Chongqing

Na Li

Public History in China: A Sketch

In the first fifteen years of the new millennium, information technology has fundamentally changed China. In 2015, with the launch of "pre-5G" technology and faster internet connection, the Chinese spent more time flipping through their smart phones, and began to access information that seemed impossible before. The number of social media users has increased dramatically, with a rough estimate of about almost 450 million, nearly one-quarter of such users worldwide. That freer flow of information represents an expanded public space for discussing many historical issues. When ordinary Chinese more critically reflect upon and react to the dominant univocal narrative, when history seems thriving outside the academy in China, when old historical materials are re-interpreted for new use, when episodes of history invite multiple interpretations, a strange paradox looms large: a lament from professional historians and history educators on the public ignorance of or indifference to the past becomes equally loud.

Are ordinary Chinese truly disengaged from the past? All sorts of forces, particularly grassroots ones, challenge the assumption that: (1) formal history education—text books, mandatory history exams, and in-class instructions—systematically indoctrinates young minds, confirms their knowledge about the past, and subsequently determines their historical consciousness; and

---

Notes for this section begin on page 140.

(2) historians and history educators play a primary role in shaping the historical consciousness of ordinary people. The term "public history" has appeared mostly outside, but also with some caveats, inside the Chinese academy. "It (public history) epitomizes a field, an attitude, a movement, and a popular culture."[1]

With emerging social media and new technologies, the public consumption of history has grown more creative. A proliferation of museums, re-vamped historical sites, memorials and monuments, historic districts and cities, for example, indicates an increasing occupation with the past. Chinese museums received 500 million more visitors in 2013 than in 2009.[2] In 1949, there were twenty-five museums when the Communist Party took control. Many were burned down during the Cultural Revolution (1966–1976) and their collections dispersed. Consequently, most of the public regard selected collections and banal presentations, accompanied with censored interpretations, as propaganda serving the Party's interest. With rapid economic growth, urbanization, and the "reform and opening up" policies since 1978, China launched a museum-building boom. Every provincial capital is constructing a new museum or renovating the ones it already has. The National People's Congress has named museum growth as a goal in both of its five-year plans since 2010. Private and industry-based art collectors often receive favorable government real estate deals for their museums.[3] And, despite the mixed motivations for founding and lack of curatorial skills, private museums also have developed exponentially. Chinese officials and museum professionals are now faced with an increasing demand from a public that is hungry to stay in touch with the past.

The expansion of public history in China, despite unearthing an uneasy relationship with some aspects of its past, can be seen as a search for citizenship and new contemporary Chinese identity. Public debates have begun to emerge over the place of the past in China, exploring the role of history in national culture and society, the role of historians and formal history education, and forms of participation in history. In turn, these discussions have raised further questions, such as: how should the past be re-interpreted? Who owns the past? How is history produced, disseminated, consumed, and shared in the public sphere? How can China create a historically based national culture?

Yet, the issue of how the scholarly world responds when history is increasingly produced and consumed by public audiences remains. A National Public History Seminar and the First National Conference on Public History that took place in 2013 demonstrated joint efforts from within and outside the academy. Both conferences confirmed that public history practices are far ahead of the academy: popular history is thriving, and the public is passionate about the past. Yet the broader inquiries for historians and history educators remain largely unanswered. As primary guardians of the past, how are they to communicate the past if they do not understand the historical sense and sensibility of the general public? How is an academic sense of history different from a public sense of history? What role should historians and history educators play in the growing public debates about the past? Which leads us, ultimately, to the question: how do ordinary Chinese think about, learn, and use the past?

History, Memory, and Historical Consciousness

Historical consciousness is an understanding of the past, present, and future, and how this understanding converges to manifest in different genres in individuals' sense-making process. The consciousness-building process breaks into three interconnected genres: collective memory, morality, and pedagogy. Though a comprehensive survey of theories about historical consciousness falls outside the scope of this chapter, the "Chinese and Their Pasts" project forms a critical initial inquiry into historical consciousness.

Hans-Georg Gadamer defines historical consciousness as a specific cultural development located in the modern era, in which contemporary societies have a full awareness of the historicity of present-day life. He further relates historical consciousness to "tradition," where "modern consciousness—precisely as 'historical consciousness'—takes a reflexive position concerning all that is handed down by tradition."[4] Amos Funkenstein connects historical consciousness and collective memory, arguing that "historical consciousness is a developed and organized form of collective memory, both of which contribute to additional historical understanding."[5] Here, individual and collective understandings of the past, the cognitive and cultural factors that shape those understandings, as well as the relations of historical understandings to those of the present and the future, all converge.

Consciousness and memories both belong to realms of human collectives, so do their representational forms or genres. If remembering is a mental activity, it has to happen within a certain social and cultural fame. Similarly, historical consciousness, expressed through narratives, makes sense only in a broader social and cultural context. The "Chinese and Their Pasts" project assumes the connection between historical consciousness and collective memory and focuses on understanding the historical consciousness of ordinary Chinese through different genres;[6] more precisely, it explores how "historical consciousness" is related to historical understanding, experience, memories, imagination, and the market-oriented quest for the past. As the Chinese generally still claim pride in their ancient origin and long history, this project also sheds light on historical consciousness at the national level, where collective memory morphs into national memory, and historical consciousness into national consciousness.

Benedict Anderson poignantly expresses that a nation is "an imagined political community," a product of an invented past that gives it esteem and a discrete narrative: "the nation is always conceived as a deep, horizontal comradeship . . . for so many people . . . willing to die for such limited imaginings, ..."[7] While Anderson's analysis focuses on the role of written and print material in laying the bases for national consciousness in profound ways, other narrative media for national consciousness, such as historic sites, monuments, museums, novels, movies, plays, and literary works also emanate a powerful national discourse. In France, Pierre Nora's monumental work on places/sites of national significance argues that an inventory of *loci memoriae* (including geographical place or locus, historical figures, monuments and buildings, literary and artistic objects, emblems, commemorations, and symbols) constitutes an imaginary process that codifies and represents historical consciousness. "If memory places are symbolic in nature it is because they signify the context and totemic meaning from which collective identity emerges."[8]

Various narrative media express in different ways how such traditions—an illusion of continuity—are translated into nationally acclaimed "tradition." It is in this connection with national tradition that historical consciousness reveals its pedagogical and moral implications. Jörn Rüsen's pioneering work attempts to understand the relationship between historical consciousness, moral values, and reasoning; it evokes the past as a mirror of experience within which life in the present is reflected and its temporal features revealed. Historical consciousness makes an essential contribution to moral-ethical consciousness: "For such a mediation between values and action-oriented actuality, historical consciousness is a necessary prerequisite."[9] One form of such morality-building is institutionalized history teaching. Built on these theoretical threads, the "Chinese and Their Pasts" project explores the material, narrative, didactic, and moral genres of historical consciousness of ordinary Chinese.

The Project: Chinese and Their Pasts

A vital inquiry from multiple perspectives, this project takes place in a social context marked by freer and unprecedented information flow, creative knowledge-sharing, and a growing consumption of history in China during the first fifteen years of the twenty-first century. Public history is contested and messy, yet it boasts incredible energy. As ordinary Chinese pursue the past actively, and make it part of everyday life, historians and history educators seem reluctant to embrace the cacophonous noises from their rigidly defined disciplinary boundaries.

Here is a series of themes and signposts for the overall historical landscape in China, which the project attempted to address:

History, tradition, and national memory/myth-making
Family history: private memory and public story
The visuals as public history
Struggling for authenticity: trustworthiness of source information
Places or sites of public history[10]
Ethnic minorities: represented or suppressed?
Voices from Taiwan: a different sense of history
History and the media
Historical consciousness and history education

Based on the above aspects, the survey breaks into six parts:[11]

1. Activities related to the Past
2. Trustworthiness of Sources of Information about the Past
3. How Connected to the Past People Feel on Certain Occasions
4. The Importance of Various Pasts
5. Importance of Places or Sites of Public History
6. Biographical Data

The project draws on a series of national and regional survey projects in the United States, a few European countries, Australia, and Canada.[12] While the project hopes to yield data that is comparable with those studies, it also realizes the limitations of those earlier works, in which nationally representative samples were collected, yet lacked in-depth analysis into the attitudes of the cross-section of the populations. Furthermore, the quantitative approach taken in those projects poses a significant methodological challenge in terms of investigating people's attitudes towards the past. Despite Rosenzweig and Thelen's ambitious survey design, ensuring that it followed the highest professional standards of academic survey research, the *Presence of the Past* project had general biases in collecting the statistical samples, especially in its use of telephone interview surveys.[13] Though the surveys in the US, Australia, and Canada used some methods employed by ethnographers and oral historians, they were neither ethnography nor oral history. All studies used computer software for coding the data, which required a certain level of uniformity in format and layout, and raised important methodological questions about coding people's emotional attachment to the past, which the researchers noted in their reflections and analysis.

In attempting to overcome these methodological challenges, the "Chinese and Their Pasts" project uses interview surveys as the basic methodology. This means a group of interviewers, with a similar background (college-level students), having received the same interview training, work in a particular geographical region, in this case, the major historic sites in the city of Chongqing.[14] As public history in China follows a different trajectory, the survey differs from the previous studies in the following ways. First, the project emphasizes place or sites of public history. One section explores people's attitudes towards these places and evaluates how public history works or fails at these places. Second, the project engages new media and digital storytelling. As the digital revolution has impacted the venues of accessing historical information, sense of history, and sense of place, so the survey, in its online format, provides an open communicative interface. Third, the project includes oral history interviews to selected questions in each section. Last, the core sample of 425 participants is complemented with thirty subsamples from Taiwan, forty subsamples from ethnic minorities, and eighty-five subsamples from one of the key museums in the city of Chongqing as a result of a year-long institutional collaboration.

Initial Findings: A Statistical Overview

The initial findings from Chongqing present a broad picture of what this project aims to achieve. A general statistical overview reveals some clear perspectives.

Historical Activities

Figure 9.1 shows the range of past-related activities in which interviewees participated. The questions investigate some past-related activities that respondents participated in during the past twelve months. A close-ended question is followed by open-ended requests for a more specific and in-depth probe. Follow-up questions aim to establish a wider social or historical context, to obtain more specific information, or to understand more about motives, emotions, and other psychological implications. For example:

> Question 1.1.1
> *During the past 12 months, have you watched any movies or television programs about the past?*
>
> Question 1.1.2
> *What kind of movies or television programs about the past do you like? What did you like about it? Or why did you think it was interesting?*

The activities fall into two main categories: one is personal, familial, and local; and the other, public, political, and organizational. More specifically,

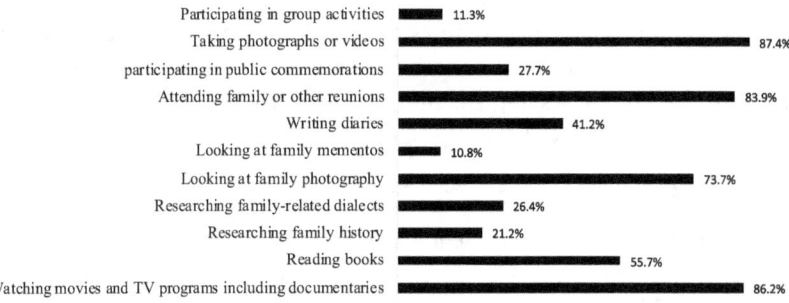

Figure 9.1. Historical activities

the first category includes watching movies and television programs (including documentaries), reading books, researching family history, telling family stories, researching family-related dialects, looking at family photographs, looking at family mementos, writing dairies, attending family or other reunions, and taking photographs or videos. The second category includes participating in public anniversaries and commemorations, and participating in past-related group activities.

The most frequently identified activities (over 80 percent) were taking photographs and videos (with looking at family photographs as its sub-category), watching movies (including documentaries) and television programs, and attending family reunions or other reunions. This hardly came as a surprise, as mass media such as films, videos, and television programs are already an integral part of ordinary people's daily life in China. The results also demonstrate how collective remembering and personal reminiscence often overlap: personal and family reminiscence are interwoven with nostalgic historical consumption, confirmed in the survey results by participants' active engagement with the past. And, overall, public activities, such as participating in public commemoration and anniversaries, and organizations about preserving the past were of secondary importance.

However, a number of issues emerged during the research which complicated the primacy of family history and popular history that was emerging, and required thought from the design team. In the pilot survey,[15] some respondents were confused about historical movies and documentaries. The word "mementos" also caused some confusion, as its Chinese equivalent, *chuanjiabao,* suggests something sacred, expensive, and invaluable. So in the survey, we explained it as something worthy of passing down to the next generation, regardless of monetary value. Moreover, not all family-related activities were ranked high, such as researching family history/heirlooms or family-related dialects. This does not necessarily indicate a lack of interest in these activities. Instead, in traditional Chinese culture, keeping family histories are deemed highly private, so it is difficult to "research" family history in cultural institutions such as public libraries, as most family keep their own heirlooms. Also, in a highly hierarchical culture, family history is usually left to the most senior ones in the family, and significant numbers of our participants do not belong to that age group.

Trustworthiness

Archives (87.79 percent), museums (85.97 percent), historic sites or monuments (83.25 percent), personal or eyewitnesses' accounts (81.20 percent) were ranked by far the most reliable source of history. The majority of respondents expressed that objects were more reliable than human interpretations, as people interpret things differently based on their motives, quality, and background. Materiality—concrete, touchable, first-hand—they agreed, means reliable:

> 'The objects in the museums, architecture in the historic districts, and etc.—I can touch and feel them. Even if they change over time, the traces still tell powerful stories about the pasts.'

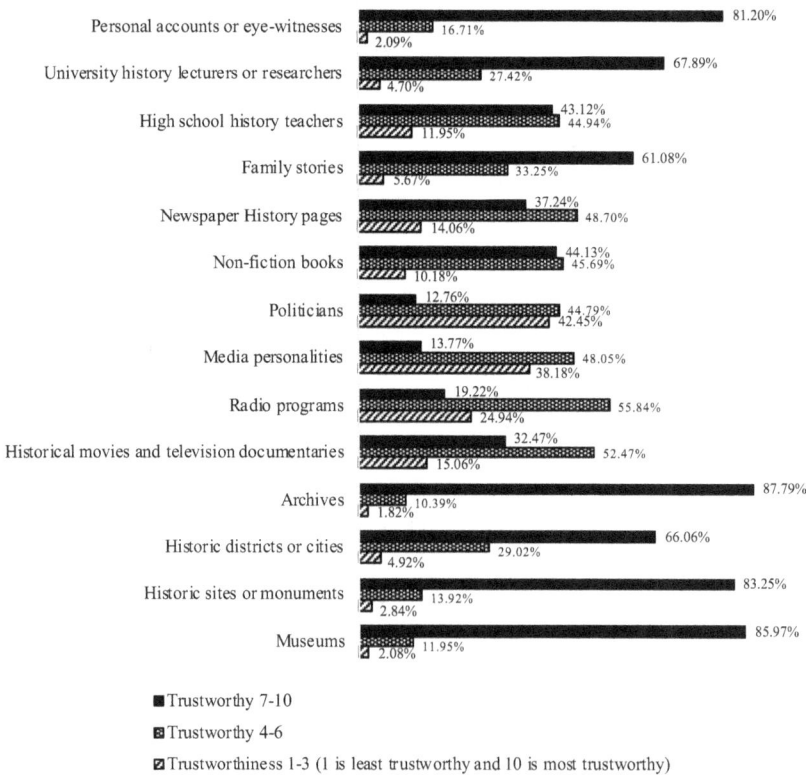

Figure 9.2. Trustworthiness of source of information about the past

'Most eye-witnesses tell true stories, because they go through those events therefore [they have the] most authority. Even with some emotions, and memory deficiency, the source from the eye-witnesses is reliable.'

Institutional authority counts heavily in the general Chinese mentality, since in China, being official often equals to being reliable. This was echoed in the views of many respondents:

'National museums are most reliable, because the central government possessed the highest authority.'

'If the source is related to our country or Chinese communist party, it cannot go wrong.'

'Many cultural institutions, such as museums and memorials, they have the responsibility for cultural continuity, therefore authority, because they service the public. Educating the public about what happened in the past is their priority, and being trustworthy is highly critical in achieving this.'

Professional authority follows. Once material culture is interpreted by professionals, it seems more reliable. This implies that professional voices actually count in the public's pursuit of reliable historical information, and scholarly authority plays an important part in shaping the public's perceptions of the past. As one respondent acknowledged, "what displays in the museums are usually rigorously researched, and carefully, interpreted by professional historians, and protected by the government, therefore reliable."

University history lectures and researchers (67.89 percent) ranked higher than high school history teachers (43.12 percent), which suggests that people have a high respect for professional historians:

'History teachers and researchers help us understand the past better, and they pursue an authentic history . . .'

'College history professors, especially those with independent and critical thinking, are trained to disseminate reliable historical information. They will not lie.'

'I believe in professional interpretations of historical events, because they are usually rigorously researched, and referenced.'

'Professional historians usually do not fabricate facts, as they are trained for scholarly justice.'

Family stories were ranked relatively high (61.08 percent), but for a different reason. People trust family stories simply because "how can my family members lie to me?" Most respondents felt that they could cup these family stories in their hands and hold them to their heart. According to this view, the very familiarity of a family story creates a natural reliability. Here, similar to personal or eye-witness accounts, most respondents confused "motives" with "results": the fact that someone does not have a motive for lying does not mean they actually lie or that their interpretations are necessarily reliable.

Unsurprisingly, politicians (12.76 percent) and media personalities (13.77 percent) were ranked the lowest. The data conveys an overwhelming mistrust about public figures. Most respondents viewed politicians and media personalities as subjective, politically biased, profit-driven, and consequently, without any integrity, or lack of any long-term vision. Some even accused politicians as "professional liars."

Connectedness to the Past

Figure 9.3 demonstrates how connected people feel when participating in certain history-related activities. Visiting history museums, historic sites/monuments, historic districts/cities were ranked highest (75.59 percent). The majority of the respondents suggested that participating in these activities was a direct, authentic historical experience, characterized by a strong sense of participation and "being-there" quality. These activities also shortened the temporal distance from historical events, especially museums built on sites, historic districts with living history, and reliving historical experiences through reenactment. The material culture spoke convincingly about what happened in the past, as one respondent said: "Monuments, for example, demonstrate how our countries come about, and some of survivors of the revolutions tell their own stories—which seems so true, and so powerful."

Celebrating public anniversaries (55.15 percent) and reading books about the past (60.48 percent) were also ranked high, but for divergent reasons. For public anniversaries, respondents cherished a sense of participation, and often, felt proud of being part of collective remembering:

'These commemorations are usually planned out and organized by professionals, and come with certain authority.'

'Public commemorations are group activities, and I feel part of a collective remembering.'

'The National Day, for example, the parade makes us feel proud, and reflective.'

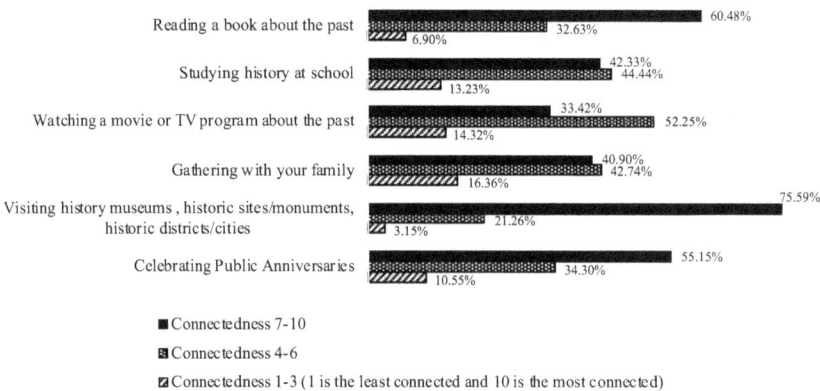

Figure 9.3. Connectedness to the past

Quite a few respondents mentioned the National Day as an important occasion for personal and collective reminiscence of national history. Sympathetic triggers included singing the national anthem, parades, and fireworks: "This year is the seventieth anniversary of WWII victory, public commemorations/pageantry evokes a strong sense of history." In China, this link with milestone historical events possesses a kernel of truth. National consciousness finds resonance in the public ground; tradition, continuity, and patriotism are all interwoven into part of contemporary life. "If some events are commemorated by the public, it must be true history—the public cannot be easily fooled, right?" said one respondent.

A high percentage of people felt connected when reading books about the past, probably because reading is easily accessible, and because books are related to a certain sort of authority, they seem a "natural" way to cultivate a sensible and informative citizenship.

That studying history at school (42.33 percent) was ranked close to the average of historical connectedness seems to indicate another venue for professional authority at work. Some respondents compared their experience of visiting history museums and studying history as school, suggesting the difference lies in approach, not the content. Instead of being contradictory, all approaches are complementary, conveying an equal sense of pride, and getting in touch with historical events or occasions.

Various Pasts

Figure 9.4 indicates respondents' attitude towards various pasts. The past of China (64.86 percent) and the past of your family (62.32 percent) were both ranked high. In fact, the majority of the respondents associated na-

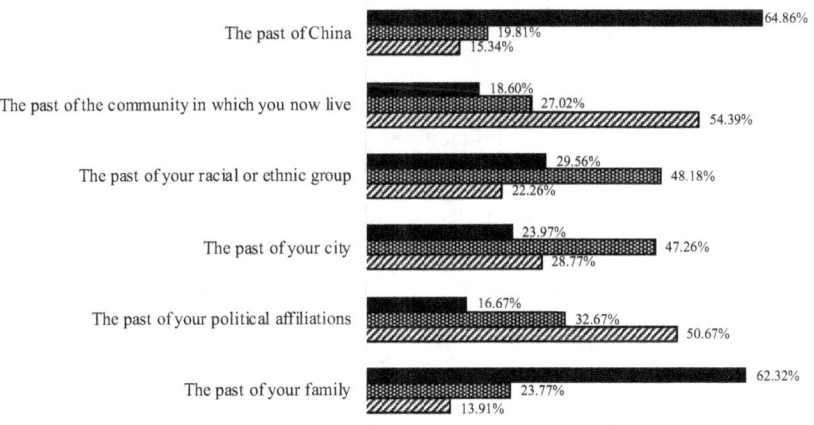

Figure 9.4. The importance of various pasts

tional history with family history. They identified with the nation as one unity, where their individual family was indistinguishable from the nation. Their commentaries are patriotic, possessive, and proud. This emotional vocabulary, built into the national fabric, is unsurprising as Chinese people are genuinely proud of their ancient origin, and an often quoted "5000-year history." The Chinese government has, tactfully and successfully, inculcated young Chinese minds with its ideological values: from straightforward patriotic education which prizes Chinese revolutionary history to a more subtle form of citizenship grounded in understanding the nation's past, patriotic spirit permeates every possible field, morals, language, history, heritage, geography, sport, and arts, to name but a few. The symbolic importance of history, in various representations, reflects new, albeit vagarious, directions in government thinking on how to use the past to create a future that serves its political agenda.

> 'We cannot separate our country (*Guo*) with our family (*Jia*).'
>
> 'Everyone is responsible for his country.' (*Tian Xia Xing Wang, Pi Fu You Ze*.)
>
> 'Wherever we go, we will be Chinese, which lies in our roots of existence.'
>
> 'I love my country, so I cherish its long and ancient history.'
>
> 'National history needs certain continuity. China is a country with a long history, for which I am immensely proud.'

About family history, one respondent said, "Family is the closest to my life. It teaches me where I am from. Family history is concrete, close, and familiar." Yet personal and family pasts are intimately connected with national consciousness. The majority of respondents thought it important for their next generations to know about national and family pasts:

> 'For cultural continuity, national history and family history will be most important to pass down to the next generation.'
>
> 'Modern Chinese history since 1840s is filled with shame and poverty, but it also a history of struggle, of change. So today, we still need to be grateful for generations of Chinese who sacrificed their individual lives to lead to where we are. These are key chapters in Chinese history, and should be remembered.'

Certain qualities, usually acclaimed as national virtue and fine tradition, were frequently mentioned by most respondents, such as morality, diligence, etiquette, hard-working, plain living, unity, spiritual continuity, and historical memories as part of a collective, national consciousness.

However, "collective" and "national" need to be qualified. The subsample from Taiwan seems to indicate a different understanding of "national history" due to historical reasons. "China is far, and I do not know much about Chinese history," said one respondent. Long regarded as one province of China, and pressured by the "one China" idea, Taiwan has had a "very different" history since the second half of the nineteenth century, especially from 1945–1949, and logically, a different historical consciousness follows. "Patriotic education," counter-intuitively, fuels nationalism on both side of the strait: Yes, I love China, but MY China is different from YOURS.

Ethnicity is also central to China's national identity. With 1.2 billion Han Chinese in mainland China alone, ethnicity and nationality seem interchangeable. Despite the government's Han-central rhetoric and its uneasy relationship with ethnic groups both home and abroad, the ceremonious respect for ethnic groups finds expression in autonomous rule over major ethnic regions, in educational preferential policy, in an unabashed claim to create a harmonious and multicultural nationhood. Since Sun Yat-Sen, who founded China's nationalist party, the idea of "common blood" has been integrated into the ruling logic: "blood is thicker than water" prioritizes unity over division. This may explain that, from the sub-sample of ethnic minorities, family past and national past were also ranked high. Yet, the statistics suggest a significant increase in importance of ethnic past. In all samples, family history was ranked high as part of cross-generational continuity.

The concept of "community" has never been specified in the Chinese context, which may explain the low percentage of the past of one's community (18.60 percent). The past of one's political affiliation was ranked the lowest. This can be explained by the fact that most respondents do not have any political affiliation in the first place. Even with the ones that do, they identify the affiliation as being merely nominal, superficial, or utilitarian.

Places/Sites of Public History

One section of this survey is dedicated to exploring places/sites of public history. Nearly 81 percent of the participants responded positively to the question, "Have you visited any place or site of public history in the past twelve months?" To probe further, the survey asks seven generic questions, and two additional site-specific questions, about people's impressions of and attitudes towards some of the key places or sites of public history in the city of Chongqing.

This part of the survey adopts focused, face-to-face oral history interviewing to generate more insights. The interviewers are all college-level students from different disciplines in Chongqing University. They all received three sessions of training and workshops about the survey, interview skills, and on-site guidance. A sub-sample from an institutional collaboration with Chongqing China Three Gorges Museum was also collected.[16] Though labor intensive, this part of the survey turned out to be the most rewarding part of the project. The textual analysis generated many rich perceptions with intriguing insights and indicates a genuine effort to reveal the human dimension of each site.

The responses we collected demonstrate a critical understanding of how history is interpreted, displayed, and disseminated at a specific place. The majority of participants responded that they learned some historical knowledge from visiting these historical places, and the experience was authentic. The reasons vary, but most suggested that they trusted the material cultures on display. Here we see a deeply ambivalent relationship between the official depiction of the past and its corresponding material, often manifest in popular historical expressions: on the one hand, the fact that most of the sites are officially designated adds another layer of authority, and for some respondents, this means being more trustworthy; yet on the other hand, with access to the previously inaccessible information, some respondents start to question the historical truth represented in these places, and a healthy skepticism prevails. The negative voices largely focused on over-commercialization. For example, at one of the nationally-designated historic districts, the attitudes towards historic preservation seemed mixed. Some sympathized with government efforts to renovate the area, to improve the quality of living for the residents, while others felt history had actually disappeared under the pretext of preservation or the vaguely defined idea of heritage:

> 'Every detail tells you the whole place is fake, devoid of history. The area represented a selected version history.'
>
> 'The government needs to balance the commercial and the historical . . .'

Conclusion: Preliminary Patterns of Public History-Making in China

The data from one city may not represent national trends, but the project scratches the surface of historical consciousness of ordinary Chinese. The initial findings suggest that despite the censorship still largely in place, there is an expanding space for public consumption of the past. Historians and history educators are facing a demanding public which has passion, interest, and capacity to engage with the past in various ways.

Some preliminary patterns of public history-making in China emerge from the survey. First, material culture stands as a convincing way of engaging the public. Places or sites of public history are highly valued in people's learning about the past. Functioning as narrative media for historical events, these places or sites possess material rhetoric and potential for public history activities. They impact the historical consciousness of ordinary people in a profound way. Second, there is a strong push towards personal, family, and local history. Family is a highly cherished place for making and doing history, and it intimately impacts people's sense of the past. Third, the public respects institutional and professional authority. Public history does not contradict professional history. Instead, it welcomes professional intervention.

What are the implications for history education in China? Historically, schools in China are public institutions that convey and disseminate historical knowledge, as an indisputable place for shaping people's historical consciousness and bolstering civic identity. The Chinese government has painstakingly tried to establish a feeling of continuity, a sense of security, however false, in "a civilization with 5000-year history"—a tradition that has been constructed, and formally institutionalized in different ways. Thus, the past is constantly reinterpreted and rewritten to chart the future. The illusion of continuity not only confirms the past as the prologue to the present, but also a prophet for the present, and indicative of the future.

However, evidence from our project finds particular faults with school-based history, which emphasizes rote learning based on a prescribed canon of historical facts, most of which are boring and irrelevant. On the other hand, it also demonstrates popular interest in intimate pasts and intimate uses of the past—first-hand, experiential, intimate, familial. As such, it is clear that Chinese historians, curriculum officials and history educators would be wise to identify and work with the patterns of public history-making, *and* integrate them into the curriculum. By encouraging creative encounters with history at school, there remains the capacity for historians and history educators to bolster civic interest in the past and develop students' historical thinking. On a final optimistic note, the survey implies that, to better tap into the historical consciousness of ordinary Chinese, and for public history to develop in China, we need well-trained public historians on the ground, to work with the public, and to intervene responsibly.

Na Li (Lina) is Research Fellow and Professor at the Department of History, Zhejiang University. She is Editor for *Public History: A National Journal of Public History,* and International Consulting Editor for *The Public Historian.* She serves on the Board of Directors for the National Council on Public History. Her research focuses on public history and urban preservation. Her first book, *Kensington Market: Collective Memory, Public History, and Toronto's Urban Landscape* (2015) incorporates collective memory in urban landscape interpretation, and suggests a culturally sensitive narrative approach (CSNA) to urban preservation. Her articles have appeared in *The Public Historian, Public History Review, The Oxford Handbook of Urban Planning,* and a number of premier Chinese journals.

Notes

1. Li and Sandweiss, "Teaching Public History," 79.
2. "Temples of delight," *The Economist,* 21 December 2013, 4.
3. Source: China Museums Association. The information is on the Chinese website, non-state-owned museums sub-committee statement. This paragraph is my interpretation of basic data from the CMA website. For more information about privately owned museum development, see *Some Advice for Promoting Privately Owned Museums,* issued by the National Cultural Heritage Administration, 2010.
4. Gadamer, "Epistemological Problems," especially pg. 9.
5. Funkenstein, "Collective Memory," especially pg. 19.
6. Chris Lorenz observes that, in competition with other representational forms of history, such as myth, literary fiction, and mature history, for example, "the media of representation have had a profound influence on the content of representation of the past. See Lorenz, "Towards a Theoretical Framework," 27.
7. Anderson. *Imagined Communities,* 6–7.
8. Nora and Kritzman, *Realms of Memory,* x. See also: Kammen, *Mystic Chords,* 689–704; Zerubavel, *Recovered Roots*; Schönle, *Architecture of Oblivion*; Hobsbawm and Ranger, *The Invention of Tradition.*
9. Rüsen, "Historical Consciousness."
10. Places/sites of public history refers to history museums (part of this research includes a collaborative project with Chongqing China Three Gorges Museum to compare how museum professionals, volunteers, and the public, experience history differently), archives, historic sites, memorials, and monuments, historic districts and cities.
11. The full survey is online at https://www.surveymonkey.com/r/ChinesePasts.
12. Rosenzweig and Thelen, *The Presence of the Past*; Angvik and von Borries, eds., *Youth and History*; Ashton and Hamilton, eds., "Australians and the Past"; Ashton and Hamilton, *History at the Crossroads*; Conrad et al., *Canadians and Their Pasts.*
13. Rosenzweig and Thelen, *The Presence of the Past,* vii, 228–31.
14. The training includes: instruction of the project; familiarity with the questionnaires; practice interviews both in class and in the field; oral history interviewing workshop, including research on the specific site to add one or two probing questions; interview skills (process, smart tips, principles); recording techniques; and ethical and legal concerns, etc.
15. From August to September 2014, I sent out the draft survey to fifty historians, history educators, and public history practitioners for advice. The majority responded with constructive suggestions. In October 2014, the project started a pilot test. This included twenty-five graduate students who enrolled in my Public History seminar at Chongqing University and a national college students' oral history program.
16. This is a separately designed survey, focusing on how, exactly, the public interpret and learn about history through museum exhibits? How to integrate the public opinions to improve museum exhibits? Three groups of people, i.e., museum professionals, volunteers, and visitors, eighty-five in total, were interviewed from April to June 2016.

Bibliography

Anderson, Benedict R. *Imagined Communities: Reflections on the Origin and Spread of Nationalism.* London: Verso, 1983.

Angvik, Magne, and Bodo von Borries, eds. *Youth and History: A Comparative European Survey on Historical Consciousness and Political Attitudes among Adolescents.* Hamburg: Körber-Stiftung, 1997.

Ashton, Paul, and Paula Hamilton. *History at the Crossroads: Australians and the Past,* 1st ed. Ultimo, NSW: Halstead Press, 2010.

Ashton, Paul, and Paula Hamilton, eds. "Australians and the Past." Special issue, *Australian Cultural History* no. 23, (2003).

Conrad, Margaret, Kadriye Ercikan, Gerald Friesen, Jocelyn Létourneau, Delphin Muise, David Northrup, and Peter Seixas. *Canadians and Their Pasts.* Toronto: University of Toronto Press, 2013.

Funkenstein, Amos. "Collective Memory and Historical Consciousness." *History and Memory* 6, no. 1 (1989): 5–22.

Gadamer, Hans-Georg. "Epistemological Problems of The Human Sciences." *Graduate Faculty Philosophical Journal* 5, no. 1 (1975): 8–52.

Hobsbawm, E. J., and T. O. Ranger. *The Invention of Tradition,* Canto ed. Cambridge: Cambridge University Press, 1992.

Kammen, Michael G. *Mystic Chords of Memory: The Transformation of Tradition in American Culture,* 1st ed. New York: Knopf, 1991.

Li, Na, and Martha A. Sandweiss. "Teaching Public History: A Cross-Cultural Experiment." *The Public Historian* 38, no. 3 (2016): 78–100.

Lorenz, Chris. "Towards a Theoretical Framework for Comparing Historiographies: Some Preliminary Considerations, professional historians are far from being the only producer of historical consciousness." In *Theorizing Historical Consciousness,* edited by Peter Seixas, 25–48. Toronto: University of Toronto Press, 2004.

Nora, Pierre, and Lawrence D. Kritzman. *Realms of Memory: Rethinking the French Past. European Perspectives.* New York: Columbia University Press, 1996.

Rosenzweig, Roy, and David Thelen. *The Presence of the Past: Popular Uses of History in American Life.* New York: Columbia University Press, 1998.

Rüsen, Jörn. "Historical Consciousness: Narrative Structure, Moral Function, and Ontogenetic Development." In *Theorizing Historical Consciousness,* edited by Peter Seixas, 63–85. Toronto: University of Toronto Press, 2004.

Schönle, Andreas. *Architecture of Oblivion: Ruins and Historical Consciousness in Modern Russia.* DeKalb: Northern Illinois University Press, 2011.

Zerubavel, Yael. *Recovered Roots: Collective Memory and the Making of Israeli National Tradition.* Chicago: University of Chicago Press, 1995.

CHAPTER 10

"They Fought for Our Language"

Historical Narratives and National Identification among Young French Canadians

Stéphane Lévesque and Jocelyn Létourneau

The teaching of history has traditionally played a central role in the shaping of citizens and the construction of national identity. Yet in a multinational society such as Canada, national history is the subject of ongoing controversies between the founding nations: French, English, and Aboriginals. The media and politicians regularly claim that Canadians in general, and youth in particular, lack proper historical knowledge of their nation. In making this deficit claim, they focus on various questions of substantive knowledge that "good" Canadians are supposed to know: Who discovered Canada? When is Confederation Day? Who was the first prime minister of Canada? What document protects the rights and freedoms of Canadian citizens? The poor performance of citizens to this type of quiz leads many to believe that the Canadian nation—and its history—are at risk. As in other countries, young people's perceived ignorance about the historical canon of their nation has been interpreted as *prima facie* evidence of the inadequacy—and even death—of Canadian history education.[1]

As researchers working in history teaching and learning, we think such questions tell us precious little about students' historical learning as they focus on the simple recall of substantive factual knowledge. While these knowledge tests are common in Canadian history education—and in Canadian society in general—they fail to capture what it is that students do know and think about the past, in other words, their historical conscious-

---

Notes for this section begin on page 157.

ness.² As such, we believe another set of questions is necessary: What stories of the collective past do young Canadians tell? What place do these stories give to original settlers, Aboriginals, women, and the "others"? What impact does regionalism and identity have on their ideas and ways of thinking historically? What role does schooling play in transmitting a national narrative? Through such questions it becomes possible to venture into the thinking of learners and their sense of historical consciousness. In our own works, we have conceptualized historical consciousness not as a series of courses and factual knowledge that people master but as "a mental structure or competence that underlies our dealing with collectively important aspects of past, present, and future."³ This competence is expressed through narratives that serve to orient people in time and space. According to Rüsen, historical consciousness functions "as a specific orientational mode in actual life situations in the present."⁴ This orientation happens in our life because we need to orient ourselves in time, so we know where we come from and where we are heading. Orientation also occurs in our own internal subjectivity, giving a self-understanding and awareness of our temporal existence beyond the limits of birth and death. Orientation, in this sense, makes people aware of the temporal dimension of the self, shaping their historical identity in reference to "a temporal whole larger than that of his/her personal life."⁵

As an attempt to operationalize historical consciousness for research purposes, we have turned to the question of "narrative competence"—the ability to understand and create historical narrations.⁶ In doing so, we have chosen to investigate in our respective works how young French Canadians create usable stories of the collective past. For the purpose of this chapter, we focus on a joint study asking students from Ontario and Québec the following: *Please tell us the history of the French in Canada, as you know it.*⁷

By asking students to tell us the history of the French presence in Canada, we wanted to investigate the structure and quality of their narratives and their sense of historical consciousness as young members of a historical community that traces its origins as far back as New France. While all Canadian schools teach national history, the "nation" is never defined in the exact same terms because the concept is not ontological. French and English Canadians have historically held different understandings of their country. These divergences have, over time, permeated the public school system, which is constitutionally divided between French-speaking or English-speaking schools.

Schooling is an important vehicle for teaching national history. But students' ideas about the collective past derive from a variety of sources, including but not limited to school. People do not construct narratives of the collective past on their own; they do so as members of particular communities. These communities, as Wineburg contends, generate stories of origins and orientation for the present that do not develop in neat concentric circles.[8] What students learn in class may contradict what they hear at home, at church, or in the media. Furthermore, several kinds of identity and narratives interplay within nation-states, notably national and ethnic ones.[9] Unfortunately, there has been limited research in Canada on how narrative ideas develop or vary within national settings. Our study provides new results on the important yet largely unexplored relationship between historical narratives, consciousness, and identity.

Theoretical Framework

Our research is based on the initial Québec study of Jocelyn Létourneau. Along with Sabrina Moisan, Létourneau[10] is the first researcher in Canada to have focused explicitly on narrative competence. His findings are surprising. Québec students are far from historically disconnected from the past.[11] Their narratives are rich and compelling but largely informed by the historical collective memory of Québec, not the more critical perspectives developed by historians and trickled down in official school curricula. Is this unique to his sample? Are Québec's Francophones distinctive in this matter? Unfortunately, Létourneau looked at a group of Québec students without consideration for other French Canadians and their own sense of identification. This limitation is critical considering the fact that French Canadians are not a monolithic group. They live in various regions and provinces having their own distinctive experiences, memories, histories, and education systems.

We think that the use of narrative competence as a methodological approach provides at least three distinct advantages to history education researchers. First, it makes it possible to investigate students' historical consciousness through a "fundamental structure of human experience."[12] Indeed, narrative has long been considered in the literature as key to organizing representation in memory and of filtering the perceptual world.[13] Narratives have also been recognized as central to historical research and consciousness.[14] Far from being an oversimplification of past realities, narrative offers a solution to how we translate knowing into telling. "Narrative," as David Carr puts it, "is at the root of human reality long before it gets explicitly told about." The reason, in his view, is because of the "closeness of structure between human action and narrative that we can genuinely be said to explain an action by telling a story about it."[15] From this perspective, our ability to make sense of the past for contemporary life purposes would inevitably be connected to "narrative acts."[16] Second, asking students to narrate the history of French Canada requires them to create meaning from the complexity of the past with a well-known cultural tool they already employ in their everyday life as storytellers.[17] So from a practical, research perspective, the prime advantage of using narrative is its familiarity. Students do not have to acquire expertise with another cultural tool to present their ideas about the collective past. Finally, through narratives students have to generate what Shemilt calls "big pictures of the past" that give orientation and perspective to the present.[18] Indeed, narratives are not a mere chorological list of everything that happened in the past. They are inherently selective and focus on significant events seen as belonging together as part of a coherent sequence. The use of narrative thus invites students to make a logical selection of past realities and arrange them in story-form through colligation.[19] It also forces them to think beyond school history because students' historical ideas come from various sources of information which are not necessarily structured in a single, coherent fashion as found in textbooks. Their responses are more likely to provide a range of stories found in Canadian society and possibly informed by various historicizing sources including, but not limited to, school history. As Wineburg et al. contend: "the history young people glean from this 'cultural curriculum' may be far more powerful in shaping their ideas about the past than the mountains of textbooks that continue to occupy historians' and history educators' attention."[20]

Methods

Our research was conducted in Ontario (ON) and Québec (QC), the two largest provinces of Canada. Both also have the largest Francophone populations in the country (ON: 600,000, QC: 6.2 million). We recruited a purposeful sample of students from thirteen high schools (ON: 6 schools, QC: 7 schools) located in various geographical settings (urban and rural, multiethnic, and homogeneous). We contacted school boards and teachers to solicit voluntary participants who had completed their compulsory national history courses (i.e., grades 10–12). The task we presented to students in class invited them to write a narrative of the history of the French presence in Canada. Students were instructed *not* to use textbooks or the internet. We indicated in our classroom instructions that we were not fishing for "correct" factual knowledge from their courses nor their ability to retrieve historical information. Our goal was broader: we sought to understand what historical knowledge and stories archived in living memory are remembered and used for structuring a narrative of the historical experiences of French in Canada. Students could write their narrative in whatever form and structure they preferred for sixty minutes. The task also included demographic and identity questions meant to measure their sense of belonging to various historical communities.[21]

A total of 635 students (ON: 250, QC: 385) completed the questionnaire in Spring 2016. Of these, 73 percent spoke French as their first language, 14 percent English, 2 percent French and English, and 11 percent another language; 48 percent were female and 52 percent male. In terms of identities, 46 percent identified as Québécois, 33 percent as Canadian, 11 percent Franco-Ontarian, 8 percent claimed dual identities, and 2 percent another identity (Acadian, American, Mexican, etc.).[22] The average age was 16.5 years old. Narratives were analyzed using an inductive-deductive coding scheme emerging from the key themes and concepts found in students' stories and informed by Canadian historiographies. Students' responses were transcribed and coded by three members of the research team using the software QDA Miner. Results presented in this chapter focus on the initial analysis of narrative themes and historical figures as well as their relation to students' sense of belonging.

Results

Initial results from our study indicate that students are far from historical amnesiacs when dealing with the collective past. Contrary to popular belief and survey results, their narratives are replete with references to events and personages of the historical presence of the French in Canada. In fact, we think that a key advantage of using narrative to probe historical consciousness is the search for historical orientation, something hardly possible with other instruments, such as surveys. Stories offer a coherent structure of meaning-making with a *mise en intrigue* (a plot), as Ricoeur puts it, which presupposes a chronological delineation, a chain of significant events linked in causal relations, and a particular orientation or purpose (objective).[23]

A Pantheon of Personages

The first striking element emerging from students' narratives is the recurring reference to key historical actors who shaped French Canada. Among these are Jacques Cartier, Samuel de Champlain, Christopher Colombus, Jean Talon, Étienne Brûlé, Maurice Duplessis, Louis Riel, René Lévesque, the Desloges sisters (Béatrice and Diane), Pierre Trudeau, James Wolfe, James Murray, Jean Lesage, and Marguerite Bourgeoys (Table 10.1). This list is telling. First, only three women are named frequently: Marguerite Bourgeoys and the Desloges sisters. Bourgeoys is the French founder of the Congregation of Notre-Dame in Montréal. She lived in Ville-Marie (now Montréal) and as of 1653, educated young girls, the poor, and Aboriginals until her death at the turn of the eighteenth century. Bourgeoys was later declared a saint by the Catholic Church. Béatrice and Diane Desloges were

Table 10.1. Key historical figures: total frequency and per province

KEY FIGURES	TOTAL FREQUENCY	NB OF CASES	FREQUENCY ONTARIO	FREQUENCY QUÉBEC
JACQUES CARTIER	148	127	45	103
SAMUEL DE CHAMPLAIN	99	92	59	40
CHRISTOPHER COLOMBUS	57	55	19	38
JEAN TALON	57	48	14	43
ÉTIENNE BRULÉ	14	13	13	0
MAURICE DUPPLESSIS	13	11	2	9
LOUIS RIEL	10	10	3	7
RENÉ LÉVESQUE	9	9	1	8
DESLOGES (BÉATRICE, DIANE)	9	9	0	9
PIERRE TRUDEAU	6	6	3	3
GEN. JAMES WOLFE	6	6	2	4
GOV. JAMES MURRAY	6	6	0	6
JEAN LESAGE	6	6	1	5
MARGUERITE BOURGEOYS	6	5	5	0

two female teachers in the city of Ottawa during the educational conflict that opposed French Catholics and English Protestants in the 1910s. After the Ontario government banned French-language education in 1912, with its controversial "Regulation 17," the Desloges refused to obey the law and persisted in their will to teach Francophone students, thanks in large part to the dedicated support of French Canadian leaders and parents. In the face of this bold act of defiance, the Ministry of Education suspended their teaching permits which forced them to teach illegally. Students appear to know a great deal about these referential figures central to Franco-Canadian collective memory:

> 'Margeritte Bourgeois was a French teacher who wanted to preserve her cultural language so she established secret French classes for young children, this is why even today she is still highly respected and many schools bear her name in her honour.'

> 'Béatrice and Diane Desloges fought for the right of French language education.'

'Regulation 17 was put in place and diminished drastically the teaching of French language in school, many historical figures fought for the cause such as Béatrice Desloges.'

The limited place of women in the narratives is indicative of the type of history that students tell. The past of Canada is very much a male affair. And not only male, but white European male. Indeed, the dominant figures are European explorers presented as part of the "discovery" of North America and founding of New France. Jacques Cartier and Samuel de Champlain are unequivocally the leading figures, with Christopher Columbus often confused in texts with Cartier and the discovery of North America. For example:

'Francophones arrived in the country after the explorations of Christopher Columbus who discovered North America.'

'In 1534, Jacques Cartier is sent to America. However, this is not the first presence of French in America. Indeed, well before Cartier, Normans and Britons came for fishing.'

'In 1608, Samuel de Champlain founded Québec city, in the province of Québec, one of the oldest settlements in Canada and with the longest past and history.'

Like intendant Jean Talon and explorer Étienne Brûlé (who is exclusively mentioned in Ontario narratives), all these personages are presented as the forefathers of French-speaking settlements in America. Their role is crucial. They help establish a sense of legacy and continuity over time, connecting the colonial past to the present of French Canada.

But the list of personages is not exclusively about French people. It contains names like General James Wolfe and Governor James Murray, both British officers who served in the colony. Wolfe is cited in reference to the infamous Battle of the Plains of Abraham which took place in 1759 between French and British armies outside the fortress of Québec. While General Wolfe died in the battle, along with his French opponent the Marquis de Montcalm, he is still remembered as the British figure who sealed the fate of New France and initiated a long period of collective hardship.

'The English took the control of New France on the Plains of Abraham under the command of General Wolf [sic]. The history of the French people that followed was turbulent under the British reign.'

James Murray, on the contrary, is presented as the benevolent governor who was appointed by the British crown following the fall of New France. Murray, a member of the landed gentry, was supportive of the agrarian, French-speaking inhabitants over the newly arrived, English-speaking merchants from the Thirteen Colonies or from Britain looking for profit. To restore peace and promote stability after the war, Murray even allowed for

French law and customs in the courts of the colony, which provoked the ire of the British settlers.

> 'The English tried repetitively to assimilate us. We had to defend ourselves and receive the help of some like Governor James Murray.'

> 'There was the War of the Conquest which the English won. Following this, the English tried to assimilated the French with the Royal Proclamation. Intendant James Murray and Guy Carleton were extremely conciliatory with the French population.'

Surprisingly, contemporary figures, such as former Prime Minister Pierre Trudeau and Québec Premiers Maurice Duplessis and René Lévesque, are not cited very frequently. Students have placed greater emphasis on the colonial past, which is possibly an effect of our narrative task itself: the implicit need to start their story at "the beginning" with limited time left in class for presenting contemporary history. Whatever the reason, students referred exclusively to a few political leaders who, in their view, affected directly the destiny of French Canadians: Duplessis for his conservatism, traditionalism, and connection with the Clergy, and Trudeau and Lévesque, emblems of Francophone modernity, for their struggles for more French-speaking presence in Canadian institutions (Trudeau) and for Québec rights (Lévesque).

> 'One day, we fell down to the dark ages of Duplessis but after came the brighter days for Québec and Francophones: The Quiet Revolution.'

> 'The Quiet Revolution brought about many changes, for example Pierre Trudeau put into place law for French as official language.'

> 'People like René Lévesque fought hard to preserve their language.'

The "Sorrows" of French Canada

Students' narratives cover an extensive period in Canadian history, ranging from first contacts with Aboriginal peoples to the modern period. This represents well over five hundred years of history in America. But saying this is not to say that students chronicled all the historical events of this vast time period. Results in Table 10.2 highlight dominant keywords found in students' narratives. Because these keywords were part of constructed stories, they are semantically connected into phrases, paragraphs, and ultimately narratives, and thus reveal important changes in the development of Francophones in Canada. When taken together in a synoptic view, these concepts represent what Shemilt calls "little pictures of the past"[24]—or what Létourneau refers to as "mythistories."[25] These are not comprehensive stories in themselves but rather small "maps" or "pictures" containing a set of ideas, events, and dates on given historical topics.

What is most striking from this table is the recurring emphasis on key episodes in Canadian history that fit what we could call the "sorrows" of

Table 10.2. Key words: total frequency and per province

KEY WORDS	TOTAL FREQUENCY	NB OF CASES	FREQUENCY ONTARIO	FREQUENCY QUÉBEC
FRENCH	1753	492	851	902
CANADA	850	361	434	416
FRANCOPHONE	831	358	420	411
ENGLISH	806	365	303	503
FRANCE	709	303	150	559
QUÉBEC	639	322	180	459
"WE"	540	189	164	376
LANGUAGE	527	260	262	265
WAR	442	247	185	257
NEW FRANCE	384	211	67	317
COUNTRY	341	203	198	143
COLONY	315	158	19	296
"OUR"	294	157	99	195
ANGLOPHONE	228	137	84	144
FIGHT	196	146	131	65
CANADIENS	196	118	80	116
SCHOOL	190	104	190	0
ABORIGINALS	185	130	16	169
RIGHT	179	125	119	60
FIRST NATIONS	142	104	57	85
FUR	137	101	0	137
QUÉBÉCOIS	118	73	0	73
FRANCO-ONTARIAN	117	61	117	0
COLONIZE	115	96	36	79
"FILLES DU ROY"	115	104	18	97
REGULATION 17	111	82	111	0
ASSIMILATE	100	85	0	85
ENGLAND	97	68	28	69
BATTLE (PLAINS OF ABRAHAM)	92	75	47	45

French Canada, in reference to the "way of sorrows" depicting the last day of Christ. In students' narratives, these little pictures (or mythistories) refer to: the French, the English, the Aboriginals, land, language, school, wars and fights, and rights. The "English" and "French" are portrayed in students' text as dichotomous cultural entities representing the dominant groups in Canada. Mostly, they are linked in a contest for control over land in America.

> 'The French and the English first immigrated to America during the 1600s and 1800s.'
>
> 'After many generations of Francophones, Québec will fall in the hands of Great Britain which is respectful. But following the war of independence in the United States, many English loyalists will immigrate to what will become Canada.'
>
> 'The French settled the land (for centuries) and later went to war with the English. After the War of the Conquest, the British took over the French possession in Canada. For years, we will continue to develop the colony and fight against Great Britain.'

Aboriginals (or First Nations) figure prominently in students' narratives when dealing with the colonial past. While few names or leaders are mentioned, students overwhelmingly consider the colonization of America by Europeans to be highly detrimental to Aboriginal peoples and their way of life. That being said, the role of Aboriginals in narratives is almost exclusively contained to the colonial past. Few references are made to First Nations in the later periods as if they had completely disappeared from history—and society. The only exception is Métis leader Louis Riel who, as a French-speaking Catholic and therefore a child of the "nation," was central in bringing the province of Manitoba into the Canadian federation but was executed for high treason for his role in the 1885 resistance to Canadian encroachment on Métis lands.

> 'The French came first, met Aboriginals and killed them with diseases. After that, they tried to convert them, engage in trade and sell liquor which led to a huge problem of alcoholism. A few years later they were invaded by the England which also tried to convert them without success.'
>
> 'The French sailed to Canada in the 1500s and 1600s. They assimilated Aboriginals or attacked them with riffles which they did not have. So the French won and built many villages and cities such as Québec and Montréal . . .'
>
> 'After the creation of modern Canada, Louis Riel was hanged because he was a 'modest francophone' who did not want his metis land to be invaded for a railroad.'

The twin concepts of "war" and "fight" are central to students' pictures of the past. They serve to represent conflicting moments in the history of French in Canada (conquest, rebellions, world wars, conscription, abolition of language rights and French schools) and the will of French-speaking communities to fight English domination and assimilation. War is thus associated with ongoing struggles for cultural survival, particularly following the conquest of New France, which is one of the most cited events in students' narratives.

> 'There was a war between France and Great Britain, the English won and took over the land settled by the French. The French population later regrouped on the same territory (Upper Canada).'

> 'During the world wars, we were forced to fight shoulder to shoulder with the British because settlers of British descent were more numerous.'

> 'Another example is the "war of the hairpins" a sort of "war" that was provoked by the closing of French schools and transfer to English schools. School teachers fought the authorities with their hairpins.'

The Template of "la Survivance"

Students' little pictures of the past do not operate as disconnected maps of the past. They are organized and embedded into "bigger" pictures of the past informed by meta-narrative assumptions about the structure, significance, and direction of their narratives. Wertsch refers to these as "narrative templates" because they represent organizing schemas that involve a temporality of events and some sort of plot that can underlie an entire set of specific narratives.[26] These templates "act as unnoticed yet very powerful coauthors when we attempt to tell 'what really happened.'"[27] What we discover from the analysis of keywords in context is the expression of a big picture template that is recurring in students' narratives: *la survivance*.

The concept of "la survivance" (survival) is well-known in French Canadian history and denotes the continuous and necessary survival of Francophone language and culture in the face of English Canadian or Anglo-American hegemony. If *la survivance* was central to French Canadian historiography up to 1970s, it is still present, as a metaphor or an implicit framework of interpretation, in some contemporary popular historical writings.[28] Above all, it remains salient in the historical collective memory of French Canadians today. Collective memory entails a set of historical references, teleological schemes, clichés, ideas, and representations through which the past, the present, and the envisioned future are decoded and anticipated. French Canadian movies, songs, theatrical plays, community events, sites of memory, beer slogans, and political discourse frequently make use of collective memory to promote agendas and muster collective support. The template of *la survivance* is arranged around the following four episodes or mythistories:

> 1. The arrival of explorers and the establishment of New France. This is the golden age of French in America with references to Jacques Cartier, Samuel de Champlain, Jean Talon, the "filles du Roy,"[29] Étienne Brûlé, and Marguerite Bourgeoys.

2. The British conquest and fall of New France. This marks the decapitation of Francophones and their culture in Canada as incarnated by General James Wolfe, Lord Durham, and other British Canadian "oppressors" who wanted to assimilate French Canadians or forced them to act against their will (e.g., abolition of French-language education, general conscription during world wars).

3. The awakening of modern French Canadian nationalism in the twentieth century following the lead of various figures who fought for the "cause" of Francophone rights (e.g., Béatrice and Diane Desloges, Jean Lesage, René Lévesque).

4. The uncertainty of the future. The momentum of the nationalist revolution is fading away. The future is unclear and possibly threatening, vigilance is de rigueur for the survival of Francophone communities.

This narrative template is often invoked in French Canadian communities in an effort to make sense of national events, both past and present, and as such it provides a plot line for the building of various regional narratives. Indeed, Québec and Ontario students do not tell the exact same stories of the history of French experiences in Canada. As discussed earlier, certain events and personages are more salient in one provincial group than the other. For example, Québec students were more likely to refer to Jacques Cartier, New France, fur trade, and war/conquest while Ontario students put more emphasis on explorer Étienne Brûlé, French-language education, and Franco-Ontarian resistance. This variation is possibly an effect of different history curricula and distinctive memories and community experiences. That being said, both groups implicitly referred to a common narrative template to structure the history of French Canada. Such a big picture template, as Wertsch suggests, acts as an interpretative framework that heavily shapes the thinking of the members of a community. Indeed, Ontario and Québec have long abandoned *la survivance* as an educational objective for their history programs. Still, many students in our study readily tell a history with reference to this big picture framework. Why?

Identifying with the Past

Interestingly, results from our study indicate that students' sense of collective identification seriously affects the use of this big picture template. In fact, as shown in Table 10.3 below, the more students identified strongly with their provincial linguistic community (e.g., Québécois, Franco-Ontarian), the more their stories followed the pattern of *la survivance* and used frequently the concepts of conquest, war, nation, assimilation, defense, and resistance. This is to say that students who identified strongly as French Canadians (or Québécois, Franco-Ontarians) more readily adopted a template informed by the mythistories of collective memory. These students were also much more likely to make use of the pronouns "We" and "Our" when talking about past events and predecessors. In doing so, they purposely established a sense

Table 10.3. Key words in relation to sense of belonging to province (Québec or Ontario), in percentage of total frequency

KEY WORDS	STRONG SENSE OF BELONGING (IN PERCENT OF TOTAL FREQUENCY)
CONQUEST	86.1
NATION	81.1
DEFEND	79.0
INDEPENDANCE (US)	77.8
REVOLUTION (FR, US)	76.9
GREAT BRITAIN	76.0
CANADIENS	75.0
ASSIMILATE	73.2
"WE"	72.7
CATHOLIC	72.2
COLONIZATION	71.9
QUÉBÉCOIS	71.7
NEW FRANCE	71.5
BATTLE (PLAINES OF ABRAHAM)	70.5
FRANCE	68.6
QUÉBEC	65.1
RÉFÉRENDUM	62.8
FIGHT	62.4
PATRIOTE	61.7

of belonging to the distant past, turning "their" experiences into "our" experiences, and connecting past changes to current national transformations.

> 'When the English took over the land, they tried to assimilate us, impose their religion, force their English language, in short to convert us. But we were strong, did not bend, and that is why we are still Francophones.'

> 'Yes, we went through traumatic events, and yes we were able to overcome these as a colony. Personally, I am proud to be a descendent of these people and to affirm that I am Québécois.'

> 'The British have always tried to assimilate us, to force us to speak English and convert us to Protestantism. I think we are a strong nation because we have resisted.'

The very fact that this pattern is so prevalent among participants both from Québec and Ontario despite the lack of a common national curriculum indicates how powerful this narrative template is in French Canadian communities. In fact, only 38 percent of our participants claimed that their stories were strongly informed by formal history education. This is important as it suggests that other forces also shape students' narrative ideas of the collective past.

Canadian school history is one among a set of agents in the formation of students' historical consciousness. Unfortunately, too often it acts as if it is the only one. Programs of study, official evaluations, approved textbooks, and even teachers continue to ignore the role and impact of external historicizing forces on students' historical learning. Our findings suggest that the relationship between formal and informal history education as well as the relationship between history and identity cannot be ignored because learners' sense of identification and meaningful real-life experiences strongly influence how they interpret history.

Conclusion: Exploring the Narrative Competence

Our study differs significantly from what captures the attention of the media and politicians: students' poor and fragmented knowledge of Canadian history. Our results indicate that by the time students graduate from high school, they have acquired an important stockpile of historical information and little pictures of the collective past that vary from one region to another. Interestingly, these little pictures are part of "bigger" pictures organized in narrative templates such as *la survivance*. These templates, as Howson and Shemilt remind us, are useful cognitive tools precisely because they act as "frameworks of knowledge"[30] intended to: (1) organize information from the past into an intelligible structure of meaning-making, (2) bridge the dimensions of time (past, present, and envisioned future) with the twin concepts of cause-effect and continuity-change, and (3) mobilize the experiences of the past for contemporary life purposes. Yet, we must recognize that narrative templates have their own limitations. Indeed, the use of one template over another directly affects the selection, the structure and arrangement, and the quality of specific historical narratives. These narratives are cultural tools affecting people's sense of orientation and identification.

In these circumstances, what should educators do? What role should narrative play in history education? Should national identification be addressed in history classes? For what purpose? There is no simple answer to these questions and, unfortunately, we have found few convincing answers so far in the literature. That being said, we believe that the current situation in Canadian education is far from satisfactory. So we propose to conclude with four possible alternatives to consider, independently or jointly, as practical applications in the context of Canadian education which could also serve as blueprint for other educational systems.

First, history educators should take into consideration students' prior narrative knowledge.[31] Recent research in the constructivist tradition indicates that new knowledge is constructed from old. Students do not simply acquire history as new imprints on a hard-drive; they learn additional information based on what they already know—or think they know. This prior knowledge is made up of thought patterns, beliefs, misconceptions, and frameworks that influence (or determine) what they take from new knowledge. Equally important, prior knowledge is shaped by various forces including, but not limited to schooling.[32] Once educators become familiar with the structure and influences on the narratives students bring to class, they are better equipped to engage these stories and call them into question. For instance, students might learn that French and English Canadians were/are not dichotomous, monolithic groups and that some English Canadians have been supportive of French-speaking rights in Canada.

Second, history educators must also reveal and teach the constructed nature of narratives. In many ways, students learn history through narratives (e.g., lectures, textbooks, movies, and oral stories). But rarely are these problematized by teachers. If we want students to "think historically," educators should explain the structure, grammar, goal, and purpose of narratives.[33] As Peter Lee and Rosalyn Ashby contend, history is always "more important than any particular story it tells."[34] It is a disciplinary way of thinking with its own procedures, concepts and rules of argumentation designed to make critical claims about the past.[35] Many stories are told in society which may "contradict, compete with, or complement one another," and this means that students should be equipped with the competencies to deal with the constructed nature of these historical narratives.[36]

Third, history educators should not lead students to develop any particular national identification but teach them to understand various historical experiences and people, in other words, to develop historical empathy. Traditionally, school history has focused on national identification as a way to promote ethnocultural assimilation and social cohesion. But in a global, multinational country such as Canada, history education can no longer pretend to promote exclusive national belonging but forms of collective attachment that are open, flexible, and plural. This means, as Barton also argues, that schools and curricula should more carefully "consider the choices they make in selecting some experiences and perspectives as representative of any particular group" as students will draw selectively from these to construct their narrative identification with the collective past.[37] They should also expand and offer more varied and balanced individual experiences to students, including those from marginalized groups.[38]

Finally, history education should provide students with the intellectual tools to know how to construct narratives of the collective past. There are many interpretations of the historical experiences of French Canadians that students should analyze and study. But narrating history plays an essential role in the formation of historical consciousness. As such, students should gradually acquire the intellectual tools necessary to develop narrative competence. Of course, students in the classroom do not have the intellectual knowledge and skills of the historians. "Given too much interpretive leeway," as Seixas warns, "students may construct and reinforce untenable views of the past and of their place in historical time."[39] But if students are given no opportunity to "do history," we believe that the formal historical narratives they learn in class may have little impact on their preconceived stories of the past.

Stéphane Lévesque is Professor and Director of the Virtual History and Stories Lab at the University of Ottawa, Canada. He has written widely on students' historical thinking, historical consciousness, and narrative competence. As Founding Director of the Virtual History Lab, his research and teaching interests also focus on digital history and the integration of technology in education.

Jocelyn Létourneau (FRSC) is Professor of History at Laval University, Québec City, where he was Canada Research Chair in Québec's Contemporary History. A former fellow of the Institute for Advanced Study, Princeton, NJ and of the Collegium of Lyon, Létourneau has been the principal investigator in the Community-University Research Alliance, *Canadians and their Pasts*. In 2010, he was Fulbright scholar at UC Berkeley and, in 2015, a Visiting Research Associate at UCL-Institute of Education. His latest publications include *Canadians and their Pasts* (2013, co-author), and *Je me souviens? Le passé du Québec dans la conscience de sa jeunesse* (2014).

Notes

This chapter is based on a larger national study conducted with Anne Gilbert (Ottawa) and Jean-Philippe Croteau (Chengdu) and financed by the Secretariat for Intergovernmental Affairs of Québec (SAIC) and the University of Ottawa. We would like to thank Raphaël Gani, Maxime Saumure, and Marc-André Lauzon for their indispensable research assistantship throughout this project. Special thanks should also go to Terry Haydn (East Anglia) and Denis Shemilt (Leeds) for constructive feedback on ideas and drafts of this chapter.

1. Granatstein, *Who Killed Canadian history?*
2. For a thorough analysis of the situation and the positive responses and interest of Canadians for history, Conrad et al. *Canadians and their Pasts*.
3. Kölbl and Konrad, "Historical Consciousness in Germany," 20.
4. Rüsen, *History: Narration, Interpretation, Orientation*, 66–67.
5. Rüsen, *History: Narration, Interpretation, Orientation*, 25.
6. See Kölbl and Konrad, "Historical Consciousness in Germany," 17–28.

7. The actual French question presented to students was the following: "Raconte-moi l'histoire des Francophones au pays comme tu la connais," (Tell us the history of Francophones in this country as you know it). By focusing more broadly on Francophones and on the concept of country we wanted our task to be as open as possible, recognizing that all investigative approaches and research tools are inherently limited and culturally bound.

8. Wineburg, "Making Historical Sense."

9. Carretero et al., eds., *History Education and the Construction of National Identities.*

10. Létourneau and Moisan, "Young People's Assimilation of a Collective Historical Memory"; and Létourneau, *Je me souviens*. Létourneau's study (www.tonhistoireduquebec.ca) has been influential in different countries, including Australia (http://hermes-history.net/remembering-australias-past-rap), Spain, Switzerland, Belgium, Germany, and France (Lantheaume and Létourneau, eds., *Le récit du commun*).

11. While Létourneau's original study includes a sample of English-speaking students (see Létourneau, *Je me souviens?*, ch. 7), our focus here is on French-speaking participants only.

12. Connelly and Clandinin, "Stories of experience and narrative inquiry," 2.

13. See Bruner, "Narrative and paradigmatic modes of thought."

14. Holt, *Thinking Historically*; Munslow, *Narrative and History*.

15. Carr, "Narrative Explanation and its Malcontents," 29.

16. Straub, *Narration, identity, and historical consciousness,* 54.

17. Barton and Levstik, *Teaching History for the Common Good,* 136.

18. Shemilt, "The Caliph's Coin," 100.

19. On the notion of colligation see the work of Thompson, "Colligation and history teaching."

20. Wineburg, et al., "Common Belief and the Cultural Curriculum," 69.

21. For these questions, students were asked to identify on a likert-scale their sense of belonging to various communities (Canada, Québec, Ontario, and "other") ranging from 0 (no sense of belonging) to 7 (very strong sense of belonging). This approach is commonly used in identity studies in which participants indicate their own self-reported sense of attachment to groups.

22. The redefinition of Québec autonomy and use of French as an official language in the province (Bill 101) have created among French Canadians a sense of national or provincial self-identify as Québécois, Acadien, or Franco-Ontarien. Since public education, health and social services are provided by provincial institutions (not federal), provincial identities are often used to identify French-language institutions. This is most particularly the case in the province of Québec.

23. Ricoeur, *Time and Narrative.*

24. Shemilt, "The Caliph's Coin," 142.

25. Létourneau, "Mythistory," 423.

26. Wertsch, "Texts of Memory and Texts of History."

27. Wertsch, "Collective Memory and Narrative Templates."

28. A recent example is Bédard's bestseller *History of Quebec for Dummies.*

29. "Filles du Roy" were young, unmarried women sometimes living in orphanages, sponsored by the King of France to immigrate to New France in order to correct the critical gender imbalance in the colony. Unlike popular mythology, they were not promiscuous women ("filles de joie") who were sent for French soldiers' and habitants' casual interests.

30. Howson and Shemilt, "Frameworks of Knowledge."

31. Létourneau, "Pour une pragmatique de l'enseignement."

32. See Lévesque, "Going beyond 'Narratives' vs. 'Competencies'"; Létourneau, "School, Textbooks and Memory."

33. Chapman, "Understanding Historical Knowing"; Lévesque, "Why Tell Stories?"

34. Lee and Ashby, "Progression in Historical Understanding," 200.

35. See Wineburg, "Unnatural and Essential"; Lévesque, *Thinking Historically*; and Seixas and Morton, *The Big Six*.
36. Lee and Ashby, "Progression in Historical Understanding," 200.
37. Barton, "School History as a Resource for Constructing Identities," 102
38. Létourneau, "Teaching National History to Young People Today," ch. 12.
39. Seixas, "The Community of Inquiry as a Basis for Knowledge and Learning," 320.

Bibliography

Barton, Keith. "School History as a Resource for Constructing Identities." In *History education and the construction of national identities*, edited by Mario Carretero, Mikel Asensio, and Maria Rodrigues-Moneo, 93–108. Charlotte, NC: Information Age Publishing, 2012.

Barton, Keith, and Linda Levstik. *Teaching History for the Common Good*. Mahwah, NJ: Lawrence Erlbaum, 2004.

Bédard, Eric. *History of Quebec for Dummies*. New York: For Dummies, 2013.

Bruner, Jerome. "Narrative and Paradigmatic Modes of Thought." In *Learning and Teaching the Ways of Knowing*, edited by Elliot Eisner, 97–115. Chicago: University of Chicago Press, 1985.

Carr, David. "Narrative Explanation and its Malcontents," *History and Theory* 47 (2008): 19–30.

Carretero, Mario, Mikel Asensio, and Maria Rodriguez-Moneo, eds. *History Education and the Construction of National Identities*. New York: Information Age Publishing, 2012.

Chapman, Arthur. "Understanding Historical Knowing: Evidence and Accounts." In *The Future of the Past: Why History Education Matters*, edited by L. Perikleous and D. Shemilt, 169–216. Cyprus: AHDR, 2011.

Connelly, Michael, and Jean Clandinin. "Stories of Experience and Narrative Inquiry," *Educational Researcher* 19, no. 5 (1990): 2–14.

Conrad, Margaret, Kadriye Ercikan, Gerald Friesen, Jocelyn Létourneau, Del Muise, David Northrup, and Peter Seixas. *Canadians and their Pasts*. Toronto: University of Toronto Press, 2013.

Granatstein, Jack. *Who Killed Canadian History?* Toronto: Harper Collins, 1998.

Holt, Thomas. *Thinking Historically: Narrative, Imagination, and Understanding*. New York: College Board Publications, 1995.

Howson, Jonathan, and Denis Shemilt. "Frameworks of Knowledge: Dilemmas and Debates." In *Debates in History Teaching*, edited by Ian Davies, 73–83. London: Routledge, 2011.

Kölbl, Carlos, and Lisa Konrad. "Historical Consciousness in Germany: Concept, Implementation, Assessment." In *New Directions in Assessing Historical Thinking*, edited by Kadriye Ercikan and Peter Seixas, 17–27. New York: Routledge, 2015.

Lantheaume, Françoise, and Jocelyn Létourneau, eds. *Le récit du commun. L'histoire nationale racontée par les élèves*. Lyon: Presses universitaires de Lyon, 2016.

Lee, Peter, and Rosalyn Ashby. "Progression in historical understanding among students ages 7–14." In *Knowing, Teaching, and Learning History: National and International Perspectives*, edited by Peter Stearns, Peter Seixas, and Sam Wineburg, 199–222. New York: New York University Press, 2000.

Létourneau, Jocelyn. "Mythistory." In *Oxford Companion to Canadian History*, edited by Gerald Hallowell, 423. Toronto: Oxford University Press, 2004.

———. *Je me souviens? Le passé du Québec dans la conscience de sa jeunesse*. Québec: Fides, 2014.

———. "Teaching National History to Young People Today." In *International Handbook of Research in Historical Culture and Education: Hybrid Ways of Learning History*, edited by Mario Carretero, Stefan Berger, and Maria Grever, 227–42. London: Palgrave Macmillan, 2016.

———. "School, Textbooks and Memory: Inside the 'History Learning Ecosystem.'" Unpublished manuscript, 2016.

———. "Pour une pragmatique de l'enseignement de l'histoire. Leçons tirées d'une recherche" [Teaching history a pragmatic way: Lessons from a research]. Accessed 30 August 2018, www.ecoleclio.hypotheses.org/.

Létourneau, Jocelyn, and Sabrina Moisan. "Young People's Assimilation of a Collective Historical Memory: A Case Study of Quebeckers of French–Canadian Heritage." In *Theorizing Historical Consciousness*, edited by Peter Seixas, 109–28. Toronto: University of Toronto Press, 2004.

Lévesque, Stéphane. *Thinking Historically: Educating Students for the Twenty-First Century*. Toronto: University of Toronto Press, 2008.

———. "Why Tell Stories? On the Importance of Teaching Narrative Thinking." *Canadian Issues* (Autumn 2014): 5–11.

———. "Going beyond 'Narratives' vs. 'Competencies': A model for understanding history education." *Public History Weekly* 4 (2016) : 12. DOI: dx.doi.org/10.1515/phw-2016-5918.

Munslow, Alan. *Narrative and History*. New York: Palgrave Macmillan, 2007.

Ricoeur, Paul. *Time and Narrative*, vol. 1. Chicago: University of Chicago Press, 1984.

Rüsen, Jörn. *History: Narration, Interpretation, Orientation*. New York: Berghahn Books, 2005.

Seixas, Peter. "The Community of Inquiry as a Basis for Knowledge and Learning: The Case of History." *American Educational Research Journal* 30, Summer (1993): 305–24.

Seixas, Peter, and Tom Morton. *The Big Six Historical Thinking Concepts*. Toronto: Nelson Publishing, 2012.

Shemilt, Denis. "The Caliph's Coin: The Currency of Narrative." In *Knowing, Teaching, and Learning History: National and International Perspectives,* edited by Peter Stearns, Peter Seixas, and Sam Wineburg, 83–101. New York: New York University Press, 2000.

Straub, Jürgen. *Narration, Identity, and Historical Consciousness*. New York: Berghahn Books, 2005.

Thompson, David. "Colligation and History Teaching." In *Studies in the Nature and Teaching of History,* edited by W.H. Burston and D. Thompson, 75–106 London: Routledge, 1967.

Wertsch, James. "Collective Memory and Narrative Templates." *Social Research* 75 (2008): 133–56.

———. "Texts of Memory and Texts of History." *L2 Journal* 4 (2012): 9–20.

Wineburg, Sam. "Making Historical Sense." In *Knowing, Teaching, and Learning History: National and International Perspectives,* edited by Peter Stearns, Peter Seixas, and Sam Wineburg, 306–25. New York: New York University Press, 2000.

———. "Unnatural and Essential: The Nature of Historical Thinking." *Teaching History* 129 (2007): 6–11

Wineburg, Sam, et al. "Common Belief and the Cultural Curriculum: An Intergenerational Study of Historical Consciousness." *American Educational Research Journal* 44, no. 1 (2007): 40–76.

Part III
Historical Consciousness and Cultural Identity

CHAPTER 11

What is Black Historical Consciousness?

LaGarrett J. King

Readers of this book are probably familiar with the nuances of historical consciousness as more than historical awareness or knowledge. As defined by Robert Thorp, the concept refers to an awareness of "how matters past, present, and future relate to each other in a way that enables the individual to create a specific kind of meaning in relation to history."[1] Historical consciousness has an important role in constructing present-day ideology, therefore, making the concept both an epistemological and ontological project. Theorizing historical consciousness, however, has a Western problem.

As Peter Seixas notes, historically, scholars have promoted through their writings the notion that "the modern West has historical consciousness, and the rest do without, until they achieve Western modes of understanding."[2] Sexias has challenged Western thought on historical consciousness by highlighting that the term should encompass not only "individual and collective understandings of the past but the cognitive and cultural factors which shape those understandings."[3] Yet Western epistemology continues to shape our thoughts concerning historical consciousness. Theoreticians of historical consciousness largely cite only Western scholarship, and if we are to take Thorp's three manifestations of historical consciousness (narrative, the use of history, and historical culture) as a barometer of how historical consciousness is developed, it is easy to identify a strong Western influence.

Notes for this section begin on page 172.

My question concerning Black historical consciousness, therefore, is largely based on those cultural factors that influence the way we interpret history. It is no secret that history's invention of Blackness operated as a key apparatus in adhering to and sustaining racial hierarchies in racial states. While school-related history has become more diverse in terms of quantitative renderings of Blackness, scholars maintain that, qualitatively, the narratives continue to maintain troublesome knowledge negating Blackness as truly legitimate. Therefore, any conversations surrounding historical consciousness that focuses on Black history, in Western contexts, should be examined more closely given that historic forms of Blackness were (and still are) based on a Western historical fallacy.

By Black historical consciousness, we should begin to think about our understanding of the historical concept of *Blackness* and how it relates to our knowledge, ideology, disposition, and treatment of present-day Black *people*. By Blackness, I am not simply referring to the history of those considered Black but more on what it means to be Black in a historic sense. This definition of Blackness is an important consideration in attempting to conceptualize Black historical consciousness, where elements of historical consciousness from Seixas are foundational but paired with the theoretical considerations from South African scholar, Stephen Biko's notion of Black consciousness.

Biko's concept of Black consciousness is an attitude and way of life that encompasses: (1) a collective agency and resistance to White oppression, (2) a redefinition of Blackness and Black humanity, and (3) group pride in themselves, their value systems, their culture, their religion, and their outlook in life.[4] I am adopting Biko's notion of Black consciousness to the field of history education in an effort to challenge and expand how researchers relate historical consciousness to how individuals and societies promote historical awareness about Black history. A Black historical consciousness entails: (1) resisting White epistemic historical frameworks, (2) redefining Black history as its own genre and set of historical contexts independent of Western knowledge, and (3) recognizing Blackness as complex and human.

The purpose of this book chapter, therefore, is to examine the current state of historical consciousness relating to Blackness and is led by the question, whether there is a need to theorize a Black historical consciousness? To do this, I look to my research as well as other salient research in K–12 Black historical studies. While my published work might not have delved specifically into historical consciousness, at its foundation are approaches that speak to and question why it is important for citizens to be historically conscious, particularly having a certain Black historical consciousness.

Conceptual Framework

As a conceptual framework, I use Thorp's three manifestations of historical consciousness to explain how K–12 Black history is imagined through pre-service history teachers, the curriculum, and media.[5] First, historical consciousness is manifested through the notion of narrative. Narratives are developed as cognitive functions that are individually assessed and derive meaning based on contexts and experiences. In history, narratives are the historical expression of what an individual understands about the past through chronicling events that tell a specific story about a person or event. Therefore, when narratives are told, the individual is attempting to make sense of history. Rüsen reminds us, however, that for individuals to be "narrative competent," their understanding of the past involves stories that are competent in content (competence of historical experiences), form (competence in historical interpretation), and function (competence in historical orientation).[6]

Creating narratives are a complex endeavor that not only involve individual interpretations but also are influenced through larger institutions and structures. Haitian scholar Michel-Rolph Trouillot notes that narratives are a result of power. Power refers to dominant or majoritarian groups and institutions who control history as a way to justify their humanity.[7] In turn, narratives of less influential groups are maintained to hold certain silences that ensure that the dominant ideology is prevalent. While it is true that some omissions or silences are inherent in narratives (due to space constraints, narratives cannot include everything), or even due to innocuous epistemological narration (I never thought to ask/include those questions/stories), silences also create a one-sided historicity of incomplete narrations.

The second way historical consciousness is manifested is through the use of history. Thorp divides the uses of history into two categories: the *what* and *how* uses of history. The *what* uses of history are about the purpose of history. In this sense, history is akin to Trouillot's notion of power, where history is used to promote certain political, existential, ideological, and scientific philosophies. The *how* uses of history explain the various methods that engage historical consciousness such as Rüsen's typology of historical narration as a guide. The first is the traditional narrative (accepting historical interpretation); second, the exemplary narrative (demonstrating single case rules and principles); third, the critical narrative (being able to critique societies and cultures and raise moral reasoning); and last, the genetic narrative (being able to historize, place into historical context, complex interpretation of an event).[8]

The third manifestation of historical consciousness is historical culture. Thorp explains that historical culture is the societal historical landscape that individuals are born into, which influences how individuals interpret historical events or facts. What this means is that the historical culture of a place is already established when a person is born into or enters said society. Yet, while the person is influenced by accepted historical culture, she or he is not without agency. People have the ability to influence and/or shift historical culture (to a certain degree) by using history to demonstrate counter narratives.

What follows is an explanation of how some of my previous research with Black history intersects with the concept of historical consciousness. While I do provide some suggestions in the conclusion, a thorough theoretical excursion into a Black historical consciousness is not provided. Based on space and brevity, this chapter explains what I found to be a consistent understanding about Black history and how those interpretations relate to the treatment of Black people. To do this, Thorp's historical consciousness concepts of narrative, uses of history, and historical culture are used to expound on how previous research has attempted to uncover what could be considered a Black historical consciousness.

Narrative

For narratives, I will focus on my work that examined how four pre-service teachers from the United States approached K–12 Black history as curriculum and pedagogy.[9] The research stated three specific goals: (1) to explore pre-service teachers' Black history knowledge, (2) to engage pre-service teachers with Black history readings and ascertain how their knowledge changed or remained the same as a result of the program, and (3) to examine how Black history was integrated in classroom instruction. A key component of this research was for the pre-service teachers to construct a Black history narrative before engaging in the reading program. One major theme that emerged was the notion of Black victimization.

For example, Amelia,[10] one of the pre-service teachers I interviewed, noted that "When you look at African Americans throughout history, you see that they were not treated as humans. They were held in slavery and treated like animals, and then they were not guaranteed any civil rights when they were free."[11] Cynthia,[12] another pre-service interviewee, echoed a similar sentiment, "African Americans could not get a break. First it was slavery, then not able to vote until decades later; there were lynching, assignations, fire hoses, and de facto segregation."[13] Similarly, Santiago was fascinated by the amount of oppression experienced by African Americans. Although his narrative about Black history was filled with stories of African American triumph, he spent a considerable amount of time during the US history class he was teaching focused on African American victimization. Santiago's narratives focused on African Americans as second-class citizens and racial violence. His class session on lynching illustrated this point when he showed an Omaha courthouse lynching and stated, "If you were a Black man during this time . . . lynching was used as a sort of reminder [of your subjected place in society] if you stepped out of line."[14]

What is interesting about the pre-service teachers' historical consciousness (through narrative) regarding Black victimization is that the majority of their narratives ignored White supremacy. Racism was narrated as acts of past transgression without a nexus to the present. In many of the narratives, the stories of Black victimization were told as if no antagonists were present. If the oppressor was mentioned, the context situated the act as the behavior of a small contingent of bad individuals who acted independently from the dominant ethos in place in the United States at the time.

Black history that does not strike a balance between oppression and agency is problematic. As West noted, "Black people have never been simply victims, wallowing in self-pity and begging for white giveaways, they have—and are—victimized."[15] Victimization narratives allow for a certain passivity of the Black experience. Victimized experiences in Black history only make sense if juxtaposed with Black agency that accompanied acts of victimization. For example, the narratives focusing on the lynching of Black bodies in the United States during the early twentieth century are problematic if not examined alongside Black advocacy such as Ida B. Wells and the NAACP.[16] To be clear, Black Americans were and still are oppressed, and the victimization narrative is salient for understanding Black historic experiences. Yet, when victimization becomes the primary Black history narrative, historical oppression desensitizes Black humanity. Oppression becomes central to Black ontology, which influences how Black history and Black people, and in effect, our society, are assessed. The Black experience becomes, as Cynthia noted, a never-ending story of abuse and leaves little space for agency and diversity—and this has important implications for Black historical consciousness.

Use of History

To illustrate the uses of history, I focus on my work with Patrick Womac on *A Bundle of Silences*.[17] *Bundle* examined a 2010 summer television series on Fox News Broadcasting that featured a public curriculum on the United States' Founding Fathers. The television show titled, *Founders' Friday*, encompassed ten shows hosted by conservative talk and radio show host Glenn Beck. We were interested in two particular shows that focused on the notion of Black Founding Fathers. While I disagreed with Beck's assertion of what a US "Black Founder" was, his recognition that Black people should be considered Founders of the United States was intriguing. For Beck and his guests, Black Founding Fathers were Black men who unquestionably believed in US egalitarian ideas and were willing to protect those principles. In contrast, I have described Black Founders, borrowing from Richard Newman, as those men and women of African descent (sometimes Africans) who helped "establish separate Black institutions, served in the military to fight for Black freedom, developed Maroons settlements, and used media to openly challenge and critique White Founders ideas on democracy."[18] Notwithstanding that our definitions were different, when viewing the show, it was clear that Beck's use of history to explain Black Founders served a purpose that revives little known Black history, and was used to provide a revisionist history on race and racism.

One of our examples centered on the show's discourse around the three-fifths provision in the US constitution.[19] The show's guest argued that the three-fifths compromise was a strategic plan by northern statesmen to eradicate slavery. The thesis as presented by show guest, David Barton, was that the three-fifths compromise reduced the southern states' power in Congress because it "cut the slavery representation to Congress in half," which made it more difficult to get a proslavery representative in Congress. Based on this premise, the show lauded the Constitution as an anti-slavery document. Womac and I made the argument that the show's premise on the three-fifth clause silenced several narratives involving the institutional aspects of racism that allowed racism to prosper for many decades. Nevertheless, *Founders* is a good example of how the uses of histories inform historical consciousness.

The *Founders* program used history to convey certain messages about US people, places, and institutions. Several arguments were presented throughout the show:

1. Racism existed but was never as bad as illustrated through history.
2. The Constitution represented the ethos of the country and that racism represented acts of a few and never was a structural phenomenon.
3. White allies were instrumental, maybe more so than Black people, who fought on behalf of victimized Black people.
4. Message to Black Americans about seeing themselves as agents, Black Founders, instead of victims, slaves.

Here, history is used to infer that Black people fought for freedom as part of the Black oppositional tradition but that their agency was tied to seeking validation from White society. The show's creators used history to tell a story of the United States as a country beyond critique and that morality succeeds despite setbacks; any suggestion of racism, as part of the institution, is an act of being mis-educated. In other words, individuals, not systems, are responsible for racism.

Historical Culture

To illustrate the dynamics of historical culture, I turn my focus to the utility of history textbooks. History textbooks are well known instruments for transmitting historical culture and are used prolifically in most Western education systems. However, history textbooks in the US in particular have a complicated and racist history with Black history. For decades, history textbooks indicated that Black people were naturally inferior, lacked morals, and contributed little to the advancements of society. Terms such as "lazy," "heathens," and "ignorant" were used to illustrate Black people's otherness. The narratives also dictated that White, middle class, heterosexual, protestant, able-bodied, and male bodies were the apex of civilization.[20] For much of the early twentieth century, historical culture indicated that Black people lacked a substantive history that did not need to be seriously considered within K–12 history education.

Black history in K–12 schools has improved over the past century. Black history is celebrated in many schools globally, textbooks have eliminated much of the outright racist terminology used previously, and there has been a shift in historical culture that affirms the legitimacy of Black history. For example, Wineburg and Monte-Sano hint that Black history has gained much from the changing historical culture.[21] In a survey of two thousand US high school students about famous Americans, their results indicated that three Black historical figures—Martin Luther King Jr., Rosa Parks, and Harriet Tubman—were the most popular answers. However, Dagbovie warns us that Wineburg and Monte-Sano's study is "intriguing, yet misleading" because the survey lacked information on student knowledge, curriculum approaches, and teacher capacity, and he believes the researchers were too optimistic about the mainstreaming of Black history in the K–12 curriculum and by teachers.[22] Other US research reveals that students' knowledge, curriculum, and classroom teaching often lacks nuance and complexity when it comes to teaching and learning Black history.[23]

The complex relationship between K–12 Black history and curriculum has extended to K–12 Black history textbooks. The publication of Black history textbooks by major textbook companies might indicate an attempt at altering historical culture about Black history but when examining the textbook narratives one could argue that historical culture has not changed in terms of how we qualitatively engage with Black history narratives. For example, in "Black History as Anti-Racist and Non-Racist ," I examined two high school Black history textbooks to ascertain how racism was explained in the texts.[24] I found that while both textbooks had different racial narratives, one textbook, in particular, was *non-racist*. By non-racist, I mean the text included narratives that describe racism as overt and highly visible behaviors of *irrational* individuals. Narratives that are non-racist marginalize how past structures influence the present. Non-racism assumes colorblindness, racial neutrality, and the possibility of racial innocence of people, policies, and ideas. Stated another way, non-racism is a polite way of not discussing the nuances of racism—it rarely challenges the status quo of White supremacy.

The Black history textbooks provide an interesting look into historical culture. Since the late nineteenth/early twentieth century, Black history has attempted to change historical culture. Early authors provided the necessary counter narratives to challenge mainstream K–12 history. These efforts at curriculum transformation helped establish multicultural education, Afrocentrism, and laws that mandate the teaching of Black history in K–12 public schools. Yet, as Thorp alludes, historical culture can only be changed to a certain degree.[25] While historical culture has changed our attitudes towards the legitimacy of Black history, the subject is still largely marginalized within K–12 history curricula and mostly regarded as an elective course with little training, support, and resources. If non-racist Black history textbooks are any indication, Black history, despite its transformative tendencies, can be used to maintain the status quo of a historical culture of Whiteness under the guise of diversity.

Conclusion

I ask the question, what is Black historical consciousness? Using my research as well as other salient scholarship in the field of K–12 Black historical studies, I attempted to understand how Black history and historical consciousness intersect through K–12 education, teacher education, and through media. If historical consciousness is closely tied to identity and how we interpret our own and others' present circumstances based on history, then to be historically conscious about what has been classified as being "Black" is really about being historically unconscious of that construct. In other words, despite efforts to quantitatively expand Black history in schools, we are continually mis-educated about the Black historical experience and the implications are as follows.

Ultimately, Black historical consciousness is centered around the notion of Black suffering—these are the narratives that highlight pain and anguish as being the very fabric of Black life histories in the US and therefore have shaped our present thinking regarding Black people's experiences. Our historical culture reifies Black suffering as narrative because in most curricula (as well as through popular culture and media) the first narratives about Black people are told through the lens of enslavement. These stories have almost neutralized Black suffering as normal and infer that Black people hold a certain passive acceptance of these conditions. As a result, the humanity of Blackness is lost within the narration. The Black suffering narrative becomes so ingrained in our historical culture that histories which challenge the Black suffering narratives are met with contention or even disbelief.

The Black suffering narrative, the way it is used as pedagogy, and its stake in our historical culture, is part of a continual mis-education about Black people that has influenced anti-Black sentiments in society. By anti-Black, I do not simply mean a tangible discrimination or even racism against Black people, but an ideology that continues to construct Black people as slaves. Michael Dumas explains anti-blackness as:

> Socially and culturally positioned as slave, dispossessed of human agency, desire, and freedom. This is not meant to suggest that Black people are currently enslaved (by whites or by law), but that slavery marks the ontological position of Black people. Slavery is how Black existence is imagined and enacted upon, and how non-Black people—and particularly whites—assert their own right to freedom, and right to the consumption, destruction, and/or simple dismissal of the Black.[26]

Within K–12 Black history spaces, anti-blackness is reciprocated through narratives that frame Black people as agentless, oppressed people who present problems to US democracy. As my research into the attitudes of pre-service teachers reveal, in many respects, Black people are seen through a sympathetic lens which nevertheless views them as victims, not as collaborators of US democratic ideas. Such historical readings critically influence not only the ways Black people and their histories are remembered, but also how those ideas and interpretations influence historical culture and historical consciousness in contemporary US society.

On the flip side, when Black agency is rendered neutral, historical consciousness encompasses what I call a White epistemic logic. White epistemic logic rationalizes Black historical experiences and ways of knowing/doing through traditional Western European perspectives. The concept allows Black agency in history to be partnered with Whiteness, allowing these narratives to appease and coalesce Whiteness, rather than be contentious of it. White epistemic logic situates history as just that, history, and not the multiple histories that help develop a historical consciousness. Black people's historical experiences (and the behaviors and ideologies that accompany those experiences) are just different. When Black and White historical experiences are told in such as a way that implies a similarity, there is a tendency for the use of history to convey a sort of racial utopia. As *Founders* inaccurately implied, the country has had some racial problems in the past, but race was not a big deal to White or Black people because the egalitarian ethos of the US, racial equality eventually won out.

So what can educators do to elicit a sort of Black historical consciousness? First, historical consciousness theoreticians need to expand the canon to explore the thoughts of non-Western thinkers. Scholars such as Franz Fanon (2004), Sylvia Wynter (1992), W.E.B. Dubois (1935/1969), Michel-Rolph Trouillot (1995), Joyce King (1992), and many others have provided much thought, while not naming it so, into notions of historical consciousness.[27] Second, as Carter G. Woodson (1929) reminds us, Black history is more complicated than it seems: to effectively teach Black history, teachers (in schools and in other institutions) have to be well prepared to not only teach *about* Black people but *through* Black people.[28] This is important to consider because featuring Black historical voices provides content that disrupts White epistemic logic. K–12 Black history should challenge the ahistorical cultural ethos, and consist of a delicate balance between themes of victimization and oppression, and perseverance and resistance, while also acknowledging Black agency through subtle forms of resistance, and recognizing the multitude of tragedies and setbacks experienced by Black people.[29] Such ideas help us understand the nuances of movements such as Black Lives Matter as not oppressive, but a liberating group that extends the legacy of the Black oppositional tradition. Without these aspects present within K-12 history, we are left with a paradigm of Black suffering viewed through White epistemic lenses that continue the oppression of Black people.

LaGarrett J. King is an Associate Professor of Social Studies Education at the University of Missouri-Columbia. His research interests include Black history education, race, social studies, and curriculum foundations. He earned his PhD from the University of Texas-Austin and has taught social studies in Texas and Georgia. His has published in several high-ranking journals including *Theory and Research in Social Education*; *Race, Ethnicity, and Education*; *Teaching Education*; and *Journal of Negro Education*.

Notes

1. Thorp, "Towards an epistemological theory," 21.
2. Seixas, *Theorizing historical consciousness*, 9.
3. Seixas, *Theorizing historical consciousness*, 10.
4. Biko, "The definition of Black consciousness," 360–63. Biko's Black consciousness is an ideology and mental attitude that developed through the Black liberation movement in apartheid South Africa.

5. Thorp, "Towards an epistemological theory."
6. Rüsen, "Historical consciousness."
7. Trouillot, *Silencing the past.*
8. Thorp, "Towards an epistemological theory," 22–23.
9. King, "Learning other people's history"; King, "Teaching black history."
10. Amelia is a pseudonym to protect the pre-service teacher's identity. Amelia was a 21-year-old history major and an education minor. She considered herself a feminist and social justice educator. She claimed that her family had helped many Exodusters (African Americans who migrated to Kansas from southern states in the late nineteenth century) move to Kansas.
11. King, "Learning other people's history," 438.
12. Cynthia is a pseudonym to protect the pre-service teacher's identity. Cynthia was a political science major with an education minor. She classified herself as an "average" white girl with little to no knowledge about Black history.
13. King, "Learning other people's history," 437.
14. Santiago is a pseudonym to protect the pre-service teacher's identity. Santiago was a history major and minor in education. Santiago, who was born in Mexico City, became a naturalized United States citizen months before the study was conducted. King, "Teaching Black history."
15. West, *Race matters,* 21.
16. See Wells-Barnett, *A Red Record;* Zangrando, *The NAACP crusade.* NAACP stands for the National Association for the Advancement of Colored People.
17. King and Womac, "A Bundle of silences."
18. King, "More than Slaves," 91.
19. The three-fifths compromise was a provision in the US Constitution that allowed enslaved Black people to be counted as three-fifths of the South's population for the purposes of congressional representation. Barton's thesis was based on a moral ethos of antislavery advocates of the North. Others argue that the three-fifth compromise upheld and protected slavery as the foundational ethos of the United States. See Marshall, "Reflections."
20. Elson, *Guardians of tradition.*
21. Wineburg and Monte-Sano, "'Famous Americans.'"
22. Dagbovie, *African American history reconsidered.*
23. See Alridge, "The limits of master narratives"; Carlson, "Troubling heroes"; Woodson, "We're Just Ordinary People."
24. See King, "Black History."
25. Thorp, "Towards an epistemological theory," 23.
26. Dumas, "Against the Dark," 13.
27. Du Bois, *Black Reconstruction;* Fanon, *The Wretched of the Earth;* Joyce Elaine King, "Diaspora literacy"; Wynter, *Do not call us Negros;* Trouillot, *Silencing the past.*
28. See Woodson, "Annual report."
29. Dagbovie, *African American history reconsidered,* 51.

Bibliography

Alridge, Derrick. "The limits of master narratives in history textbooks: An analysis of representations of Martin Luther King, Jr." *Teachers College Record* 108, no. 4 (2006): 662–86.
Biko, Stephen. "The definition of Black consciousness." In *The African Philosophy Reader,* edited by P.H. Coetzee and A.P.J. Roux. London: Routledge, 1998.
Carlson, Dennis. "Troubling heroes: Of Rosa Parks, multicultural education, and critical pedagogy." *Cultural Studies↔Critical Methodologies* 3, no. 1 (2003): 44–61.

Dagbovie, Pero Gaglo. *African American history reconsidered.* Urbana: University of Illinois Press, 2010.
Du Bois, W.E.B. *Black Reconstruction in America, 1860–1880.* New York: New York University Press, 2001.
Dumas, Michael. "Against the Dark: Antiblackness in Education policy and discourse." *Theory into practice* 55 (2016): 11–19.
Elson, Ruth Miller. *Guardians of tradition, American schoolbooks of the nineteenth century.* Lincoln: University of Nebraska Press, 1964.
Fanon, Frantz. *The Wretched of the Earth.* New York: Grove Press, 2004.
King, Joyce Elaine. "Diaspora literacy and consciousness in the struggle against miseducation in the Black community." *The Journal of Negro Education* 61, no. 3 (1992): 317–40.
King, LaGarrett J. "More than Slaves: Black founders, Benjamin Banneker, and Critical intellectual Agency." *Social Studies Research and Practice* 9, no. 3 (2014): 88–105.
King, LaGarrett J. "Learning other people's history: Pre-service teachers' developing African American historical knowledge." *Teaching Education* 25, no. 4 (2014): 427–56.
King, LaGarrett J. "Teaching black history as a racial literacy project." *Race Ethnicity and Education* 19, no. 6 (2016): 1303–18.
King, LaGarrett. "Black History as Anti-Racist and Non-Racist." In *But I Don't See Color, The Perils, Practices, and Possibilities of Antiracist Education,* edited by Terry Husband, 63–79. Rotterdam: Sense Publishers, 2016.
King, LaGarrett J., and Patrick Womac. "A Bundle of silences: Examining the racial representation of Black founding fathers of the United States through Glenn Beck's founders' Fridays." *Theory & Research in Social Education* 42, no. 1 (2014): 35–64.
Marshall, Thurgood. "Reflections on the bicentennial of the United States Constitution." *Harvard Law Review* 101, no. 1 (1987): 1–5.
Rüsen, Jörn. "Historical consciousness: Narrative, structure, moral function, and ontogenetic development." In *Theorizing historical consciousness,* edited by Peter Seixas, 63–85. Toronto: University of Toronto Press, 2004.
Seixas, Peter. *Theorizing historical consciousness.* Toronto: University of Toronto Press, 2004.
Thorp, Robert. "Towards an epistemological theory of historical consciousness." *Historical Encounters* 1, no. 0 (2014): 20–31.
Trouillot, Michel-Rolph. *Silencing the past: Power and the production of history.* Boston: Beacon Press, 1995.
Wells-Barnett, Ida B. *A Red Record: Tabulated Statistics and Alleged Causes of Lynchings in the United States, 1892-1893-1894.* Salt Lake City: Project Guttenberg, 1895.
West, Cornel. *Race matters.* Boston: Beacon Press, 1993.
Wineburg, Sam, and Chauncey Monte-Sano. "'Famous Americans': The changing pantheon of American heroes." *The Journal of American History* 94, no. 4 (2008): 1186–202.
Woodson, Ashley. "We're Just Ordinary People: Messianic Master Narratives and Black Youths' Civic Agency." *Theory & Research in Social Education* 44, no. 2 (2016): 184–211.
Woodson, Carter G. "Annual report of the director." *Journal of Negro History* 14, no. 4 (1929): 361–70.
Wynter, Sylvia. *Do not call us Negros: How 'multicultural' textbooks perpetuate racism.* San Francisco: Aspire, 1992.
Zangrando, Robert. *The NAACP crusade against lynching, 1909–1950.* Philadelphia: Temple University Press, 1980.

CHAPTER 12

"There Are Current Lessons from the Holocaust"

Making Meaning from Jewish Histories of the Holocaust

JORDANA SILVERSTEIN

Leading the memory studies boom, the history of the Holocaust and its aftermaths has proved to be of great interest to scholars internationally, generating large amounts of scholarship. For me, the interest in taking up a study of Holocaust memory in Jewish communities in Melbourne and New York, and in examining the ways in which histories of the Holocaust are taught in Jewish schools in those two cities, began when I was in my Honours year, and had its roots in my being a member of the third generation: the granddaughter of two Holocaust survivors. Having undertaken a year of Holocaust studies as part of my Jewish studies education at a Jewish high school in Melbourne in the closing years of the twentieth century, and having been profoundly moved by the experience—both emotionally, and in terms of the future direction of my studies—I was curious to turn my tertiary historical training back onto what I had previously learned.

And so I took up my PhD in this field as I tried to understand the work that Holocaust education does in Jewish schools, a project which over the following decade would lead to the production of a book on the topic, *Anxious Histories: Narrating the Holocaust in Jewish Communities at the Beginning of the Twenty-First Century*. In the final manuscript, I began by quoting Theodore Adorno: "The premier demand upon all education is that Auschwitz not happen again. Its priority before any other requirement is

---

Notes for this section begin on page 183.

such that I believe I need not and should not justify it,"[1] and it was this approach which guided me through my research. What does a Holocaust pedagogy, memory, and history which is oriented towards ensuring an end to genocide and mass violence look like? How, in this way, does Holocaust education—a form of *lieux de memoire*—become public facing and acting?

Over the course of the interviews I conducted with teachers of the Holocaust it became evident that for some, this was crucial. Many of them oriented their teaching towards producing a different future for their students: it was of serious concern to some of them that their students think about what these lessons of the past meant for Jews, but also, for a few of them, for all people. For all of the teachers though, the construction of a narrative of the Holocaust, and the passage of this to their students, was fundamentally produced by a concern over the place of Jews in the world at the beginning of the twenty-first century. Could another Holocaust happen again to the Jews? Holocaust pedagogy, I would come to understand, functioned as both a symptom of the fear that it could, as well as a working-through of that fear, or that anxiety. The narratives taught were saturated with a concern for how the Western world feels about Jews.

Indeed, a governing concern of Holocaust pedagogy for one teacher in New York was that "we're dealing with how do these students live and work with this memory and what are they supposed to do about it."[2] Memories of the Holocaust, for this teacher as for others, are something one carries with them; they require work to be understood and incorporated; and they require the carrier to undertake some action. But the carrying of these memories also makes a difficult demand on the teacher: how to formulate memories—or histories—of the Holocaust such that the students are able to live, work, and *do* something with them.

The book that I wrote was thus formulated around a series of questions: What work are the histories of the Holocaust that are being taught in these Jewish schools in Melbourne and New York undertaking? What lessons are being taught? What identities are being negotiated and formulated? How are the deep, terrifying horrors of the Holocaust and their after-effects being managed? What is the Holocaust being made to mean in these Jewish schools? Histories of the Holocaust taught in these conditions are not mere dispassionate histories. For many, they are not lessons of a foreign land or a foreign people. When teachers in these Jewish schools teach their students about the Holocaust they *feel* that they are teaching something of themselves and their students. This, importantly, determines what is being taught.

As well as being *lieux de memoir,* these teachings are fundamentally instances of postmemory, a term coined by US literary theorist Marianne Hirsch to describe the belatedness of those memories carried by those of us who came *after*. Postmemory "characterizes the experience of those who grow up dominated by narratives that preceded their birth, whose own belated stories are evacuated by the stories of the previous generation shaped by traumatic events that can be neither understood nor recreated." Moreover, "postmemory is distinguished from memory by generational distance and from history by deep personal connection. Postmemory is a powerful and very particular form of memory precisely because its connection to its object or source is mediated not through recollection but through an imaginative investment and creation."[3] The teachings, therefore, carry this postmemory, producing Jewish memories of the Holocaust into the future and thereby creating a traumatically imbued historical consciousness for this Jewish public.

Jewish schools serve an important role in Jewish communities around the world. Acting as a place for the learning of Jewish history, culture, and religion, as well as enabling certain formations of Jewish sociality, they provide a space for the creation of both new Jewish cultures and the transmission of older memories and histories. While they occupy a different place in New York than Melbourne—substantially more Jews in Melbourne, as a proportion, attend Jewish dayschool than those in New York—in both locations they play an important role in passing on an awareness of the ways that global Jewish life and history was fundamentally changed by the Holocaust.

The work I undertook in *Anxious Histories* was not to provide a history of Holocaust education, nor to suggest ways that the Holocaust could be "better" taught. That is however, important and interesting work that needs to be undertaken. What would a new high school history of the Holocaust look like, one which engages substantially with current thinking in academic Jewish history and global history? One which is oriented further towards the complexities of the Holocaust, rather than providing a simplified chronological narrative, as so many of the teachers provide? And, more profoundly, one which is particularly *of this moment* (which is, it is clear, one of a rising right-wing sentiment in both the United States and Australia)? How will the Trump presidency, for instance, change Holocaust education, and change the types of historical consciousness which teachers feel they need to pass on to their students? This is a vital topic of discussion, with the parallels between Trump and the Nazi regime—and the importance of these parallels occupying space within public discourse—already being widely discussed.[4]

The project instead was focused on thinking historiographically and was in large part an excursion in critique. In it I provided a close, deconstructive analysis of a series of texts—and located these texts within broader collections of historical literature—in order to unravel and understand a body of historical narration. My intention therefore was not to describe an objective truth, or reading, of what teachers are teaching. Instead, I wanted to open a series of questions, to complicate the narratives, and not to provide definitive answers. I was interested in how the discourses that the teachers pursue are productive: what do they say? What do they produce, or help to constitute? Some of the teachers, I should note, probably did not recognize themselves in my analysis of their teachings: this was perhaps an inevitable outcome of the methodologies I used. In the text I also attempted to show the difficulties involved in constructing a narrative of the Holocaust which can be taught in history classes in schools: there are many impossibilities involved in such pedagogical pursuits.

The historical narration, or historiography, that I explored in the project was predominantly based on curricula collected from, and a series of interviews conducted with, teachers of the Holocaust in a selection of Jewish dayschools in Melbourne and New York in 2006. In this way, as I mentioned above, I was not presenting a longitudinal study of Holocaust education: this was more of a snapshot, or a glimpse at an archive captured during one year in time. Curricula were collected where available: four schools in Melbourne and three in New York supplied curricula. Interviews were conducted with teachers of the Holocaust in five schools in Melbourne and seven schools in New York.[5] Some of these schools were co-educational, and some were all-girls schools. No all-boys schools participated in the study—teachers were either too busy to participate, did not return phone calls or emails, or explained that they do not teach about the Holocaust, as they teach only "modern Jewish history (nationhood to present)."[6] For that reason, the conclusions that I presented were not intended as totalizing or final. The project did not present information about the general state of Holocaust education at that moment in time, but rather moved through some questions and ideas that arose through interactions with these twelve schools, and the fifteen teachers at the schools, involved in the research. Some of these conclusions could have applied to the teaching at other schools entirely, others may not have. In undertaking the project in this way, I was looking to understand those ways in which Holocaust awareness and understanding can operate, and to get a sense of the kinds of things that can be passed on to students.

While my intention was never to be representative in my sampling, I did want to try to understand any important differences that would be created by the different religious or political approaches to Judaism or Jewishness carried by the schools. At the same time, I was limited by the problem of a lack of response from some schools, as well as the availability of different types of schools in the two cities. As reflects the make-up of Jewish dayschools in New York, the schools I engaged with there were overwhelmingly Orthodox-oriented.[7] One non-Orthodox school participated in the study, and this was a non-denominational school.[8] To be an Orthodox school means that the school is associated with the Orthodox Jewish movement, which, in brief, entails a belief that the Torah was written by God and that it must therefore be strictly followed.[9] I spoke with teachers at schools in three different boroughs of New York City, thus gaining an understanding of the different geographical communities. The schools in Melbourne included a Progressive school, two Modern Orthodox schools, one Orthodox school, and one secular school. The Progressive school is associated with the Progressive movement, which entails a particular idea of the modernization of Judaism, involving not only different understandings of the ways in which the Torah and Talmud should function, but also a belief that Judaism should be molded to a degree with the secular societies in which it exists.[10] The secular school in Melbourne and the non-denominational school in New York both predominantly focus on Jewishness as cultural and nationalistic, rather than religious. While Jewish religious festivals are observed to a degree, the emphasis is placed on history and culture rather than religion.

The schools which participated are overwhelmingly Ashkenazi in orientation—the student body at these schools, as well as the understandings put forward in the teachings, come from Eastern European origins. There was only one school which was explicitly predominantly Sephardi, wherein the students and families which make up the school body are descended from Jews from Spain and the Iberian Peninsula. One school in Melbourne is—according to an interviewee—largely made up of families with Russian backgrounds, as is one of the schools in New York. Even though there is this dominance of Ashkenazi people and frameworks, and the majority of the events of the Holocaust took place within the geographic confines of Ashkenazi Jewish life, I felt that when considering the formative importance of these histories in Jewish historical consciousness, it was important to consider what this hegemonic status meant. As part of the broader project of problematizing the ideas, histories, and methodologies of the Holocaust which were being taught and the Jewish identities which are thus created, I sought to align this project with those other deconstructions of Jewishness that seek to dislodge hegemonic Ashkenazi histories and identities from their dominant positions within US and Australian Jewish historiographies.[11] In other words, in developing this project I came to realize that the sense and understanding of Jewish history carried by large populations in these two cities is formed through Eurocentric historical narratives. What would it do to histories of the Holocaust if this Eurocentrism were challenged? How could this produce a new sense of Jewish history? This is a question I was able to touch on by bringing to the surface some of the groups—such as women, and non-Jewish victims of the Holocaust—who are often left out of dominant narratives. But there remains a great deal of work to be done in furthering this project, which would, I think, serve to create new perspectives on what a public historical Jewishness entails.

Most of the schools in Melbourne are dominated by descendants of survivors of the Holocaust, although there are certainly also students from other national and ethnic backgrounds. In New York the schools all contain some students who are descendants of survivors of the Holocaust, however not to the same degree as in Melbourne. This is largely due to the different histories of the two cities, wherein the vast majority of Jews migrated to New York from Russia and other parts of Eastern Europe at the turn of the twentieth century, whereas Melbourne had its biggest influx of Eastern European Jews after the Holocaust.

Indeed, there is quite a bit which makes these two Jewish communities different: their size, diversity, longevity, political histories, relationships to non-Jewish society, make up just a few. One of the interesting things I learned, given all these differences, was that the ways that they taught about the Holocaust differed only to a very small degree between the two cities. When substantial differences in teaching occurred, it was based much more on the individual teacher, or the particularities of the school. For instance, a teacher at an all-girls Orthodox school in Melbourne told me that she tells her students about the importance of remembering by reflecting on their tasks as religious Jewish women. She said that she uses:

> a few different articles, one about Pesach, one about Hanukkah, and one about Shabbat, and I think that there's a significance, that the girls will relate to them; because not all of them, but many of them, sing every Friday night, every Shabbat. . . And so we talk about how meaningful it must have been that it continued on even if it was only ordinary soup with potato peel in it. And what that woman had done in order to get that.[12]

This teacher said that she tells the students that she has:

> a very strong Jewish identity, and sometimes when I'm cooking for Shabbat on a Friday afternoon, or when I'm in [synagogue], and I think, even if I wanted to stop doing it, I just don't think that I could because of the obligation to keep it going after what happened. And I think that's okay, you know. I think that that's a part of it but partly we're teaching it so they know, but also partly because of the *mitzvah* [good deed] of *zachor* [remembrance].[13]

In this way, it was her search for a connection with her students that enabled her to create a particular approach to her teachings. This particularity was echoed by a teacher in New York, who told me that, because she had done work interviewing survivors for Steven Spielberg's archive, she had ready access to numerous survivor testimonies. She would regularly bring these testimonies into the classroom, she told me, in order to have her students understand the people at the heart of the stories. This was unique amongst the teachers—all of them used survivor testimonies at different times (and indeed an exploration and critique of the use of testimony became a significant part of the project)—but no others used testimony to such a substantial degree.

What was of fundamental interest to me was the way that a narrative of the Holocaust had come to appear to be settled on, across the two cities. A teacher at a school in New York explained that in her teaching she begins with stories of antisemitism in Europe prior to the Holocaust, then discusses:

> the rise of Nazi Germany and Hitler's agenda against the Jews, the platform of the Nazi party, the SA, the development of the youth movement . . . and how Hitler developed his concentration camps to the SS, the one-day boycott of Jewish shops and services, and the expulsion of Jews from universities, the development of the Gestapo, the public book burning in Berlin, the Nuremberg Laws, and explaining how there was a steady development of Nazism within Germany and Jews were not necessarily prepared for how it would peak eventually, they thought that this was an isolated circumstance.[14]

She described the continued rise of Nazism, Kristallnacht, the Kindertransport, the political situation throughout Europe, the experiences of Jews in different parts of the Nazi Reich, the Einsatzgruppen, the massacre at Babi Yar, the Wannsee Conference, the death camps and concentration camps, before coming to the Allies invading Europe and liberating the camps. Jewish responses to the Holocaust are then explored through an examination of music, writings, sculpture, and other forms of artistic response. This is a representative example of the chronological summary of the Holocaust which the vast majority of the history teachers interviewed present to their students. It is a modernist narrative, which progresses towards the "happy ending" of liberation, and, normally, of the creation of the Jewish State of Israel. Across the interviews, teachers repeatedly told me about strikingly similar narratives being taught.

What was meant by this seemingly settled narrative, which made a comparison between the two locations possible? I came to the conclusion that a comparative reading of these two very different communities was thinkable for two reasons: because both communities are located within settler colonial states,[15] and because every teacher at every school who participated in this study expressed strong Zionist feelings and ideas as a basis for the school and their teachings, yet this Zionism is one which coexists with the maintenance of Jewish communities outside Israel. These two ideologies serve to structure the histories which are taught. Moreover, as a result of years of the public production of Holocaust narratives—in popular culture, museums, teacher education courses, and the like—teachers in these two locations had developed a narrative for a young Jewish public. It was a narrative which would draw on testimony and primary evidence, on traumatic memory and historical research, but would be based on modernist tropes and would serve to produce a sense of a Jewish communal history, memory, and future.

As I touched on above, the teachers consciously wanted to transmit to their students a sense that they inhabited a Jewish history which would shape their relationship to the world. This was reflected throughout the interviews, as with the teacher quoted above who pondered what students are "supposed" to do with the memories they "live and work with." For another teacher, the "number one" thing she wanted her students to learn from studying the Holocaust:

> is that for students today, our Jewish children today, to understand that as much as America is a very democratic society, life in the dawning years of the Holocaust was just as democratic in the respective societies, and the calamity of the nature of the Holocaust was able to transpire. I think it is important for our kids to understand that complacency and that easiness with which they [have] begun to regard American society in the twenty-first century is actually quite a myth. And they need to understand the factors that enabled the Holocaust to take place, they need to understand the conditions, they need to understand the reactions or lack of reactions coming from the outside world. They also have to understand what the victims of the Holocaust lost.[16]

Another teacher in a school in Brooklyn explained that she wants the students to understand the Holocaust as a:

> loss. It's not just an abstract 'Oh, once upon a time there were Jews who resided here,' but we want them to feel the loss. We want them to know what was lost. There was a rich and vibrant life in Eastern Europe and Western Europe. And it's hard to say, but the 'Never Again' idea, which is problematic but nevertheless we want the kids to understand that this is what was lost and *don't ever think that it can't happen again* because we're living in a very dangerous world and *the kids today feel that*. And the slogan 'Never Again,' is that in fact a reality? And lots of the kids feel that today we're living in a dangerous world and that I think that you have to be ever-vigilant about antisemitism and be aware that there are current lessons from the Holocaust.[17]

Comments like these echoed through the interviews. It was evident that the teachers, like others throughout Jewish communities and Jewish studies faculties around the world, are grappling with the ways that the histories of the Holocaust which occupy Jewish life and thought can be used to produce a sense of history that students can carry with them as they go about their lives.

In recent texts such as *Probing the Ethics of Holocaust Culture,* which acts as a follow-up to the foundational volume Saul Friedländer edited in 1992, *Probing the Limits of Representation: Nazism and the 'Final Solution,'* historians and literary theorists have worked to understand the different ways in which the Holocaust can be understood and narrated, and the teachers in the schools I explored in my *Anxious Histories* project provide a way for these ideas to reach larger audiences.[18] While oftentimes not consciously drawing on academic theorizations, these teachers and their pedagogies are clearly part of these broader conversations regarding the function and place of the Holocaust in Jewish life. Examining the teachers' words and curricula in this light makes it clear that there is no truly adequate way to teach about the Holocaust. Every narrative, every system of representation, falls short in some way. The problems of representation, of containing history within a narrative or relying on a set of signifiers, forever remain. Regardless, this research provided the possibility of learning something new about the ways that Jewish identities in Melbourne and New York at the beginning of the twenty-first century are thoroughly informed by Jewish histories of the Holocaust. It became apparent that by examining these new histories and historiographies being created we can understand much about how migrant groups, and post-genocide groups, negotiate their marginality, and we can thus grasp some of the pain—and some of the possibilities—imbricated in such marginality.

Jordana Silverstein is a Postdoctoral Research Associate with the ARC Laureate Fellowship Project, "Child Refugees and Australian Internationalism, 1920 to the Present," led by Professor Joy Damousi. As part of this project, Jordana is investigating the history of Australian Government policy directed towards child refugees from 1970 to the present. Her previous research has focused on questions of belonging, nationalism, identity, historiography, sexuality and memory, which she has primarily investigated through the lens of Australian Jewish history. She is the author of *Anxious Histories: Narrating the Holocaust in Jewish Communities at the Beginning of the Twenty First Century* (2015) and a co-editor of *In the Shadows of Memory: The Holocaust and the Third Generation* (2016).

Notes

1. Adorno, *Can One Live after Auschwitz*, 19. Cited in Silverstein, *Anxious Histories*, 1.
2. Interview with Teacher A at School NYA, 16 November 2006. All of the teachers and schools were referred to anonymously. Within this schema, a school in Melbourne was designated with an "M" and a school in New York with an "NY."
3. Hirsch, *Family Frames*, 22.
4. See, for instance, Lubchansky et al., "Never Again?"
5. While there are countless Jewish schools in New York, there are only seven in Melbourne that teach at a high-school level. For that reason, a comparative number of schools in New York were involved in this study.
6. Email from Principal A at School NYH, 28 November 2006.
7. This is representative of the composition of Jewish schools in New York and the US more generally. Marc Lee Raphael explained that "in 2005, approximately 205,000 students were enrolled in 760 schools (elementary and secondary)—about two-thirds in New Jersey and New York—an increase of more than 10 percent in the past five years. Of these students . . . more than 80 percent are affiliated with Orthodox institutions, and Orthodox-affiliated schools are growing at a slightly faster rate than the non-Orthodox schools. This is in part the result of an insistence in most Orthodox synagogues today that boys and girls attend Jewish day schools as well as of a higher fertility rate among the Orthodox." Raphael, "Introduction," 11.
8. There are schools in New York which are organized by the Conservative movement, but they did not participate in the study.

9. See Prell, "Triumph, Accommodation, and Resistance," 124–6; Neusner, ed., *The Alteration of Orthodoxy*.

10. See Kaplan, *American Reform Judaism*; Neusner, *The Reformation*.

11. Ella Shohat, writing with reference to the use by European Jews of the texts of the Cairo Geniza—that great storehouse of Egyptian Jewish life and culture, which was emptied out and its contents taken to England—writes of the "asymmetrical power relations" that exist between the Egyptian worlds that are documented in these texts, and the European scholars who use the texts to write histories. She claims that "[w]ithin these asymmetrical power relations, Euro-Jewish scholars infused the colonized history with national meaning and telos, while, ironically, Arab-Jews were simultaneously being displaced and, in Israel, subjected to a school system in which Jewish history textbooks featured barely a single chapter on their history." Shohat, *Taboo Memories,* 227.

12. Interview with Teacher A at School MC, 27 April 2006.

13. Interview with Teacher A at School MC, 27 April 2006.

14. Interview with Teacher A at School NYB, 10 November 2006.

15. See Wolfe, "Logics of Elimination."

16. Interview with Teacher B at School NYB, 28 November 2006.

17. Teacher A at School NYD, 26 October 2006. Emphasis added.

18. Fogu et al., *Probing the Ethics*; Friedlander, ed., *Probing the Limits*.

Bibliography

Adorno, Theodor W. *Can One Live after Auschwitz? A Philosophical Reader*. Edited by Rolf Tiedemann. Translated by Rodney Livingstone et al. Stanford: Stanford University Press, 2003.

Fogu, Claudio, Wulf Kansteiner, and Todd Presner, eds. *Probing the Ethics of Holocaust Culture*. Cambridge, MA: Harvard University Press, 2016.

Friedlander, Saul, ed. *Probing the Limits of Representation: Nazism and the 'Final Solution.'* Cambridge, MA: Harvard University Press, 1992.

Hirsch, Marianne. *Family Frames: Photography, Narrative and Postmemory*. Cambridge, MA: Harvard University Press, 1997.

Kaplan, Dana Evan. *American Reform Judaism: An Introduction*. New Brunswick: Rutgers University Press, 2003.

Lubchansky, Matt, Lisa Rosalie Eisenberg, Leela Corman, Eli Valley, and Sarah Glidden. "Never Again? Five Jewish cartoonists on the use of Holocaust imagery in Trump's America." *The Nib*. The Response. 15 March 2017. Retrieved 16 March 2017 from https://thenib.com/never-again.

Neusner, Jacob. *The Reformation of Reform Judaism*. New York: Garland Publishing, Inc., 1993.

Neusner, Jacob, ed. *The Alteration of Orthodoxy*. New York: Garland Publishing, Inc., 1993.

Prell, Riv-Ellen. "Triumph, Accommodation, and Resistance: American Jewish Life from the End of World War II to the Six-Day War." In *The Columbia History of Jews and Judaism in America*, edited by Marc Lee Raphael, 114–41. New York: Columbia University Press, 2008.

Raphael, Marc Lee. "Introduction." In *The Columbia History of Jews and Judaism in America*, edited by Marc Lee Raphael, 1–17. New York: Columbia University Press, 2008.

Shohat, Ella. *Taboo Memories, Diasporic Voices*. Durham, NC: Duke University Press, 2006.

Silverstein, Jordana. *Anxious Histories: Narrating the Holocaust in Jewish Communities at the Beginning of the Twenty-First Century*. New York: Berghahn Books, 2015.

Wolfe, Patrick. "Logics of Elimination: Colonial Policies on Indigenous Peoples in Australia and the United States." (University of Nebraska Human Rights and Human Diversity Initiative monograph series 2, no. 2.) Lincoln, NE: University of Nebraska-Lincoln, 2000.

CHAPTER 13

The "Realness" of Place in the Spiral of Time

Reflections on Indigenous Historical Consciousness from the Coast Salish Territory

MICHAEL MARKER

While I have always tried to be practical in my thinking about the questions of Indigenous inclusion in interpretations of the past, I have learned from Elders and knowledge holders that Indigenous meanings of history include realities beyond what Western minds consider to be historical truth. Events in the past, particularly in cross-cultural colonial contexts, have multiple and shifting interpretations. For example, treaties and negotiations between settlers and Indigenous leaders raise questions regarding communication between language and thought systems that were vastly different from each other. It is likely that people across this divide misunderstood each other more than they understood each other.

In this cross-cultural context, history not only contains multiple accounts and interpretations of events, but also multiple forms of consciousness for experiencing the reality of events. If history is concerned with what is "real" (as it must be), then, for Indigenous people, the real is a layered condition that includes metaphysical relationships with plants, animals, and more-than-human entities. The "realness" of events includes elements of landscapes and relationships that contain these metaphysical forms. This realness is a fundamental condition of Indigenous knowledge systems and therefore central to an Indigenous historiography. It is perplexing to merge Indigenous cultural

Notes for this section begin on page 197.

understandings about place and metaphysics into a practical conversation about the meaning of history.

It is nonetheless crucial, as I will explain here, that historians and educators try to include Indigenous interpretations of history in the curriculum beyond simply introducing creation stories and myths. These stories are sometimes introduced at the beginning of a history textbook, before the *real* history is started. The mythic aspect of Indigenous relationships to land does not show up anywhere else in these books. It drops out before real time begins, essentially before the story of colonization. I think it is actually quite a practical and important question to ask if the metaphysical aspects of Indigenous narratives about the past are a historical narrative of truths rather than fictions. Many Elder narratives contain challenges to mainstream assumptions about categories of knowledge. What does it mean to take the words of Elders seriously and follow the threads of ideas about the meanings of the past?

My experience teaching and studying in Coast Salish communities and my efforts to translate Indigenous ideas about land, spirituality, and time to colleagues at universities have led me to conclude that conversations about the meaning of history are not so much plagued by disputes about the factuality of past events—although there is certainly plenty of dispute about "facts" regarding the past. It is more that the two worlds, Indigenous and Western, maintain separate discussions in separate languages. Even with English as the common academic language, the Indigenous concepts make more sense in Indigenous languages. I must be clear that I do not mean to narrowly invoke the controversial discussions of the Sapir-Whorf Hypothesis[1] asserting that worldviews and languages are non-translatable across cultural and epistemological divides. Yes, there are aspects of language/thought disconnects that are at work in these *oceans apart* regarding historical consciousness; but to put it more directly, it seems that each knowledge system is concerned with different questions and therefore require different kinds of conversations that reflect toward different purposes.

What is now called *decolonizing* involves delineating differences in ways of knowing between Indigenous and Western knowledge systems, toward reclaiming suppressed visions of Indigenous life. In Canada, the "Truth and Reconciliation Commission Report" has presented the most recent information on the reality of residential schools and government policies resulting in the destruction of languages, ecological knowledge systems, supportive family relations, and community health. This report has prompted a national conversation that has pulled *history* out of the past and placed it center stage for a discomfiting panoply of inquiries regarding Canadian identity. The toxins of this history of residential schools as well as other forms of colonization continue to poison Indigenous life in the transference of trauma through time. The meaning of the past—*history*—is something Indigenous communities have an enormous stake in.

Indigenous and de-colonial scholars have been foremost in emphasizing the past being located in the present. Emerging curriculum reform/development movements across Canada aim to place Indigenous history and culture prominently in classrooms, correcting texts where Indigenous people were often portrayed as primitive others outside the story of western civilization— a "people without history."[2] When leaders of settler nations that colonized Indigenous lands make public apologies for such nefarious projects as residential schools, as in the case of Canada and Australia, we must think historically and imaginatively about such confessions of national regret. It implies a rethinking of a moment in the past, a kind of time-travel to arrive in that past with a different and countervailing mindset regarding the choices of that moment. It also implies that *new minds* in leadership roles have evolved from that time into the present moment that could and would make different choices regarding the treatment of both Indigenous peoples and Indigenous lands. However, without understanding specific forms of Indigenous consciousness and identity, dominant interpretations of what constitutes history (for example, a story of the "progress" of the nation state) are likely to reproduce the values associated with colonization and industrial exploitation of land. Such exploitation has meant ecological devastation on Indigenous lands from pipeline oil spills, contaminated rivers and lakes from mining operations, among countless other industrial poisonings for the sake of profit and globalized economic competition. The apologies for policies of cultural genocide that were part and parcel to "nation building" are perfunctory and empty with regard to a *reconciliation* between Indigenous and Western knowledge systems.

I enter into this conversation carefully. I would not, and could not, give a cogent account of a universal Indigenous historical consciousness. Such a thing does not exist outside of the unique proportions of each Indigenous peoples' territory. However, I can offer an account of my own experience and observations regarding Coast Salish time and place: the learnings from these communities, and the people who have shared ideas with me. This includes concepts of the ever-emerging traces and sediments of human, and the more-than-human, relationships with the natural world, welding layers of metaphysical and physical reality together.

The Preeminence of Place over Time: The Maiden of Deception Pass

This writing will focus broadly on what I consider to be the two most essential elements of an Indigenous historical consciousness that are difficult to integrate into conventional Western ideas of the methods and meanings of history. They have to do with: (1) the essential "place-ness" of Indigenous history, and (2) the ways that the past is soaked with metaphysical actuality. With regard to place-ness, much of Vine Deloria's work emphasizes that when it comes to making meaning of the past, Indigenous people were never as concerned with *when* an event occurred as *where* it occurred: "It was not what people believed to be true, but what they experienced as true. Hence, revelation was seen as a continuous process of adjustment to the natural surroundings and not as a specific message valid for all times and places."[3] So, in this way of understanding time and space, it is always space, or place, that contains the meaningfulness of reality placed in time. This moves the conversation about an event always into the realm of what the "sentient landscape that listens and responds to human indiscretion" is *speaking* to with regard to animals, plants, geologic forms, winds, tides, and more-than-human entities in intricate contexts of balance.[4]

Daniel Wildcat, following from Deloria, has put it well:

> The big picture in Indigenous thinking is informed by the lands, by other living species (the trees, the animals, and the birds), and by the unique ecological and environmental features of the continents; in short, the custom of 'viewing life in its totality' informs Indigenous thinking. It means that the distinctions we make and the categories we form function very differently from those found in modern Western civilization.[5]

The second element of Indigenous historical consciousness that is inextricably interwoven with the considerations of place is what I call the metaphysical imperative. Elders and Indigenous knowledge holders narrate the meanings of the past referencing the sacred and metaphysical dimensions of their territory—without a sharp division between material and mythical occurrences. Narrations of that which occurred before the present include interstitial zones where human and more-than-human entities etched the morality of the cosmos enacted not just *in* a place, but rather *by the consciousness, agency, and holism* of a place injected into human concerns. As Deloria suggests, "space generates time, but time has little relationship to space."[6]

All of these contemplations about time and place have practical influences in a number of public policy and social contexts, especially in schools and teaching. When I was a history teacher for Coast Salish high school students in the 1980s, I struggled continually with the curriculum and the expectations about what I would be teaching. What was history? What gets contained inside history and who decides this? The high school program, integrated into the tribal college located on the Lummi reservation in Northwest Washington State, was, at that time developed to parallel the local public school curriculum—such that students could transfer between the two systems. I was supposed to teach a required course named Washington

State History. However, Elders and parents invited me to ask deeper questions about some historical categories and borders that would be dissolved by a Coast Salish inquiry into the meaning of events in places, in time.

First of all, the Coast Salish territory includes British Columbia and Washington State, but these are lines drawn by colonizing agents, not by Salish minds and understandings of the territory. So, a history of both British Columbia and Washington State—the Salish world—would make more sense given the location of the tribal college and the realities of the students who had relatives on both sides of a colonial border. The textbooks of the local school district were simply useless: the information on Indigenous life was isolated, scant, and inaccurate because of gross simplification of intricate knowledge systems. After consulting with Elders, I assembled a collection of readings from books in anthropology, geography, and even ethno-botany of the Pacific Northwest. The students produced writings on topics that focused on human relationships to the Coast Salish territory with an emphasis on the changes and choices for people over time. We called it "history class" and didn't name it further.

I was trying to understand what history meant—particularly the meaning of a history of this place that would develop consciousness from inside the territory rather than only reference the views of outsiders/settlers who were chronicling Coast Salish space gazing from a trespasser's perspective. Where does history begin? How do we think about beginning a narrative that is historical? Such a narrative always collects from the narratives of a previous-ness. One of the central problems of the history discipline, from an Indigenous perspective, is that its sequential rationality is structured in a linear fashion. Indigenous understandings of the past are that the movement of time is not linear, but rather circular or a spiral motion. Vine Deloria's explication about the difference between Western and Indigenous concepts of time is useful for thinking about the challenges for history's sequential cumulative quality: "Time has an unusual limitation. It must begin and end at some real point, or it must be conceived as cyclical in nature, endlessly allowing the repetition of patterns of possibilities."[7]

When I was at the tribal college, I worked with Elders and language teachers who continually referenced the stories that contained the moral and spiritual meaning of the Coast Salish universe. In the Northern Straights Salish Lummi language (Xwelemi chosen) the word *sche'lang'en* is used to mean the sacred proportions of time and space that are woven together with a moral recipe for the peoples' survival. To use the word *sche'lang'en* is to invoke the ancient way of life as shown in the narratives about humans and more-than-humans in the past. The foundation of history then, from a Lummi position, is *sche'lang'en*. The Coast Salish understanding of this metaphysical and physical blending in the narratives about the past is enormously complex. Keith Thor Carlson notes, "Stó:lō people classify their historical narratives into two categories: *squélqwel,* often translated as 'true stories' or 'real news' which seem to tell of recent happenings; and *sxwōxwiyám,* which often appear to describe the distant past."[8] However, while Carlson finds this classification useful to make *some* distinctions between narrative forms, he also warns against thinking of a dichotomy between mythical pasts and a recent past since this would be an inadequate representation of Coast Salish knowledge systems and beings who move between these realms in time and place. In other words, conventional Western divisions between mythic, primordial time, and recent events evade comprehending that Salish "history is filled with significant points of interpenetration between the two dimensions."[9]

One of the accounts that I heard during my time as a history teacher was the story of the Maiden of Deception Pass.[10] This story is attributed to Samish people. Like so much of the Coast Salish world it interweaves with many communities and places in the Salish Sea. Linguist Brent Galloway analyzed and translated the version told in the Samish language by Victor Underwood at Tsawout Reserve on Vancouver Island in the 1980s.[11] The story is of a young woman, named *q^alasalwal* or sometimes spelled *Ko-kwahl-alwoot* who, while bathing near the shore, is spotted by the undersea headman or leader of a family group, a more-than-human being. Exuding the coldness of another world, he comes to the village, enters the longhouse, and asks to marry the young woman. He announces that he is the being who controls all the food from the undersea world. Starvation and death will come to the village if the girl's family refuses his request. In return, the undersea headman assures a continued flow of fish, clams, mussels, and the resources of life from the sea. The family must sacrifice their daughter to this other world of beings that percolate back and forth through the layers of an interconnected reality that provides the resources for survival. The daughter comes to the land for yearly visits but, after enough time in the undersea world, she undergoes transformations that produce barnacles on her face and seaweed growing for hair. Her father tells her that she should not return to her own people any longer. He comforts her that her village and family will continue to live in prosperity with the resources from the undersea world that her sacrifice has insured. The story has an element of deep sadness as the family loses a loved one to a realm from which she cannot return.

This narrative is profusely indexed with culturally specific signals—especially for youth—as it shows a deep-rooted truth about the ecological conditions that both merge and separate human and natural ecologies. This report from the *previous-ness* of a specific Coast Salish place provides information about being in the natural world that contains mythic time and the interface humans have with the natural world. Indeed, the food resources of the Salish

Sea, the salmon and shellfish, were provided by natural systems so incomprehensively intricate and vast that these *sxwōxwiyám* were the methodology for historical knowledge of an ecological primordial familiarity.

The Elders told me, "this is our history; this is our *sche'lang'en*." From the Elders I recognized that the best way to engage this history—as real history and not a fictional "legend" or "myth"—was to take the students to the place where the story exists on the land. This positions the *sche'lang'en* as the meaning of a place *where something happened*. The sacred narrative from the landscape continues to renew the story allowing it to exist in a previous time but also maintaining itself in the present space and time. The event/story both happened at a specific place and a less specific time, yet also exists as a recurring theme for the larger morality of the Coast Salish world. Keith Basso's work with the Cibecue Apache is chronicled in his well-known book, which takes for its title the axiom of Indigenous knowledge: "wisdom sits in places."[12] Likewise, in the inquiry about an Indigenous historical consciousness, it would seem that history also sits in places. Basso describes how Apache Elders use place names to cause the appearance of landscapes that contain the ancient moral substance from the past to enter a person's consciousness:

> So her mind went to those places, standing in front of them as our ancestors did long ago. That way she could see what happened there long ago. She could hear stories in her mind, perhaps hear our ancestors speaking. She could recall the knowledge of our ancestors.[13]

So it was that I wanted to bring the fifteen high school students to this important story from the history of the Coast Salish land and water. I drove the van of high school students to Deception Pass for an all-day field trip. Our classroom was not the place to talk about this story and the distance between the College and Deception Pass was only forty miles. Elsewhere, I have shown how Elders will refuse to discuss certain events in the past if the inquiry occurs in a place where the history does not belong, and instead take individuals on journeys to the place where an important story is said to dwell in a landscape.[14] When we arrived and walked around the rocks and ledges we looked into the waters below to see the eelgrass waving in the vigorous current. This is said to be the hair of the Maiden of Deception Pass. The Elders do not say that it *is symbolic* of her hair or that it is some other distanced meaning from the actuality of *being* the hair of an ancestor from a parallel realm. The Elders recognize that this is a linguistic sensibility from the *sxwōxwiyám* layer of reality. Back at the classroom, the students and I talked about how this condition is one where the eelgrass can *be* hair in a larger view of reality and language. Not all the students were engaged with the concept of being in the place where the story dwells, but at later times

I did utilize the story as a reference for the deep ecological minds of Coast Salish ancestors. And, I do think that travelling to the place where the story exists in the landscape produced some form of psychic glue that made the story more potent and real for the students. Elders assert these stories are part of an historical consciousness that was intact in the minds of the Coast Salish people as they first encountered the Europeans who arrived to *map* their already well-mapped lands.

Universalizing History, Colonization, and the Moral Dimensions of Landscape

Was I teaching history and developing historical consciousness by taking students to the site of an ancient story and then discussing the meaning of the story in a cross-cultural context? Until recently, historians and social scientists would have placed the account of the Maiden of Deception Pass in the category of a myth or legend—a fiction segmented away from real history and even as a "non-history." After all, history is supposed to be a truth-telling of the past, an empirical, evidence-based account of what happened. And yet, as Sherry B. Ortner has explained, "history is not simply something that happens to people, but something they make—within, of course, the very powerful constraints of the system within which they are operating."[15] A growing number of scholars in history, science, and social science are coming to understand that Indigenous knowledge systems contain intricate and advanced information. They are not primitive fictions, but innovative expressions of ancient wisdom in places.

The idea of progress compresses and universalizes the meaning of history. In a linear account of history, Indigenous people become objects in the dominant narrative of the creation of settler states. In this constriction, they can only exist as "Other," a victim of the inevitability of modernity's advancement. Historical knowledge, like other forms of Western knowledge, is organized and controlled as a discipline. Academic disciplines decide what counts as valid and universal knowledge—within their disciplinary boundaries. Indigenous and de-colonial scholars such as Nakata (et al.) describe, "the role of the disciplines in constructing a corpus 'about' the Indigenous, which continues to shape and re-shape understandings and knowledge production 'about' and 'by' the Indigenous in the present." Meanwhile, they continue, "Indigenous critique of the universalising Western standpoint announces that there are other epistemologies and other standpoints from which Indigenous people come to know the world and from which we understand and analyse our more recent encirclement by Western knowledge over the last few centuries and its legacies."[16]

The separating and bordering of knowledge into disciplines has had a silencing effect on Indigenous expressions of meaning, especially historical meaning. Making space for an Indigenous historical consciousness within the discipline of history will require major revisions of some taken-for-granted assumptions regarding evidence about the past. Geographer Jeff Olliver, writing about the "diverse and sometimes eclectic sources" he employed to describe the Stó:lō landscape of the *contact zone* in the nineteenth century Fraser Valley, notes that "approaching history from this angle has also meant a significant departure from more conventional plotlines."[17]

Indigenous views of life were expressed without making Western-style distinctions between categories of knowledge. The holism of Coast Salish understandings of time and space were contained in totalizing, but not universalizing, words like *sche'lang'en*. Such knowledge standpoints still belonged only to the Indigenous territory but they were complete expressions of reality *within* that landscape. Vine Deloria has described the tension between Western disciplinary modes of thought and Indigenous expressions. His comments, while unique to Sioux modes of thought, are consistent with what I have found in Salish views of life and knowledge:

> Unlike Western thinkers, for example, the Sioux did not separate their thoughts into categories and disciplines. Everything was practical, economic, political and religious all at once. Indeed, they had a word to describe this totality, *wounicage*, which simply meant 'our way of doing things.' They accorded other people the right to have their own ways also. Although Sioux people did not develop 'disciplines' as ways of sorting knowledge and inquiry, they nonetheless had an observational and analytical approach that generated knowledge of the world. Their view of life was holistic. All experiences were carefully analyzed and remembered, and beliefs always had an empirical referent.[18]

Deloria's explication of the holism of Indigenous knowledge as described by the word *wounicage* matches the ways Elders used the Xwelemi chosen word *sche'lang'en* to explain the deep meaning of placed historical accounts in the Coast Salish world. There are a number of moral teachings that are conveyed in this narrative about events that happened in a place that still circulates the story of the people living in ecological balance with the natural forces of their territory. For Coast Salish youth, there is a message of caution about the zone between water and land as between the zones of life and death. The story recognizes certain physical and spiritual danger in interstitial zones both in the physical and metaphysical realm.

The beaches of the Salish Sea and the banks of the rivers are potent spaces between worlds. There is also a profound significance in the young woman's sacrifice and transformation from human to a more-than-human being for her people's survival. The meanings of this story are not simple, though: there is a sublime ambiguity in this narrative about the nature of reality that has layered dimensions interpenetrating each other. A narrative like the Maiden of Deception Pass provides the empirical referents that Vine Deloria notes, since the ecology of the place was experienced at the same time the narrative about human life was absorbed. The morality of the story makes more sense the more one understands relationships between tides, animals, plants, and humans as whole ecosystems.

With regard to the *metaphysical* imperative of this account, it would be a mistake to equate such Indigenous knowledge of the past with a religious belief. The truth of the story requires an understanding that while wisdom might sit in places, there are aspects that "travel" to other dimensions of reality as well. There is a growing body of scholarly work in traditional ecological knowledge and Indigenous science that sees the metaphysical blurring of Indigenous place-based narratives as consistent with quantum physics and the way reality behaves differently at the subatomic level.[19] The metaphysical aspects to some historical accounts do bend time and space in ways that correspond to the work of physicist David Bohm and his idea of an "implicate order" to the universe. Bohm viewed mind and matter as two expressions of an energy that resist understanding by Western modes of thought, but this knowledge has been available to Indigenous people through their language systems and distinctive ontologies.[20] As Deloria observed, "In physics the subatomic particles begin to take on a less substantial aspect until they can only be described in a set of relationships that seem to have spiritual or mental characteristics."[21] Metaphysical questions that are asked in the format of physics have a very different character than the credenda of religious groups.

While I did not bring quantum physics into my history classes with the students at the tribal College at that time, I have acquired more information since then and I certainly would introduce these ideas to students now. In that classroom, we used the story of the Maiden of Deception Pass and other stories as part of a decolonizing framework to consider their ancestors' ways of perceiving and thinking about time and space in that era when the settlers were first arriving in the territory. We considered languages and ideas from Coast Salish leaders as contrasted with those of the nineteenth-century settler minds. This led to more expansive conversations about epistemological divides and the multiple meanings of treaties and other negotiations of that era. One of the students in this high school group continued to study closely with Elders and traditional knowledge specialists. He presently teaches the Lummi language at the nearby public high school and is a researcher for the Lummi Nation in history, place names, and cultural reclamation.

Multiple Accounts, Multiple Realities, Metaphysics

Keith Carlson has described metaphysical aspects of Stó:lō historical consciousness and the multi-world condition of Coast Salish places in straightforward language that corresponds with my questions of what history might be from inside this knowledge system. He does not refer to the variegated reality of the Coast Salish world as being bizarre, or a fiction. For example, the descriptions of mystical tunnels in Salish space and time are simply part of the cosmological holism of the real world:

> Special tunnels link various sites on the Indigenous landscape of southwestern British Columbia's lower Fraser River watershed. Although they cannot be found on government-produced maps, and are not readily visible to casual travellers, for those who know the history and know where to look, the tunnels are real. Local Native Elders explain that you do not need to be Aboriginal to find them, nor do you even need to believe in their reality to be affected by them. People occasionally travel through these mystical portals, but the journey is inevitably dangerous. . . . Travel through these tunnels is almost instantaneous, and as such their existence shapes Indigenous views of the physical landscape by bending time.[22]

In 1936 Katzie Elder Old Pierre referred to these tunnels, translated from Halkomeylem as "underground channels," in what anthropologist Diamond Jenness titled the *Katzie Book of Genesis*.[23]

Supernatural components in history are not simply relegated to the primordial past. Carlson writes that Indigenous oral histories, containing metaphysical elements, sometimes offer contrasting interpretations from newspapers and other documentary sources regarding early twentieth century events and meetings with settlers. For example, contemporary Stó:lō oral tradition relates the way the leader Simon Pierre, trained in Coast Salish shamanism, "conjured a small bird and caused it to circle repeatedly less than a metre above his head during a dinner meeting with senior British and Canadian government officials."[24] This was intended as a display of Simon Pierre's spirit powers and was said (in Indigenous oral accounts) to have impressed the officials greatly. Written accounts of this 1906 event, on the other hand, make no mention of this display of spirit powers and portray the Aboriginal guests as being awed by the power of British and Canadian superiority instead. Carlson does not question the "truth" or *factuality* of what might have occurred at this moment in the past, but certainly this event raises many unresolved questions regarding what people from epistemological divides experience and pay attention to because of cultural expectations about how reality functions.

University education must navigate teachers and curriculum into deeper waters of the mind and spirit in considering Indigenous reality. Carlson maintains "when viewed across both temporal and cultural divides, the subtleties of Indigenous ways of knowing are difficult to appreciate, but this does not mean that they are impossible to discern, nor does it absolve us from the task of trying."[25] In the Truth and Reconciliation Commission Calls to Action, one of the expectations is that government will make "curriculum on residential schools, Treaties, and Aboriginal peoples' historical and contemporary contributions to Canada a mandatory education requirement for Kindergarten to Grade Twelve students."[26] If the curricula and teacher training that is developed does not examine the ways that Indigenous people understood—and understand—the universe through advanced knowledge systems and deep ecological consciousness, the history of residential schooling may reveal only the darkness of racism and cultural genocide and fail to show the light of Indigenous wisdom that was devastated by the catastrophes of colonization.

When students learn about residential schools, it is now imperative that they be presented with an Indigenous standpoint on this history. Elsewhere, writing about the Coast Salish history of residential schooling, I have stated, "removing children from their land was, from this Indigenous ethos, an act of ecological violence."[27] Understanding that Indigenous communities developed nuanced and refined ways of knowing about the ecologies of places and the possibilities of the human spirit reveals the irony, paradox, and tragedy of colonization and "progress." What was lost was not just lost to Indigenous others; the catastrophe of the residential schools and coordinated policies of colonization suppressed and collapsed a knowledge of the natural world that is now a much-desired contemporary wisdom for diverse groups of new paradigm thinkers toward planetary survival.

New/Old Spaces and In-Between Spaces for Meanings of the Past

As a tribal college history teacher I was learning to open a thought portal into the past that would take me away from linear settler narratives of progress. For Coast Salish people, the flow of time swirls forward holding the metaphysics of the landscape in narratives of both human and more-than-human ancestors. Their history is not transportable; it belongs in these sacred places and continues to reveal the truth from the past nurturing the knowledge of the present. Wanting to respect a Coast Salish standpoint, I simply had to take the words of the Elders seriously about the meaning of history. It was more than *their* history as in some proprietary sense; it was the land's history and they were the holders of this knowledge, the narrators.

I came to understand that the meaning of the events of the past does travel in a circle—or perhaps a spiral—into the present to inform an understanding of identity in place for Coast Salish people. As the Elders said to me, "this is our sche'lang'en." In a sense *sche'lang'en* is a Salish teleology. Trying to respond to Elder requests to expand my thinking about my thoughts, I came to see the points of interpenetration from metaphysical and physical dimensions in narrations about the past that shape the peoples' understanding of the sacred geography. Without enacting the place-ness of this history by taking the students to an important site in their traditional territory, I would not have been able to build an epistemological foundation with them for comparative thinking about the minds of their ancestors in contrast to those of the colonizers. However, I must be clear that I do not wish to assert simple binary divisions between Indigenous and Western ways of knowing, portraying them as incommensurable.

In my experience in the Coast Salish territory, I have learned that the landscape contains the meaning of history and that this meaning is part of a layered reality with multiple points of metaphysical interpenetration. If the students of the future learn about Indigenous mindscapes as they learn about the history of colonization that shattered sustainable ways of life, they may gain new insights about the possibilities for being in innovative relationships with plants, animals, humans, and the more-than-humans. Expanding the parameters of historical consciousness to include Indigenous ontologies can propel a paradigm shift in educational possibilities.

Michael Marker is Associate Professor in the Department of Educational Studies at the University of British Columbia and the director of Ts"kel Indigenous Graduate Studies. Previously, he was Teacher Education Director at Northwest Indian College at the Lummi reservation in Washington State. He has published works related to Aboriginal education in *Paedagogica Historica, History of Education, History of Education Review, International Journal of Qualitative Studies in Education, Canadian Journal of Native Education, Harvard Educational Review*, and *Anthropology & Education Quarterly*. His present research brings to light ecological education and place-based pedagogies in the Coast Salish region. His forthcoming works are focused on Indigenous traditional knowledge in higher education, and place as research methodology.

Notes

1. See Fee, "The Sapir-Whorf Hypothesis."
2. See Wolf, *Europe and the People Without History*.

3. Deloria, *God is Red*, 67.
4. Cruikshank, *Do Glaciers Listen?*, 142.
5. Wildcat, "Indigenizing the Future," 423.
6. Deloria, *God is Red*, 71.
7. Deloria, *God is Red*, 71.
8. Carlson, *The Power of Place*, 63–64.
9. Carlson, *The Power of Place*, 65.

10. Deception Pass was named by George Vancouver in 1792 because he felt that the watery landscape had deceived him. What he thought was a peninsula turned out to be an island. Vancouver named Whidbey Island for his naval officer who found the channel. This history of colonial naming/mis-naming shows fundamental Eurocentric misunderstandings of Indigenous emplaced history. It is ironic that a Coast Salish place of revelation is now named a place of deception. Many aspects of Colonial toponomy in Indigenous landscapes reveal these kinds of dark ironies.

11. Thompson and Egesdal, eds., *Salish Myths and Legends*, 395–400.
12. Basso, *Wisdom Sits in Places*.
13. Basso, *Wisdom Sits in Places*, 83.
14. Marker, "Indigenous Voice, Community."
15. Ortner, "Theory in Anthropology," 403.
16. Nakata et al., "Decolonizing Goals," 124.
17. Olliver, *Landscapes and Social Transformations*, 201.
18. Deloria, *C.G. Jung and the Sioux Traditions*, 7.
19. See Meyer, "Indigenous and Authentic."
20. Bohm, *Wholeness and the Implicate Order*.
21. Deloria, *C.G. Jung and the Sioux Traditions*, 78.
22. Carlson, *The Power of Place*, 7.
23. Jenness, *The Faith of a Coast Salish Indian*, 11.
24. Carlson, *The Power of Place*, 267.
25. Carlson, *The Power of Place*, 272.
26. *Truth and Reconciliation of Canada*, 7.
27. Marker, "Borders and the Borderless Coast Salish," 483–4.

Bibliography

Basso, Keith. *Wisdom Sits in Places: Landscape and Language Among the Western Apache*. Albuquerque: University of New Mexico Press, 1996.

Bohm, David. *Wholeness and the Implicate Order*. London: Routledge and Kegan Paul, 1980.

Carlson, Keith Thor. *The Power of Place, The Problem of Time: Aboriginal Identity and Historical Consciousness in the Cauldron of Colonialism*. Toronto: University of Toronto Press, 2010.

Cruikshank, Julie. *Do Glaciers Listen?: Local Knowledge, Colonial Encounters, & Social Imagination*. Vancouver: UBC Press, 2005.

Deloria, Vine. *God is Red: A Native View of Religion*. Golden Colorado: Fulcrum Publishing, 1994.

Deloria, Vine. *C.G. Jung and the Sioux Traditions: Dreams, Visions, Nature, and the Primitive*. New Orleans: Spring Journal Books, 2009.

Fee, Margery. "The Sapir-Whorf Hypothesis and the Contemporary Language and Literary Revival among the First Nations in Canada." *International Journal of Canadian Studies* 27, no. 1 (2003): 199–208.

Jenness, Diamond. *The Faith of a Coast Salish Indian*. Anthropology in British Columbia, Memoir, no. 3. Victoria: British Columbia Provincial Museum, 1955.

Marker, Michael. "Indigenous Voice, Community, and Epistemic Violence: The Ethnographer's 'Interests' and What 'Interests' the Ethnographer." *International Journal of Qualitative Studies in Education* 16, no. 3 (2003): 361–75.

———. "Borders and the Borderless Coast Salish: Decolonizing Historiographies of Indigenous Schooling." *History of Education* 44, no. 1 (2015): 480–502.

Meyer, Manulani A. "Indigenous and Authentic: Hawaiian Epistemology and the Triangulation of Meaning." In *Handbook of Critical and Indigenous Methodologies,* edited by Norman K. Denzin, Yvonna S. Lincoln, and Linda T. Smith, 217–32. Thousand Oaks: Sage Publications, 2008.

Nakata, N. Martin, Victoria Nakata, Sarah Keech, and Reuben Bolt. "Decolonizing Goals and Pedagogies for Indigenous Studies." *Decolonization: Indigeneity, Education & Society* 1, no. 1 (2012): 120–40.

Olliver, Jeff. *Landscapes and Social Transformations on the Northwest Coast.* Tucson: University of Arizona Press, 2010.

Ortner, Sherry B. "Theory in Anthropology." In *Culture, Power, History: A Reader in Contemporary Social Theory,* edited by Nicholas B. Dirks, Geoff Eley, and Sherry B. Ortner. Princeton: Princeton University Press, 1994.

Thompson, M. Terry, and Steven Egesdal, eds. *Salish Myths and Legends: One People's Stories.* Lincoln: University of Nebraska Press, 2008.

Truth and Reconciliation Commission of Canada: Calls to Action. Winnipeg, Manitoba: Truth and Reconciliation Commission of Canada, 2015.

Wildcat, Daniel R. "Indigenizing the Future: Why We Must Think Spatially in the Twenty-first Century." *American Studies* 46, no. 3/4 (2005): 417–40.

Wolf, Eric. *Europe and the People Without History.* Berkeley: University of California Press, 1982.

CHAPTER 14

Intergenerational Family Memory and Historical Consciousness

ANNA GREEN

For the past thirty years or so my research has concentrated upon oral history and "history from below" in diverse historical contexts of labor conflict, everyday life in a community, environmental disaster, and the family. During that time approaches to oral history underwent transformative interpretive change, led by the Italian historians Luisa Passerini and Alessandro Portelli. Both identified, although arriving at this position from different perspectives, the distinct value and "credibility" of subjective memory.[1] Alongside these developments in oral history a new scholarly interest in the relationship between memory and history also led researchers to Maurice Halbwachs' sociological concept of "collective memory." Halbwachs developed his theory of collective memory in the 1920s, and seven decades later it re-emerged to dominate the burgeoning multidisciplinary field of memory studies.[2] This approach to the social construction of memory had particular resonance for research into national commemoration and memorialization, a major scholarly focus of memory studies at the time. But as an oral historian, studying personal autobiographical memory, I became increasingly concerned about the limitations of one particular aspect of Halbwachs' mnemonic model for oral history narratives.[3]

To recapitulate briefly, Halbwachs argued that memory is fundamentally socially-framed, and from childhood through to adulthood memories are created within specific social contexts and through active engagement with other human beings. That remembering does not take place in a vacuum,

Notes for this section begin on page 209.

but is embedded in social and cultural contexts, is paralleled in the later work of Passerini and Portelli. But reflecting the influence of his mentor, Émile Durkheim, Halbwachs further argued that collective memory performed a socially integrative function, and that while individuals remembered, it was the social group that determined which memories would survive. Halbwachs identified the family as the original mnemonic community, applying his theory, first of all, to the distinct, affective "framework of domestic memory." He argued that family stories are compressed, constructed narratives that demonstrate general attitudes and physical or moral qualities perceived to be inherent within the family. From the time we are born, he suggested, "the family is the group within which we pass the major part of our life, family thoughts become ingredients of most of our thoughts. Our kin communicate to us our first notions about people and things."[4] Halbwachs' approach is consistent with recent work in social psychology that draws attention to the positive, generative function of family stories.[5]

Halbwachs' insight into the social and cultural importance of family memory is central to my current research. But other dimensions of his approach to collective memory have come under critique. The first concerns the relationship between the individual and the collective. As James Fentress and Chris Wickham asked, does Halbwachs' theory "render the individual a sort of automaton, passively obeying the interiorised collective will"?[6] Secondly, what happens to memories that do not accord with the dominant social memory of the group? These do not disappear, as Halbwachs appears to suggest, and the sociological emphasis upon the functional role of memory in securing social cohesion neglects dissenting memories or those that appear to emphasize the painful or mendacious dimensions of human relationships. The final question relates more to reception: to what extent can we assume that collective memory, even when sanctioned by the state, is necessarily received by members of the public in the ways intended? Consequently, as an oral historian, I began to think about alternative ways to theorize family memory that did not begin from the functional premise of cohesion and could encompass the reflective, conflicting, and dissenting dimensions of remembering.

During the 1990s I became increasingly interested in bringing oral history into the public forums of history and curated an oral history museum exhibition constructed around sound as much as sight.[7] Introduction to the literature in public history and heritage further opened up questions around audience reception and public perceptions of the past. In this context, *The Presence of the Past* by Roy Rosenzweig and David Thelen (to which I will return a little later), and Peter Seixas's edited volume on *Theorizing Historical Consciousness*, particularly addressed the questions in which I was interested. The first concerned the limitations of "collective memory." To paraphrase the question Peter Seixas posed in the introduction to *Theorizing Historical Consciousness*, what could the concept of historical consciousness contribute to our understanding of oral history that Halbwachs' idea of collective memory could not?[8] Here, I am taking the definition of historical consciousness that emerged in West German pedagogical research in the 1970s, which emphasized the importance of the "life world" in framing everyday thinking about the past. This form of historical thinking contrasted with professional Rankean historiography in that it did not draw an impermeable line between past, present, and future. In everyday life, it is argued, we all move between these temporal dimensions in order to plan our lives and activities.[9] Originally published in 1979, the following definition of historical consciousness makes these psychological temporal connections between past, present, and future in historical thinking explicit: "Historical consciousness encompasses the inter-connection between an interpretation of the past (*Vergagenheitsdeutung*), an understanding of the present (*Gegenwartsverständnis*) and a prospect for the future (*Zukunftsperspektive*)."[10]

The key dimension of historical consciousness, as subsequently defined both by Jürgen Straub and Jörn Rüsen, is that of psychological orientation.[11] In other words, definitions of historical consciousness begin with each individual's need to orient him or herself cognitively, morally, and temporally to the world around them. And in contrast to collective memory, the relationship between the individual mind and the social context is envisaged in ways that does not exclude those diverse, dissenting, or conflicting voices of historical memory that the search for social cohesion tends to repress.

There are two further reasons why the concept of historical consciousness has now come to frame the way I approach family memory. The first is the use of the word "historical." Memory and history are often perceived to represent completely divergent thinking about the past. Many historians remain deeply sceptical about the value of memory as a historical source, and this is especially true in the context of family history, where quantitative demographic methodologies hold a particularly strong influence. This scepticism can lead to the neglect of the valuable, subjective dimensions of human thought, as Passerini and Portelli pointed out. Through the methodology of oral history, it is possible to access aspects of the phenomenological dimensions of family life. And, as I have argued elsewhere, memories of the emotional life and exercise of power and authority within the family should surely be included in the remit of historical enquiry.[12] The second reason is the use of the word "consciousness." Most research into human subjectivity pays little attention to the conscious, reflective individual. Poststructuralist, psychoanalytic, and other models of society and culture emphasize the collective, unconscious dimensions of human thought. As an oral historian I am also interested in the conscious dimensions of historical thinking, and the ways in which those I interview reflect upon their lives and the meanings they attach to experiences in the past. Are they passive automatons "obeying the interiorised collective will," or engaged, thoughtful, and sometimes rebellious historical actors?

Research into historical consciousness initially focused more narrowly upon the acquisition of national historical knowledge through formal education, and that remains an important strand of inquiry. But, as the British historian Raphael Samuel also concluded, "History has always been a hybrid form of knowledge, syncretizing past and present, memory and myth, the written record and the spoken word."[13] This cultural hybridity, the intersection between diverse forms of knowledge about the past—formal and informal, collective and private, accepted and contested—in historical thinking is one of the conceptual strengths of historical consciousness. It also signals the importance of learning how people actually think about the past, and why. But I would argue that despite this recognition of the diverse roots of historical consciousness the fundamentally powerful role of family narratives has been neglected. Two studies of family memory in Germany and Russia, conducted in the context of traumatic pasts and potential fear of historical moral responsibility, demonstrate that family memory can be deeply influenced by the dominant role of the state.[14] But is this also the case in pluralist democratic societies, or "postcolonial" nations? Very little research into family memory in these contexts has been done.

A national survey of popular history-making, by Roy Rozenzweig and David Thelen, *The Presence of the Past,* explored participation in history or heritage activities in the United States. It was followed by similar projects in Australia and Canada, and all three projects had a wider remit than family memory. Yet survey respondents in each country indicated that they placed more trust in family memory than in other forms of historical knowledge.[15] Why should this be so, when scepticism about the level of historical accuracy and seemingly arbitrary nature of memory is generally widespread? If exact verisimilitude is not what many appear to expect in family stories, what is being sought? One of the co-authors of the American study, David Thelen, argued that his participants' interest in the past concerned, above all, "the tension between individual and circumstances, and how individuals struggled, sometimes successfully and sometimes not, to take responsibility for those around them and those who come after them."[16]

Thelen's statement encapsulates the essence of family stories, but much more needs to be done to tease out the implications for historical consciousness. In the following discussion I will start this process and draw upon oral history interviews conducted in 2008–2010 for my first project on multi-generational family memory in Devon and Cornwall, England.[17] The majority of participants were found by random sampling of the electorate lists in two comparatively deprived communities: the first around a naval dockyard, and the second with a large rural hinterland. Contacting potential interviewees through random sampling generated an oral history cohort that expanded beyond community elites, maximized socioeconomic diversity, and avoided attracting only those with well-established genealogical interests. Twelve families ranging from two to four generations were recorded, and since evidence of transmission of family stories across the generations was a core question in the research, interviews were conducted separately with each participant. The interviews followed an interviewee-driven, interactive approach, leaving the narrative trajectory as open as possible.

In this this chapter I will briefly touch on three core dimensions of orientation evident in these oral history family narratives. The first two dimensions, the temporal connections between past, present, and future, and moral values, are regarded as key components of the orientation process in historical consciousness. I would also like to suggest a third, which relates to the physical world: defined as place, nature, environment, or landscape. Orientation to place has considerable antecedents in a substantial literature among geographers about the construction of identities.[18] To illustrate these three dimensions of historical consciousness in family memory I will draw upon the stories recounted by one family within the oral history cohort. This family consisted of a mother and daughter: Betty, born in 1937 and Alison, the original respondent to the random sample letter, was born in 1966. Earlier male generations of the family included seamen, gardeners on the local Cornish aristocratic estate, and skilled tradesmen, while one great-grandmother had run a dairy shop in Helston and another had become a dressmaker. Betty and Alison had held a variety of jobs from "lollipop lady" to factory worker. Their family stories traversed family experiences in the past of both hardship and economic security, and Betty's narrative also included trickster tales and mystical experiences. Her stories appeared to belong to an earlier rural existence, closer to the natural world and older village customs and beliefs. She possessed effective rhetorical oral storytelling skills, using variations in tone, pauses, repetition, a rich Cornish vocabulary, and humor to great effect.

Let us turn first to the question of time, that of past, present and future, which is at the heart of the concept of historical consciousness. Although Betty and Alison's family had not undertaken any genealogical research, their stories extended back beyond "living memory" in that they talked about forebears whom neither had ever known. It has been argued that most family (or social) memory extends to three generations, or ninety to one hundred years, but in this English family cohort stories about great-grandparents were not uncommon.[19] Family memory could, therefore, extend back into the mid to late nineteenth century. This was the case with Betty, and the following story stands as a key to the family narrative as a whole:

> But Great Grandfather L, he died in the flu epidemic in London, and the ship had to be sold [a hundred ton three-masted schooner] and all the debts paid. Then, of course, Great Grandma, she had to come into town; she came into Walsingham Place, and of course no help in those days, and she started a milliners and dressmaking business because she had four children.[20]

Subsequently Betty talked about the hardships and difficulties of family life after this unexpected death of the family breadwinner, such as her grandmother being sent into service as a child. She concluded: "They were tough, in they days. They had to be. I mean if they weren't tough, you know, it's survival, the weakest went to the wall, the strongest they survived. No help in they days, not when our grandmas was."

In this part of the interview Betty employs a more conventional linear narrative, moving from past to present. But, unusually, some of Betty's stories also included references to a comforting supernatural ancestral presence in the present.

> It's like I said, looking at the family tree they're all names. But listening to my father talk about his grandmother, it's made it a real person for me. The same with Auntie Liz, I mean people might say it's my imagination that sometimes I can feel her smooth my hair or put her hand on me shoulder . . . they think you're daft if you say you've seen something like ghosts or anything.[21]

In this way time itself is transcended, as manifestations of a particularly loved ancestor remains accessible to the human senses in the present. In so doing, this story challenges modern notions about death and the irrevocable passage of time.

Another aspect of time in these family oral histories relates to generational differences. Older and younger generations placed themselves in the stream of time facing in opposite directions. For the older generations, perspectives on family stories were framed through the lens of a life already lived; they looked back on the lives of earlier family generations, sometimes with satisfaction and often with regret. In four families out of the twelve, this regret led to elements of counterfactual thinking, the "what if" of memory and imagined alternative presents.[22] In contrast, the youngest generation recounted family stories as a counterpoint to their hopes for the future, for their lives yet to come. While aware of and acknowledging the family stories about poverty, lack of trust, disloyalty, or violence, they hoped to build a very different future for themselves and their children. One younger participant, in her late twenties, considered the stories about hardship valuable in reminding younger generations who grew up in more prosperous or emotionally settled times and circumstances that it is possible to survive misfortune: "if your family has survived, I don't know, horrible things, it's worth just knowing you could survive. . . . it keeps you grounded a bit more, I think."[23] This, indeed, may be the purpose of these stories.

None of the interviewees structured their family narratives around the nineteenth or twentieth century "history of historians," although there were discrete references to World War I and II, early campaigns for women's rights, the Depression of the 1930s, the trade union movement, and the rise of the Welfare State and social security.[24] The family stories do not lack a historicist dimension, and each participant at some point actively reflected upon the differences between past and present. But the driving agent in many family stories, that which generated the peripeteia around which the family narrative revolved, were less the external events and more the reactions or behavior of a specific forebear. Consequently, family stories, as signalled by Thelen, often derived their meaning from the attribution of personality traits and character to family forebears that had affected the lives of future generations, and/or were inherited by them. These stories were imbued with moral values and judgments about social relationships, the second dimension of historical consciousness briefly considered here.

For many participants in this project, family stories revolved around behavior that put the family at risk, such as grandfathers who gambled, were abusive, or abandoned the family. The word "survival" arose frequently when thinking about the family past.[25] But survival may take many forms, and Betty's family narrative includes both a conventional narrative of economic survival by her great-grandmother, and trickster tales, or the magical interventions of gypsies (Romani). Her father and mother both told her these family stories, and she in turn has passed them on to her daughter Alison. Many related to rural, village life earlier in the twentieth century, such as a trickster story about earning a shilling catching a vicious cockerel. Other stories were about specific forebears, and Betty described what she called a "trait" of "eccentricity . . . that I think did come through the family." In this story, two sisters passed their older cousin Jack on their bikes without responding to his greeting. When they later asked him, on the way back, to repair a puncture in Ethel's tyre, he responded: "You didn't know me last time and I don't know you now. And that is a characteristic of the P's, you cross them, like a Romani, you fall out with them . . . goes right through the family and not only that, it's carried on for generations, which I think is ridiculous."[26] This story demonstrates the existence of a perceived shared family identity based on an inherited personality trait, but rather than building cohesion it highlights a characteristic that pushes the family apart. Secondly, this also demonstrates another way in which family memory often contrasts with "the history of historians" through the attribution of inheritance. The perception of sharing personality traits with earlier generations tends to emphasize continuity between past and present, rather than change over time.

The third dimension of historical consciousness, that of spatial or environmental orientation, was also evident in a number of the family narratives. In many cases it related to the search for a place of family origin, but it could extend beyond that to the natural world, or landscape in general. Both Betty and Alison explicitly emphasized their sense of belonging in Cornwall. Both had visited sites of family memory such as the gardens where forebears had worked or houses where they had lived. Both mother and daughter also talked about their emotional attachment to the countryside as children: Betty described how "you'd go for a walk, and you'd see all sorts in the hedge, like different flowers, the shapes of twigs. They call it daydreaming now I suppose, but you could see and it'd give you pleasure . . . but you did, you notice little things like that, like trees and flowers, and first snowdrops coming out."[27] And Alison talked about catching magpies, and going ferreting, rabbiting, picking mushrooms or whimberries, and making sloe wine with her grandfather.[28] While both Betty and Alison wondered about the relevance of the stories about their rural childhoods for the next generation, the landscape and natural world enter into many of the family stories. Does this indicate that there is an element of emotional and/or cognitive orientation to the physical world that should be included in the conceptualization of historical consciousness?

Conclusions

This family memory project in England demonstrated, first of all, that family stories about the past are transmitted across generations, and that the youngest generation actively engage with them when thinking about their own lives and plans for the future. In terms of temporal orientation, the family stories extended to between three and five generations, and in some cases beyond living memory.

The participant generations, however, located themselves in time facing different ways. Older family members used family stories to look back and trace family fortunes to the present, while younger generations deployed the same stories as either jumping off points, or counterpoints, for their plans and hopes for the future. There is also a strong dimension of continuity in family stories, in contrast to the professional historical goal of explaining change over time. Through underlying assumptions about both inherited personality traits and constant cultural norms of ethical behavior, our interviewees emphasized elements of continuity between generations. Change in the external environment was given much less prominence in the narration of family fortunes. Finally, in one family story ghostly traces of forebears could be sensed as a benign presence in the present. In all these ways the past lived on in the present in meaningful and emotionally powerful ways. It is, perhaps, time to think about Bill Schwarz's suggestion that memory may represent a fourth dimension of time.[29]

In terms of social and moral orientation, the family stories were structured around the norms of ethical or proper behavior towards those within the family and without. The personality traits of forebears were at the forefront of the stories, and their failures to meet the moral family norms of trust, loyalty, affection, and support function as the peripeteia in many family narratives. These stories were not about building family cohesion, as Halbwachs suggested, since they rest upon the behavior or actions that tore the family apart and contributed to ongoing problems in the present. While the scope for personal agency is diminished in much recent scholarly theorizing over the past decades, within family stories individual agency—for good or ill—remains the driving force in the narrative. The English family stories, therefore, reflected a wider unresolved tension over the extent of human autonomy or self-determination.

Two further questions relating to the relationship between family memory and historical consciousness are those of gender and place. Rosenzweig and Thelen touched upon the significance of gendered participation in their national survey. Most volunteers participating in this research were women, and women may be culturally perceived as responsible for ensuring that family memory is preserved and transmitted to the next generation. If this is the case, what are the implications of gender for family stories? Are women transmitting, through family stories, gendered moral rationalities?[30] Finally, I would argue for the inclusion of spatial or environmental orientation in historical consciousness. The importance of place varied between families and individuals in this project, but emotional attachment to local landscapes, urban or rural, were a consistent thread throughout many of the oral histories.

While the early work in historical consciousness focused upon the acquisition of historical knowledge through formal education systems, family stories at times appear to operate in a parallel universe, attached by a relatively slender thread to the "history of historians." This disjuncture between public and private narratives about the past dismays many historians, and further oral history research into family intergenerational memory may be able to illuminate the connections between collective or national narratives and family stories. This is one goal in my current research into Pākehā (New Zealand European) family intergenerational memory in New Zealand.[31]

The relationship between private and public narratives is particularly important in a "settler" nation coming to terms with its past. In this much larger project, with fifty multigenerational families located through a similar random sample of the General Electoral Rolls, I hope to address the questions raised in this chapter, including those relating to temporal frameworks, moral tensions, gendered narratives, and place or environment in family stories. One question that could not be addressed through the English oral history cohort concerned the implications of genealogical research for family memory and historical consciousness. In contrast to the English families, early signs indicate that the New Zealand participants have a much more extensive interest in genealogy.

These questions take on an additional dimension in the context of a colonial/postcolonial society, and the New Zealand study is the first investigation into European colonial family memory. The forebears of those we are currently recording came as migrants in the nineteenth century, many as soldiers, carpenters and builders, or impoverished agricultural labourers. They were fleeing, for example, the potato famine in Ireland, the English rural Depression of the 1870s, or Prussian military conscription in Denmark towards the end of the century. But the flood of European migrants led to the dispossession of Māori and ultimately contemporary political and partial economic restitution through the Waitangi Tribunal. How does Pākehā family memory navigate this complex colonial past?

The English family memory research demonstrated the ways in which family members drew on family stories to orient themselves in terms of time, moral values, and place. In the New Zealand family memory project, we will also be exploring the relationship between family stories and other sources of information about the past, including both genealogy and changing national narratives. I hope to be able to suggest a provisional answer to the question: in what ways and to what extent is family intergenerational memory the lens through which knowledge about the past, understandings of the present, and hopes for the future are refracted in everyday historical consciousness?

Anna Green is an Associate Professor in the Stout Research Centre for New Zealand Studies at Victoria University, Wellington. She is editor of *The Journal of New Zealand Studies,* and teaches history and theory at postgraduate level. Her publications include, with Kathleen Troup, *The Houses of History: A Critical Reader in History and Theory,* 2nd ed. (2016). Currently she is leading a national Marsden-funded research project investigating New Zealand European/Pākehā intergenerational family memory: www.family memory.nz.

Notes

1. Passerini, "Work Ideology"; Portelli, *The Death of Luigi Trastulli,* 51.
2. Halbwachs, *On Collective Memory.*

3. Green, "'Individual' and 'Collective' Memory"; Green, "Can Memory Be Collective?"
4. Halbwachs, *On Collective Memory*, 61–2.
5. See de St. Aubin et al., *The Generative Society*.
6. Wickham and Fentress, *Social Memory*, ix.
7. Green, "The exhibition that speaks for itself."
8. Seixas, ed., *Theorizing Historical Consciousness*, 8.
9. See Jensen, "Usable Pasts," 48–50.
10. Jensen, "Usable Pasts," 50.
11. Straub, "Telling Stories"; Rüsen, *History*.
12. Green, "Intergenerational Family Stories," 397–8. This research was funded by a European Commission Marie Curie Reintegration Grant MIRGCT-2007-205289.
13. Samuel, *Theatres of Memory*, vol 1, 443..
14. Welzer, Moller and Tschuggnall, "*Opa war kein Nazi*"; reviewed by Le Faucher, H-Net Reviews. Figes, "Private Life in Stalin's Russia," and *The Whisperers*.
15. Rosenzweig and Thelen, *The Presence of the Past*; Hamilton and Ashton, *History at the Crossroads*; Conrad et al., *Canadians and Their Pasts*.
16. Thelen, "But Is It History," 43.
17. Green, "Intergenerational Family Stories," 389–401.
18. See Taylor, *Narratives*; and Massey, *For Space*.
19. Assman, "Memory," 213.
20. F3, Betty, 2 February 2009, 7.21–7.52. Names are pseudonyms, and the recordings are in the possession of the author.
21. *Ibid.*, 1.09.19-1.10.12.
22. Green and Luscombe, "Family Memory."
23. F2, Vera, 16 February 2009, 1:15.00-20.00.
24. This phrase is from Ricoeur, 397.
25. Green, "Intergenerational Family Stories," 397.
26. F3, Betty, 2 February 2009, 28.25-31.02.
27. F3, Betty, 2 February 2009, 1:07.00-1:09.10.
28. F3, Alison, 19 January 2009, 44.30-46.25.
29. Schwarz, "'Already the Past.'"
30. Duncan and Edwards, "Lone Mothers."
31. The New Zealand family memory project "The Missing Link: Pākehā intergenerational family memory" is funded by the Royal Society of New Zealand Marsden Fund, 2016–2019. For further information see www.familymemory.nz.

Bibliography

Assman, Aleida. "Memory, Individual and Collective." In *The Oxford Handbook of Contextual Political Analysis,* edited by Robert E. Goodin and Charles Tilly. Oxford: Oxford University Press, 2006.

Conrad, Margaret, Kadriye Ercikan, Gerald Friesen, Jocelyn Létourneau, Delphin Muise, David Northrup, and Peter Seixas. *Canadians and Their Pasts*. Toronto: University of Toronto Press, 2013.

de St. Aubin, Ed, Dan P. McAdams, and Tae-Chang Kim. *The Generative Society: Caring for Future Generations*. Washington, DC: American Psychological Association, 2004.

Duncan, Simon, and Rosalind Edwards. "Lone Mothers and Paid Work—Rational Economic Man or Gendered Moral Rationalities?" *Feminist Economics* 3, no. 2 (1997): 29–61.

Figes, Orlando. *The Whisperers: Private Life in Stalin's Russia*. New York: Picador, 2007.

Figes, Orlando. "Private Life in Stalin's Russia: Family Narratives, Memory and Oral History." *History Workshop Journal* 65 (Spring 2008): 117–37.

Green, Anna. "'Individual' and 'Collective' Memory: theoretical presuppositions and the contemporary debates." *Oral History* 32, no. 2, Autumn (2004): 35–44.

———. "The exhibition that speaks for itself: oral history and museums." In *The Oral History Reader*, 2nd ed., edited by Robert Perks and Alistair Thomson, 416–24. London: Routledge, [1998] 2006.

———. "Can Memory Be Collective?" In *The Oxford Handbook of Oral History*, edited by Donald A. Ritchie, 96–111. New York: Oxford University Press, 2011.

———. "Intergenerational Family Stories: Private, Parochial, Pathological?" *Journal of Family History* 38, no. 4 (2013): 387–402.

Green, Anna, and Kayleigh Luscombe. "Family memory, 'things,' and counterfactual thinking." *Memory Studies* (June 2017). doi:10.1177/1750698017714837.

Halbwachs, Maurice. *On Collective Memory*. Edited and translated by Lewis A Coser. Chicago: University of Chicago Press, 1992.

Hamilton, Paula, and Paul Ashton. *History at the Crossroads: Australians and the Past*. Sydney: Halstead, 2010.

Jensen, Bernard Eric. "Usable Pasts: Comparing Approaches to Popular and Public History." In *People and their Pasts: Public History Today*, edited by Paul Ashton and Hilda Kean, 42–56. Basingstoke: Palgrave Macmillan, 2009.

Le Faucheur, Christelle. Online review of *"Opa war kein Nazi": Nationalsozialismus und Holocaust im Familiengedächtnis*, by Harald Welzer, Sabine Moller, and Karoline Tschuggnall. H-Net Reviews, H-German, April 2004. Retrieved 30 September 2013 from https://www.h-net.org/reviews/showrev.php?id=9159.

Massey, Doreen. *For Space*. London: Sage, 2005.

Passerini, Luisa. "Work Ideology and Consensus under Italian Fascism." *History Workshop Journal* 8, no.1 (1979): 82–108.

Portelli, Alessandro. *The Death of Luigi Trastulli and Other Stories: Form and Meaning in Oral History*. New York: State University of New York Press, 1991.

Ricoeur, Paul. *Memory-History-Forgetting*. Translated by Kathleen Blamey and David Pellauer. Chicago: University of Chicago Press, 2004.

Rosenzweig, Roy, and David Thelen. *The Presence of the Past*. New York: Columbia University Press, 1998.

Rüsen, Jörn. *History: Narration, Interpretation, Orientation*. New York: Berghahn Books, 2005.

Samuel, Raphael. *Theatres of Memory, vol. 1: Past and present in contemporary culture*. London: Verso, 1994.

Schwarz, Bill. "'Already the Past': memory and historical time." In *Memory Cultures: Memory, Subjectivity and Recognition*, edited by Susannah Radstone and Katharine Hodgkin, 135–51. New Brunswick, NJ, Transaction: 2006.

Seixas, Peter, ed. *Theorizing Historical Consciousness*. Toronto: University of Toronto Press, 2006.

Straub, Jürgen. "Telling Stories, Making History: Toward a Narrative Psychology of the Historical Construction of Meaning." In *Narration, Identity, and Historical Consciousness*, edited by Jürgen Straub, 44–98. New York: Berghahn Books, 2005.

Taylor, Stephanie. *Narratives of Identity and Place*. London: Routledge, 2010.

Thelen, David. "But Is It History?" *The Public Historian* 22, no. 1 (2000): 39–44.

Welzer, Harald, Sabine Moller, and Karoline Tschuggnall. "'Opa war kein Nazi': Nationalsozialismus und Holocaust im Familienged." Frankfurt: Fischer Taschenbuch Verlag, 2002.

Wickham, Chris, and James J. Fentress. *Social Memory: New Perspectives on the Past*. London: ACLS Humanities E-Book, [1992] 2008.

CHAPTER 15

Researching Identity and Historical Consciousness

CARLA L. PECK

I first encountered the term "historical consciousness" when I began my PhD studies with Dr. Peter Seixas at his newly opened *Centre for the Study of Historical Consciousness* (CSHC) at the University of British Columbia. The CSHC, which had opened in 2001, was a dynamic nexus of academic conversation, stimulation, and debate that included professors and students from across campus, as well as visiting scholars and students from across Canada and the world. Together, and over time, we discussed and debated the meaning of historical consciousness, encountered in various ways in the writings of Jörn Rüsen, Martin Jay, Hannah Arendt, Zygmunt Bauman, Walter Benjamin, Vivian Sobchack, Maria Grever, Mario Carretero, Jocelyn Létourneau, and Timothy Stanley, among many others.

When I moved to Vancouver in 2003, I had just completed my Master's of Education at the University of New Brunswick where I had researched twelve and thirteen-year-olds' understandings of ethnic diversity. Grounded in citizenship and critical multicultural education literature, and now living in one of Canada's most diverse cities, I quickly became interested in how I might build on that work through an exploration of students' historical thinking and historical consciousness. My critical, multicultural leanings shaped my thinking and led me to question how ethnically diverse students were responding to the Canadian history they were learning in school. More specifically, I was interested in exploring how students' ethnic identities shaped the ways they understood, and constructed, narratives of Canada's

Notes for this section begin on page 221.

past. Ultimately, this has important implications for how students locate themselves in the nation's past, present, and future. As I began this research I wondered, as Bannerji writes, if students saw themselves as an "insider" or an "outsider" to the Canadian nation?[1] Thus, for me, historical consciousness is inextricably tied to questions of identity and belonging, both of which have important implications for citizenship.

By citizenship, I am not referring to one's official status as a citizen of a nation. Rather, I am influenced by Benedict Anderson's understanding of "nation" as an "imagined community,"[2] and am therefore interested in one's sense of belonging to a community or communities (which may or may not be "the nation") as well as the relationships one builds with the people, places, and institutions (including historical narratives) of the community(ies) in which one lives. In this sense, citizenship can be local, national, and even international or cosmopolitan, and it certainly has the potential to be fluid and plural.[3]

Researching History, Identity, and Citizenship in Canada

To understand my approach to research, it is important that I explain the context in which I work. Canada is a highly diverse, sparsely populated nation composed of Indigenous peoples, people born in Canada, and immigrants who may or may not seek Canadian citizenship. Complicating this mix is the existence of sub-state Indigenous and Francophone (Québec) nations. The latest reliable census results for which statistics on diversity are available show that Canada's population continues to diversify, although certainly the majority of the people continue to claim Canadian, French, or British roots.[4] While the percentage of overall visible minorities seems small at a national level (16.2 percent of total population), the story is quite different when we look at the population figures in some of Canada's urban centers. For example, Calgary, Montreal, Toronto, and Vancouver have all witnessed significant increases in their visible minority[5] population, with the latter two cities approaching the 50 percent mark. What is so interesting about the 2006 Census is that, for the first time, all respondents were allowed to enter up to six ethnic backgrounds on the form—so whether someone identified as a visible minority or not, 12.9 million Canadians (almost a third of the population) self-identified using multiple ethnic background indicators.

Canadian political philosopher Will Kymlicka contends that Canadian multiculturalism is unique in terms of:

(a) the complexity of the diversity within its borders, namely, immigrant groups, sub-state nations, and Indigenous peoples. Kymlicka argues that Canada is unique in that it has (and has had) all three groups existing simultaneously;

(b) the constitutional protections for diversity provided by the *Charter of Rights and Freedoms;* and

(c) the extent to which multiculturalism has been woven into narratives told about Canada, both internally and externally (that is, how Canada is seen by other nations).[6]

This complexity has influenced what Canadian history is taught in schools. Because the Canadian constitution gives authority for education exclusively to provincial governments, educational policy and curricula are developed at the provincial or regional level which means there is little consistency from province to province in terms of what is taught. Whereas students in Manitoba learn about Métis leader Louis Riel and the *resistance* he led against the Canadian government, students in other parts of the country learn about Riel's *rebellion*. This is but one of many, many examples of how (in this case, regional) identity plays out in history or social studies curricula across the country.

Previous research that explored intersections of identity and historical thinking has demonstrated that "positionality" influences how one understands history.[7] This work was critically important to history education research because it demonstrated that one's gender, religion, or ethno-cultural identity may shape how one thinks about history. However, in this previous work, researchers did not provide opportunities for students to contribute to the discussion on how their ethnicity, religion or gender may influence the ways in which they understand history. Rather, previous researchers assigned students a label ("African American," "Franco-Ontarian," "Protestant," etc.) without acknowledging the diversity that exists within such categories and only rarely did researchers ask students to reflect on how their identity may have shaped their historical understandings. Nor did this research attend to the question of intersectionality, that is, how is one's historical consciousness might be shaped by the intersections of, for example, ethnicity and gender?

What Do I Mean by "Identity"?

Before going further, it is necessary to situate myself theoretically in terms of "identity" generally and "ethnicity" in particular. Although space does not allow for a full exploration here, and while there are no clear-cut definitions of ethnicity or ethnic identity—indeed, Pryor et al., describe ethnicity as a "conceptual maze"—there is a certain level of agreement in the literature about certain aspects of the concept.[8] First, ethnicity is fluid and potentially plural in nature. The articulation of one's ethnic identity may change depending on the social, political, and/or cultural context in which one finds oneself. Second, the development of ethnic identity is both a personal and social process, which occurs through inter- and intra-group boundary formation. Individuals look not only within themselves, but also within-group for clues to their ethnic identity. Individuals also take cues from the larger society, including people, social, and political institutions to define their identity. Finally, some of the markers associated with ethnic identity include language, religion, appearance, ancestry, regionality, nonverbal behavior, values, beliefs, cultural symbols, and practices.[9]

Given the complexity of ethnic identity, and in order to better understand and do justice to the students in our classrooms, it is critical that educators take the question of students' self-identifications (ethnic or otherwise) seriously. According to Cummins and Early, "the ways in which teachers negotiate identities with students can exert a significant impact on the extent to which students will engage academically or withdraw from academic effort."[10] Sociologist and cultural theorist Stuart Hall argues "that we all speak from a particular place, out of a particular history, out of a particular experience, a particular culture, without being contained by that position. . . . We are all, in that sense, *ethnically* located and our ethnic identities are crucial to our subjective sense of who we are."[11]

Complex Methods for Complex Work

An important feature of my research that differentiates it from similar previous work is the data I collected on students' perceptions of their ethnic identities. As a White researcher, I did not want to make assumptions about students' ethnic identities, nor did I wish to lump students into broad categories.[12] Therefore, I had students complete a questionnaire that asked questions about their ethnic and cultural ancestry or origins, their religious affiliations, languages spoken, and so on. These are fairly basic demographic questions that have led other researchers to then place a label on students—labels such as "Franco-Ontarian," "African American," or "European American." In reading this research in preparation for my own study, I was troubled by these labels that cast every person assigned the label in exactly the same light. Wanting to avoid such simplistic labels, I decided to ask students to respond to an additional question, which was based both on Kymlicka's framework of diversity in Canada and on a question asked by Statistics Canada on the *Ethnic Diversity Survey*[13] administered in 2002:

> I would now like you to think about **your own** identity in ethnic, cultural and/or national terms. This identity may be the same as that of your parents, grandparents or ancestors, or it may be different. Your ethnic, cultural and/or national identity is the ethnic, cultural and/or national group or groups to which you feel you belong.
>
> Using the information you have provided so far, as well as any other personal information that will help you, please write a paragraph describing **your** ethnic, cultural and/or national identity.
>
> It is possible that you could describe yourself has having more than one type of (cultural, ethnic or national) identity. For instance, one person might describe his or her identity as "Greek," even though they were born in Canada. Another person might describe their identity as "Canadian," even though he or she was born in Greece. Someone else might decide that they are both of these: "Greek-Canadian." There are no wrong answers—describe yourself the way that makes the most sense to you.

This strategy proved fruitful and worthwhile because many students' descriptions of their ethnic identities were different than their responses to closed questions related to identity on the questionnaire.

In addition to writing a description of their ethnic identity, the students worked in small groups to create a timeline of Canadian history. They had thirty events to choose from and were allowed to select only ten. These events were selected from the curriculum the students had studied in grades eleven and twelve, and were carefully selected to include a range of ethnicities, genders, time frames, geographic locations, and so on. During the small group and individual interviews, I asked students if they wanted to add, delete, or change any of the events selected by the group and told them that they weren't restricted to what they'd learned in school. In the individual interviews, I also asked students which one of the events in Canadian history was the most important to them in terms of their ethnic identity (using the description they provided on the questionnaire). In what follows, I explore connections between students' ethnic identities and their historical thinking about Canada's past, in short, their historical consciousness.

Munny

On the questionnaire, Munny listed "Cambodian" as his ancestral origins.[14] However, on the extended questions that asked about his ethnic identity, Munny wrote: "I feel like I am a Canadian and also a Cambodian. So basically a Cambodian-Canadian. I was born in Canada but my roots are Cambodian. I've never been to Cambodia before. I've been in Canada all my life."

When I asked Munny which of the events was most important to him in terms of his self-described ethnic identity, he said, "The multiculturalism one [Multiculturalism Act]—that one affects me because, even though I'm Canadian, you know the Japanese got mistreated even though they were Canadians too, right, so that affected [my decisions] because it wasn't a positive thing for me . . . and also, since I'm . . . Cambodian, like, I felt sympathy for the Japanese and the Chinese [who were recruited to build the Canadian Pacific Railway] so—I guess that affected my decision too."

In this example, Munny has made a connection with Japanese and Chinese immigrants through his ethnic identification as Cambodian-Canadian. An examination of history and social studies textbooks shows that topics such as the Japanese internment and the recruitment of Chinese workers to build the railway receive minimal attention—sometimes they merit a single page in some textbooks—yet for Munny, these events left a lasting impression on him—and not a positive one—because of the connections he drew between his ethnic identification and the immigrants involved in the selected events. For Munny, the past is not past. In some ways, he's doing what every history teacher wishes her students would do—make connections between the past and present. However, the kinds of connections Munny made remain a mystery unless we find ways to uncover his thinking, which is what I tried to do in my research.

Sam

Sam listed "Eastern Chinese" on the portion of the questionnaire that asked about his ancestral origins. On the extended written response, he wrote:

> I still feel my pride as a Chinese. I defend Chinese history. I am still living in a typical Chinese family, eating typical Chinese food and learning the history of China. But as I live in Canada longer, I think I also have absorbed some Canadian North American culture. But here comes a question: what is Canadian culture? I think it is multiculturalism. So as I become more Canadian, I am more and more tolerant to other cultures. I promote both Canadian and Chinese cultures. So it would be best to describe me as a Chinese-Canadian.

What is most interesting about Sam's description, in addition to the specific markers he references (food, family, "Canadian, North American" culture, tolerance towards diversity) is his perception that his ethnic identity is undergoing change the longer he lives in Canada. When asked how his ethnic identity may have impacted the decisions he made during the timeline task, he had the following response:

> As I was deciding on these pictures I was kind of putting myself in the mindset of a Canadian instead of a Chinese. So I fought for the events that are important for Canadians in general—they may not be typical Chinese-Canadian, but Canadian in general—so like all the native born people or the immigrants from Britain/France . . . So that partly explains why we didn't . . . why I didn't

choose a lot of minority rights because . . . I don't think there's any . . . my Chinese background had any influence on my decisions.

However, as he thought more about this question his response became more intricate and revealed his understanding of the complicated relationship between his ethnic identity and the decisions he made about historical significance: "So in some ways during the process of choosing these I shifted my own identity, so not a lot of these things really represent my true identity." Importantly, Sam also added that, "it's not like [I'm] Chinese and Canadian. I am in between—but I'm actually, I'm constantly shifting between the two."[15] The notion that one's ethnic identity is always a process—that it is not fixed—is apparent in Sam's reflections on the relationship between his ethnic identity and his ascriptions of significance to events in Canada's past and is a clear reflection of the theoretical work on ethnic identity discussed briefly earlier.

Ariana

Ariana reported that her ancestors were coastal First Nations and referred specifically to the Nuu-Chah-Nulth Nation and the Cowichen Tribe. Ariana provided multiple responses to the question about her ethnic identity: "An urban Aboriginal who learns about other Aboriginal culture because my own isn't offered. Multi-cultural Canadian Aboriginal I see myself." Although brief, Ariana's response indicates that she is aware of several aspects of her identity: First, she specifically identified herself as an *urban* Aboriginal, indicating that she lives in a city and does not live in a rural Aboriginal community (or reserve). Second, she uses the term "multicultural" to describe herself in addition to identifying herself as Canadian and Aboriginal. These latter terms imply some sort of national identification on Ariana's part although it is not clear to what extent she identifies herself as both Canadian and Aboriginal.

When asked how her ethnic identity may have affected her decisions during the timeline task, Ariana commented that "I didn't really know how to identify myself [on the questionnaire] but I knew I'm Aboriginal but that's all I knew. . . . The choosing of the timeline was hard too because . . . I'm not really sure who I am, you know . . . I'm lost." Ariana's statement reveals much about the connection, for her, between ethnic identity and history. Castenell and Pinar argue that, "'We are what we know.' We are, however, also, what we do not know. If what we know about ourselves—our history, our culture, our national identity—is deformed by absences, denials, and incompleteness, then our identity—both as individuals and as [Canadians]—is fractured."[16]

As I noted above, identity is a complex, fluid, and subjective concept and the descriptions the students provided should be regarded as provisional. That is, students' perceptions of their own ethnic identity likely changed over the course of the study and will have continued to develop since that time. Therefore, before beginning the final stage of data collection (the individual interviews) I conducted member-checks with students and provided opportunities for them to elaborate on their identity descriptions as desired. VanSledright, Kelly, and Meuwissen advise that, while no method for collecting biographical information is infallible, "the effort must be made, as a means of providing some sociocultural context within which to situate" the data.[17]

Through my research, I have attempted to address the methodological shortfall identified at the beginning of this chapter through a relatively simple step: I ask students to provide detailed descriptions *of their own* ethnic identities, rather than assigning students a label myself. The data from my study demonstrate that students' perceptions of their ethnic identities are complex and fluid. Even those who described themselves in terms of a single ethnic identity drew on several factors to explain themselves and some indicated that they recognized that their identity was "in process" and still developing. Many of the students who described themselves in terms of multiple ethnic identities articulated complicated notions of their identities, and some referenced particular "sides" to their identity or expressed that a particular aspect of their ethnic identity was more dominant than other aspects when they interpreted various aspects of Canadian history. As a result, my research incorporated complex and shifting notions of what it meant for students to be Chinese-Canadian, or Aboriginal, or first-generation Canadian, for example. Through this work, I hope to have highlighted students' own malleable understandings of their ethnic identities and the potential of this methodological innovation for future researchers who undertake similar studies. I have since used the same questionnaire with teachers and with students as young as twelve and have found them very capable of responding in complex ways to questions about their ethnic identity.

Secondly, by encouraging meta-cognition as an active part of the research process, I brought students' own complex definitions of their ethnic identities into dynamic interplay with their historical thinking: "Historical thinking provides students with a means to not only construct historical narratives, but also to sift through the layers of identity that influence their own understandings and interpretations of history. . . . Thus, historical thinking, with an explicit focus on identity, can lead to a shared quest for understanding from where the other person speaks."[18] This insight lies at the core of history education not only in Canada but throughout all multicultural societies in a world increasingly shaped by globalization.

What I did not do, and this is something I still wonder about, was examine the intersections of ethnicity with other identity categories. For example, some of the young women in my study occasionally spoke about connections they perceived between their gender identity and certain events in Canadian history. (Interestingly, none of the young men did so.) I chose not to explore those connections in any depth because my focus was on ethnicity; this had the consequence of isolating ethnicity from other identity categories, something that is typical in a research study, but which belies the messiness of identity.

Concluding Thoughts

In multicultural democratic societies, it is vital that we recognize that we are all located in relation to many others—that, according to Charles Taylor, our identity is fundamentally dialogical in nature.[19] Gutmann agrees, and argues that "if human identity is dialogically created and constituted, then public recognition of our identity requires a politics that leaves room for us to deliberate publicly about those aspects of our identities that we share, or potentially share, with other citizens."[20] Gee contends that individuals use "identity kits" with which they "live out [their] social lives as different and multiple kinds of people."[21] Identity kits involve socio-culturally situated identities, the performance of identities, the use of cultural tools and particular ways of acting and interacting with others.[22]

Human identity, in addition to being dialogically created and constituted, is also fundamentally rooted in the past. Children grow up, listening to stories from their parents and grandparents; mothers pass on traditions to daughters (and fathers to sons); Indigenous elders teach youth about the importance of following protocol during ceremonial gatherings. The purpose of this informal and formal tutelage is not only to ensure that the past lives on but also to help younger generations develop a sense of identity built on the past. Thus, our individual identity has a role to play in how we construct the past, present, and future.

However, if we teach history only for the development of identity, it is inevitable that consequences will follow. One such consequence is the development of grand narratives, which, according to Ahonen, "were developed in a way that ignored the experiences of each 'nation's' ethnic and social minorities."[23] As a result, members of these groups cannot use school history to the same extent as majority group members to develop their identity. Minority group members thus become further excluded, as they are not able to contribute to the development of a common narrative: "Those with no place or role in the grand narrative will be excluded from the historical community."[24] Other consequences included the use of history to strain already tenuous relationships—lines drawn along ethnic or religious boundaries are further solidified or breakdown altogether; identity politics descend into cultural relativism; immigrants are pitted against non-immigrants in a fight over what it means to be a "citizen."

Socio-cultural studies in education emphasize the need to understand the social, cultural and political positions from which students approach learning and, I believe, provide a way forward for this work.[25] Knowing what frameworks students use to make sense of what they are learning in history is important, particularly for teachers working in schools within a multicultural society: "By understanding how young people from different racial or ethnic groups interpret history and contemporary society . . . teachers and policymakers can make more informed decisions about what and how to teach social studies subjects to diverse groups of students."[26] None of this is easy work, yet I feel strongly that we must do it.

Carla L. Peck is Professor of Social Studies Education in the Department of Elementary Education at the University of Alberta. Her research interests include students' understandings of democratic concepts, diversity, identity, citizenship, and the relationship between students' ethnic identities and their understandings of history. She has held several major research grants and has authored and co-authored numerous journal articles, book chapters, and books related to this work, including *Education, Globalization and the Nation* (2016) and *Teaching and Learning Difficult Histories in International Contexts* (2018).

Notes

Portions of this chapter are based on Carla L. Peck, "'It's Not Like [I'm] Chinese and Canadian. I Am in Between': Ethnicity and Students' Conceptions of Historical Significance," *Theory & Research in Social Education* 38, no. 4 (2010): 574–617. Reprinted with permission. See also Peck, "Multi-ethnic high school students' understandings of historical significance."

1. Bannerji, *The Dark Side of the Nation,* particularly the chapter, "Geography Lessons: On Being an Insider/Outsider to the Canadian Nation," 63–86.
2. Anderson, *Imagined Communities,* 5–7, 36–46.
3. Osler and Starkey, "Learning for Cosmopolitan Citizenship."
4. Under the Harper government, the mandatory "long-form" Census was cancelled in 2010 and was replaced by a voluntary survey in 2011. Many researchers do not consider the voluntary survey a reliable source of census data.
5. A Statistics Canada term for Person of Color.
6. Kymlicka, "Canadian Multiculturalism."
7. For an in-depth review of this research see Peck, "National, Ethnic, and Indigenous Identities."
8. Pryor et al., "Measuring Ethnicity," 215.
9. Bentley, "Ethnicity and Practice"; Stasiulis, "Theorizing Connections"; Berry and Laponce, *Ethnicity and Culture in Canada*; Nagel, "Constructing Ethnicity"; Jenkins, "Ethnicity Etcetera"; Isajiw, *Understanding Diversity.*
10. Cummins and Early, eds., *Identity Texts,* 24.

11. Hall, "New Ethnicities," 94.
12. Carr and Lund, eds., *The Great White North*; Delpit, *Other People's Children*; Tyson, "Research, Race, and Social Education."
13. Kaddatz, "The Ethnic Diversity Survey."
14. All student names are pseudonyms.
15. This quotation from Sam served as inspiration for my *TRSE* article, Peck, "'It's Not Like [I'm] Chinese and Canadian.'"
16. Castenell and Pinar, "Introduction," 4.
17. VanSledright et al., "Oh, the Trouble We've Seen," 227.
18. Peck, "Peering through a Kaleidoscope," 71.
19. Taylor, "The Politics of Recognition."
20. Gutmann, "Introduction," 7.
21. Gee, *An Introduction*, 33.
22. See also: Wertsch, *Voices of Collective Remembering*.
23. Ahonen, "Politics of Identity," 180.
24. Ahonen, "Politics of Identity," 190.
25. Barton, "A Sociocultural Perspective"; Epstein, *Interpreting National History*; Nieto, "Critical Multicultural Education."
26. Epstein, "Racial Identity," 42.

Bibliography

Ahonen, Sirkka. "Politics of Identity through History Curriculum: Narratives of the Past for Social Exclusion—or Inclusion?" *Journal of Curriculum Studies* 33, no. 2 (2001): 179–94.

Anderson, Benedict. *Imagined Communities: Reflections on the Origin and Spread of Nationalism*. London: Verso, 1983.

Bannerji, Himani. *The Dark Side of the Nation: Essays on Multiculturalism, Nationalism and Gender*. Toronto: Canadian Scholars' Press Inc., 2000.

Barton, Keith. "A Sociocultural Perspective on Children's Understanding of Historical Change: Comparative Findings from Northern Ireland and the United States." *American Educational Research Journal* 38, no. 4 (2001): 881–914.

Bentley, G. Carter. "Ethnicity and Practice." *Comparative Studies in Society and History* 29, no. 1 (January 1987): 24–55.

Berry, John, and J. A. Laponce. *Ethnicity and Culture in Canada: The Research Landscape*. Toronto: University of Toronto Press, 1994.

Carr, Paul R., and Darren E. Lund, eds. *The Great White North? Exploring Whiteness, Privilege and Identity in Education*. Rotterdam: Sense Publishers, 2007.

Castenell Jr., Louis A., and William F. Pinar. "Introduction." In *Understanding Curriculum as Racial Text: Representations of Identity and Difference in Education*, edited by Louis A. Castenell, Jr., and William F. Pinar, 1–30. Albany: State University of New York, 1993.

Cummins, Jim, and Margaret Early, eds. *Identity Texts: The Collaborative Creation of Power in Multilingual Schools*. Staffordshire: Trentham Books, 2011.

Delpit, Lisa. *Other People's Children: Cultural Conflicts in the Classroom*. New York: The New Press, 1995.

Epstein, Terrie. "Racial Identity and Young People's Perspectives on Social Education." *Theory into Practice* 40, no. 1 (Win 2001): 42–7.

Epstein, Terrie. *Interpreting National History: Race, Identity, and Pedagogy in Classrooms and Communities*. New York: Routledge, 2009.

Gee, James Paul. *An Introduction to Discourse Analysis Theory and Method*, 2nd ed. New York: Routledge, 2006.

Gutmann, Amy. "Introduction." In *Multiculturalism: Examining the Politics of Recognition*, edited by Amy Gutmann, 3–24. Princeton: Princeton University Press, 1994.

Hall, Stuart. "New Ethnicities." In *Identities: Race, Class, Gender, and Nationality*, edited by Linda Martín Alcoff and Eduardo Mendieta, 90–95. London: Blackwell Publishing, 2003.

Isajiw, Wsevolod W. *Understanding Diversity: Ethnicity and Race in the Canadian Context*. Toronto: Thompson Educational Publishing Inc., 1999.

Jenkins, Richard. "Ethnicity *Etcetera*: Social Anthropological Points of View." *Ethnic and Racial Studies* 19, no. 4 (October 1996): 807–22.

Kaddatz, Jennifer. "The Ethnic Diversity Survey: Measuring Ethnic Ancestry, Ethnic Identity and Ethnic Salience in Canada." Association of Canadian Studies Conference: Ethnic Diversity Survey and the Future of Ethnic Identification in Canada, Toronto, Ontario, 2005.

Kymlicka, Will. "Canadian Multiculturalism in Historical and Comparative Perspective: Is Canada Unique?" *Forum Constitutionnel/Constitutional Forum* 13, no. 1/2 (2003): 1–8.

Nagel, Joane. "Constructing Ethnicity: Creating and Recreating Ethnic Identity and Culture." *Social Problems* 41, no. 1 (February 1994): 152–76.

Nieto, Sonia. "Critical Multicultural Education and Students' Perspectives." In *Critical Multiculturalism: Rethinking Multicultural and Antiracist Education*, edited by Stephen May, 191–215. London: Falmer Press, 1999.

Osler, A., and H. Starkey. "Learning for Cosmopolitan Citizenship: Theoretical Debates and Young People's Experiences." *Educational Review* 55, no. 3 (Nov 2003): 243–54.

Peck, Carla L. "National, Ethnic, and Indigenous Identities and Perspectives in History Education." In *The Wiley International Handbook of History Teaching & Learning*, edited by S. Metzger and L. McArthur Harris. Hoboken, NJ: Wiley-Blackwell, forthcoming.

Peck, Carla Lee. "Multi-ethnic high school students' understandings of historical significance" Implication for Canadian history education." PhD diss., University of British Columbia, 2009.

Peck, Carla Lee. "Peering through a Kaleidoscope: Identity, Historical Understanding and Citizenship in Canada." *Citizenship Teaching and Learning* 5, no. 2 (2009): 1–15.

Peck, Carla Lee. "'It's Not Like [I'm] Chinese and Canadian. I Am in Between': Ethnicity and Students' Conceptions of Historical Significance." *Theory & Research in Social Education* 38, no. 4 (2010): 574–617.

Pryor, Edward T., Gustave J. Goldmann, Michael J. Sheridan, and Pamela M. White. "Measuring Ethnicity: Is 'Canadian' an Evolving Indigenous Category?" *Ethnic and Racial Studies* 15, no. 2 (April 1992): 214–35.

Stasiulis, Daiva. "Theorizing Connections: Gender, Race, Ethnicity, and Class." In *Race and Ethnic Relations in Canada*, edited by Peter S. Li, 269–305. Toronto, ON: Oxford University Press, 1990.

Taylor, Charles. "The Politics of Recognition." In *Multiculturalism: Examining the Politics of Recognition*, edited by Amy Gutmann, 25–73. Princeton: Princeton University Press, 1994.

Tyson, Cynthia A. "Research, Race, and Social Education." In *Research Methods in Social Studies Education: Contemporary Issues and Perspectives*, edited by Keith C. Barton, 39–56. Greenwich, CT: Information Age Publishing, 2006.

VanSledright, Bruce, Timothy Kelly, and Kevin Meuwissen. "Oh, the Trouble We've Seen: Researching Historical Thinking and Understanding." In *Research Methods in Social Studies Education: Contemporary Issues and Perspectives*, edited by Keith C. Barton, 207–33. Greenwich, CT: Information Age Publishing, 2006.

Wertsch, James V. *Voices of Collective Remembering*. New York: Cambridge University Press, 2002.

EPILOGUE

Why Historical Consciousness?

MARIA GREVER

Contemplating the way people deal with history has become more urgent than ever in the current political landscape with increasing populism and the use of new media in many countries around the world. The recent violent clashes over a contested past, such as the war of monuments in Tallinn, Charlottesville, and Johannesburg, underline this need. Today Putin, Trump, Erdogan, and other authoritarian political leaders stimulate the circulation of fake histories and frozen images of the nation, using populist rhetoric with the aim to mobilize the masses behind their politics of intolerance towards migration and those considered to be foreigners. Their rhetoric and performance enhance the idea that we live in a post-truth society. Public debates are increasingly framed by appeals to emotion; factual rebuttals do not matter. According to British conservative politician Michael Gove: "People in this country have had enough of experts."[1] At the same time parades and reenactments in contested regions commemorate past victories as part of current struggles and fundamentalist religious movements cherish "events" from a distant past as though they happened yesterday, resulting in the coalescing of past, present, and future. Supported by information technology, manipulated stories and images of some desired past are constantly re-mediated in newspapers, television, the internet, Twitter and other social media, reaching millions of people.

The instrumental ways of dealing with time and the growing resistance to differentiate history from the here-and-now might subvert the importance of orientation in time and weaken the awareness of reality. Hence the

---

Notes for this section begin on page 229.

volume *Contemplating Historical Consciousness: Notes from the Field* appears at the appropriate time.

Since the 1970s, a large body of theoretical and empirical research on the meaning and development of historical consciousness has been published. Contributors to this field have different ideas about the elaboration and application of the concept. Historians and social studies experts, particularly those who research history and civic education, often consider historical consciousness as hybrid and "slippery."[2] Perhaps one of the reasons is that the concept evolved in two different research cultures: philosophical and historiographic studies on the one hand and research into history education on the other.[3]

Philosophical studies of the continental tradition emphasize the *historicity* of human beings. In terms of H.G. Gadamer's hermeneutics: we are thrown into a world that has a historical context to which we somehow consciously or unconsciously relate in a process of changing meanings. Understanding the world is historically effected means understanding that it is always situated in time. There are limits to which we can be aware of historical effect; we can never make our historicity completely transparent to ourselves.[4] Paul Ricoeur refers to "the fundamental and radical fact that we make history, that we are immersed in history, that we are historical beings."[5] In sum, historical consciousness implies an awareness of the fundamental historical character of human behavior, knowledge, institutions, events, and developments in the world, including one's own position.[6] In this sense, historical consciousness is a temporary outcome of a changing *state of mind* concerning orientation in time of human beings who are involved in transforming, sometimes overlapping mnemonic communities.[7] Related to the philosophy of history, historiographic studies explore how, in society, a growing awareness of the differences between past, present, and future, and an increasing sensitivity to anachronisms since the late seventeenth century have influenced historiography and the rise of the historical discipline, resulting in the construction of new forms of historical periodization and the use of new temporal concepts, such as "revolution," "progress," "development," "future," "transition time" (Reinhart Koselleck's "Sattelzeit"), "century," and "epoch."[8] The educational approach primarily focuses on the operationalization of historical consciousness for empirical research and its applications in concrete educational practices. This approach is a mixture of German philosophy and Anglo-American analytical and empirical research, with the publications of German cultural historian Jörn Rüsen as most influential.[9] A significant development was the general shift in the reflections on history teaching in several countries in the late 1970s. History teaching should no longer focus on memorizing facts or fostering beliefs but on the ability of "people to think historically themselves, and thereby to be able to reflect upon (and clarify) their personal as well as collective historical identity."[10] Hans-Jürgen Pandel provided a practical definition of historical consciousness, particularly widely used in Germany, consisting of seven dimensions. Three dimensions are specific for history as a discipline (see Carla van Boxtel's chapter in this volume): the awareness of time (then, today, and tomorrow), reality (facts and fiction), and historicity (continuity and change).[11] Four other dimensions refer to the complexity of society: awareness of identity, and political, economical and moral awareness. Recently, Andreas Körber has critically assessed this model in his overview of conceptual developments in German history didactics. In his view historical consciousness must be understood as "the set of capabilities, dispositions and skills necessary to undertake the required operations. Historical Consciousness then is a competence—a competence to think historically."[12]

In the wake of this line of thought, historical thinking and reasoning seem to be one of the roads to develop historical consciousness as a competence, involving verbally expressed, cognitive dealings with the past and embodied expressions of how people experience, use, and perform the past.[13] Although discussions about the operationalization of historical consciousness tend to lose themselves in making all kinds of abstract schemes with ever more specifications, this approach has stimulated interesting large scale surveys in Europe, the US, Australia, and Canada,[14] as well as local, community, and transnational projects (see several chapters in this volume).

★ ★ ★

Indebted to Peter Seixas' well known *Theorizing Historical Consciousness* (2004), the editors of this volume have done a wonderful job to bring these worlds together. They attempt to synthesize the different theoretical approaches and empirical research on historical consciousness. Several authors retrospectively reflect on the genesis of their own research and how they value the concept of historical consciousness despite its hybrid character. All authors more or less engage with Rüsen's description of historical consciousness as *making sense* of the past, where "the past is interpreted for the sake of understanding the present and anticipating the future."[15] Some authors, particularly Alan W. McCully and Keith Barton, confess that they are more interested in a practical approach than in "the theoretical landscape of history and historical consciousness," because these distinctions have rarely helped them to understand students' educational experiences in Northern Ireland. Nevertheless, they acknowledge that their research in this deeply divided society gains insight from being theorized. Indeed, conceptualized insights are helpful to investigate other comparable contexts and are the means to communicate with other researchers.

All authors directly or indirectly agree that historical consciousness relates to and expresses itself in different domains: school education, historical scholarship, public history, media, family and community histories, heritage, and museums. Particularly in the Australian case of the "stolen generation," analyzed in the chapter by Anna Clark, the intersections between public and private encounters with the past reveal the tensions between the official and the intimate. The conversations about the different perspectives and stories not only show how people remember and make sense of the contested past, but also how they become aware of history's subjectivity. Several authors also point to the public performance of remembrance: acts in the present (speech, movement and gestures, art or bodily form) to remember an historical event which tries to resist erasure or oblivion by evoking the past.[16] This active and often collective engagement with the past can have an incredible impact on current perceptions of people. A telling example is how in Northern Ireland, families have traditional patterns of religious and cultural loyalties that are passed down from generation to generation. McCully and Barton explain that these loyalties are reinforced through symbolic representations in the respective communities: "Marches, banners, commemorations, and wall murals display sectional loyalty through the use of imagery associated with historical events and figures from the past." Perhaps the authors could have emphasized more that performative acts of remembrance which shape and reiterate collective identities often inculcate selective and dichotomous versions of the past in people's minds.

All these informal sources of historical consciousness might enlighten the changes in how young and new generations deal with the past. But we need much more research to understand the relationship between *formal* history education and these *informal* ways of dealing with the past, either public or intimate. To what extent and how does school history interact with history encountered in families and in the community? What are students' appropriations of history and what impact do these have on developing their historical consciousness? Or is there no interaction at all? What is the impact of historical tourism?[17]

We also have to take into account that historical consciousness is not limited to the nation-state, as argued in the chapter of Kaat Wils and Karel Van Nieuwehuyse, nor to the Western world, see the chapters of LaGarrett King, Michael Marker, and Na Li. Future research should focus more on these issues, which also implies a reflection on moral dimensions. An inspiring starting-point are the published papers of an international workshop, "Towards an integrated theory of historical and moral consciousness." The papers point to a blank spot in the existing research and argue that the intersections between historical and moral consciousness remain very much unexplored. Studying ethical values in history education or the way museum exhibitions deal with sensitive pasts in society are highly relevant for contemporary political and social concerns, because "education of historically informed and morally engaged citizens would greatly benefit from understanding how people interrelate the past, the present and the future, how they handle complex dilemmas, and . . . how they ponder on implications of historical moral dilemmas for the present and the future."[18]

Another related, increasingly influential source of historical consciousness—hardly explored in this volume—is the expanding field of virtual popular historical culture with huge audiences: video games, augmented reality, selfies, instagrams, and YouTube vloggers.[19] These new media stimulate what Jerome de Groot calls historioglossia: a multiplicity of hybrid discourses accruing around a single historical person or event, with overlapping genres all of which might be simultaneously in operation.[20] The immediacy of these media gives the viewers the feeling that they are really part of the story in the medium without any form of mediation between the medium and the viewers. It creates an immersive historicity, an atmosphere of being personally involved in experiencing history in a virtual world as time travellers.[21] These new media accelerate the democratization process of producing and consuming history, blurring the boundaries between academic historians and "hobbyists" or ideological activists, between critical history and myths, between producers and consumers, and between representation and interaction by people, groups and institutions.[22] It can go even so far that the immersive simulations "withhold us from experiencing a break between the past and the present."[23]

Finally, the chapters of Mario Carretero, Michael Marker, and Anna Green in this volume stress the importance of researching the impact of spatial environmental orientation on historical consciousness. Indeed, the perception and experience of territories and place are together with temporal orientation basic elements to understand historical consciousness. This research would benefit much from publications on global warming and the current planetary crisis of climate change. Dipesh Chakrabarty argues that anthropogenic explanations of climate change spell the collapse of the age-old humanist distinction between natural history and human history. Human beings are no longer simple biological agents, but manifest themselves as a geological force. Chakrabarty considers the anthropocene as a new period and advocates to think of humans as a form of life, as a species, and to look "on human history as part of the history of life on this planet."[24] Because "humans constitute a particular kind of species they can, in the process of dominating other species, acquire the status of a geological force. Humans, in other words, have become a natural condition."[25] The distance between geological time and chronology of human histories has been breached, consequently the climate crisis requires a new collective and universal awareness. Not in Hegelian terms. The awareness points to a shared sense of a possible catastrophe and to a different perception of humanity as a species on the planet. What this means for further development of historical consciousness we do not yet know. But it is certainly an urgent issue that should be on the research agenda of those who are engaged with history and civic education.

Maria Grever is Professor of Theory & Methodology of History, Director of the Center for Historical Culture, and Head of the History Department, Erasmus University Rotterdam (the Netherlands). Her research interests are historical consciousness, theory of historiography, heritage, and memory. Currently, she is research leader, together with co-applicant Stijn Reijnders, of the program *War! Popular Culture and European Heritage of Major Armed Conflicts*. She co-edited several books: *Transforming the Public Sphere* (2004), *Beyond the Canon* (2007), *Sensitive Pasts* (2016), *Palgrave Handbook of Research in Historical Culture and Education* (2017); published many articles and book chapters. She is a member of the Netherlands Royal Academy of Arts and Sciences.

Notes

1. Brown, "The idea of a 'post-truth society.'"
2. Clark and Peck, this volume.
3. Grever, "Experiencing war"; Clark and Grever, "Historical Consciousness."
4. Veith, *Gadamer and the Transmission of History*, 113; Gadamer, *Truth and Method*. See also Lukacs, *Historical Consciousness*.
5. Ricoeur, *Hermeneutics*, 274.
6. Grever and van Boxtel, *Verlangen naar tastbaar verleden*, 20.
7. Grever, "Experiencing war"; Clark and Grever, "Historical Consciousness."
8. Koselleck, *Vergangene Zukunft*; Blaas, "Het paradigma van de eeuwwende"; Grever and Jansen, eds., *De ongrijpbare tijd*; Bevernage and Lorenz, "Breaking up Time."
9. For example, Pandel, "Dimensionen der Geschichtsbewußtseins"; Rüsen, "The Didactics of History in West Germany"; Rüsen, "Historical Consciousness"; Straub, ed., *Narrative Identity*; Lee and Ashby, "Progression of historical understanding"; Lee, "'Walking Backwards into Tomorrow'"; Wineburg, *Historical Thinking*; Seixas, "Introduction"; Seixas, "Historical Consciousness"; Grever and van Boxtel, *Verlangen naar tastbaar verleden*; Wilschut, *Images of Time*.
10. Körber, "Historical Consciousness."
11. See also Grever and van Boxtel, *Verlangen naar tastbaar verleden*, 83–84.
12. Körber, "Historical consciousness," 19.
13. Clark and Grever, "Historical Consciousness," 193.
14. Angvik and von Borries, eds., *Youth and History*; Rosenzweig and Thelen, *Presence of the Past*; Ashton and Hamilton, *History At The Crossroads*; Conrad et al., *Canadians and Their Pasts*.

15. Rüsen, "Tradition."
16. Winter, "Introduction."
17. Clark, "Teaching the Nation's Story"; Stone and Sharpley, "Consuming dark tourism"; Ribbens, *Strijdtonelen*; Grever, "Teaching the War."
18. Ammert et al., "Bridging historical and moral consciousness," 6.
19. Kingsepp, "Immersive Historicity"; Van den Heede et al., "Replaying Today's Wars?"; Adriaansen, "Smiling in Auschwitz."
20. De Groot, *Consuming History*, 13.
21. Kingsepp, "Immersive Historicity," 61, 68.
22. Grever and Adriaansen, "Historical Culture"; Van den Akker, "Antiquarianism and Historical Consciousness," 68.
23. Van den Akker, "Antiquarianism and Historical Consciousness," 67.
24. Chakrabarty, "The Climate of History," 213.
25. Chakrabarty, "The Climate of History," 214.

Bibliography

Adriaansen, Robbert-Jan. "Smiling in Auschwitz. The Semiotics of Instagram Selfies at Holocaust Memorial Sites." Paper presented at the conference, Image, History and Memory. Genealogies of Memory in Central and Eastern Europe. Warsaw, 8 December 2017.

Ammert, Niklas, Silvia Edling, Jan Löfström, and Heather Sharp. "Bridging Historical and Moral Consciousness: Promises and Challenges." *Historical Encounters: A Journal of Historical Consciousness, Historical Cultures, and History Education* 4 no. 1 (2015): 1–13.

Angvik, Magne, and Bodo von Borries, eds. *Youth And History: A Comparative European Survey On Historical Consciousness And Political Attitudes Among Adolescents*. Hamburg: Körber-Stiftung, 1997.

Ashton, Paul, and Paula Hamilton. "At Home with the Past: Background and Initial Findings from the National Survey." *Australian Cultural History* 23 (2003): 5–30.

———. *History at the Crossroads: Australians and the Past*. Sydney: Halstead Press, 2010.

Bevernage, Berber, and Chris Lorenz. "Breaking up Time—Negotiating the Borders of Past, Present and Future. An Introduction." In *Breaking up Time. Negotiating the Borders between Past, Present and Future*, edited by Chris Lorenz and Berber Bevernage, 7–38. Göttingen: Vandenhoeck & Ruprecht, 2013.

Blaas, P.B.M. "Het paradigma van de eeuwwende." In *De burgerlijke eeuw. Over eeuwwenden, liberale burgerij en geschiedschrijving*, edited by P.B.M. Blaas, 15–23. Hilversum: Verloren, 2000.

Brown, Tracey. "The idea of a 'post-truth society' is elitist and obnoxious," *The Guardian*, 19 September 2016. Retrieved 3 January 2018 from www.theguardian.com/science/blog/2016/sep/19/the-idea-post-truth-society-elitist-obnoxious.

Chakrabarty, Dipesh. "The Climate of History." *Critical Inquiry* 35 (2009): 197–222.

Clark, Anna. "Teaching The Nation's Story: Comparing Public Debates And Classroom Perspectives On History Education In Australia And Canada." *Journal of Curriculum Studies* 41, no. 6 (2009): 745–62.

Clark, Anna and Maria Grever. "Historical Consciousness: Conceptualizations and Educational Applications," In *International Handbook of History Teaching and Learning*, edited by S.A. Metzer and L. McArthur Harris, 177–201. New York: Wiley-Blackwell Publishers, 2018.

Conrad, Margaret, Kadriye Ercikan, Gerald Friesen, Jocelyn Létourneau, Delphin Muise, David Northrup, and Peter Seixas. *Canadians and Their Pasts*. Toronto: University of Toronto Press, 2013.

De Groot, Jerome. *Consuming History. Historians and Heritage in Contemporary Popular Culture.* London: Routledge, 2009.
Gadamer, Hans-Georg. *Truth and Method.* London: Continuum Impacts, 2006.
Grever, Maria. "Experiencing war. Sensitive heritage in popular culture." Paper presented at the Deusto University Bilbao, Spain, 27 April 2015.
———. "Teaching the War. Reflections on Popular Uses of Difficult Heritage." In *Teaching and Learning Difficult Histories. Global Concepts and Contexts. A Critical Sociocultural Approach,* edited by Terrie Epstein and Carla Peck, 30–44. New York: Routledge, 2017.
Grever, Maria, and Robbert-Jan Adriaansen. "Historical Culture: a Concept Revisited." In *Palgrave Handbook of Research in Historical Culture and Education,* edited by Mario Carretero, Stefan Berger, and Maria Grever, 73–89. Basingstoke: Palgrave Macmillan, 2017.
Grever, Maria, and Harry Jansen, eds. *De ongrijpbare tijd. Temporaliteit en de constructie van het verleden.* Hilversum: Verloren, 2001.
Grever, Maria and Carla van Boxtel. *Verlangen naar tastbaar verleden. Erfgoed, onderwijs en historisch besef.* Hilversum: Verloren, 2014.
Kingsepp, Eva. "Immersive Historicity in World War II Digital Games." *HumanIT* 8 (2006): 60–89.
Körber, Andreas. "Historical Consciousness, Historical Competencies—and Beyond? Some Conceptual Development within German History Didactics." *Pedocs,* 2015. Retrieved 3 January 2018 from www.pedocs.de/volltexte/2015/10811/pdf/Koerber_2015_Development_German_History_Didactics.pdf.
Koselleck, Reinhart. *Vergangene Zukunft: Zur Semantik geschichtlicher Zeiten.* Frankfurt am Main: Suhrkamp, 1979.
Lee, Peter. "'Walking Backwards into Tomorrow': Historical Consciousness and Understanding History." *International Journal of Historical Learning, Teaching and Research* 4, no. 1 (2004): 1–46.
Lee, P., and R. Ashby. "Progression of historical understanding among students ages 7–14." In *Knowing, teaching, and learning history: National and international perspectives,* edited by P.N. Stearns, P. Seixas, and S. Wineburg, 199–222. New York: New York University Press, 2000.
Lukacs, John. *Historical Consciousness: The Remembered Past.* 3rd ed. New York: Schocken Books, 1985.
Pandel, Hans-Jürgen. "Dimensionen der Geschichtsbewußtseins: Ein Versuch, seine Struktur für Empirie und Pragmatik diskutierbar zu machen." *Geschichtsdidaktik* 12, no. 2 (1987): 130–142.
Ribbens, Kees. *Strijdtonelen. De Tweede Wereldoorlog in de populaire historische cultuur.* Rotterdam: EUR / NIOD, 2013.
Ricoeur, Paul. *Hermeneutics And The Human Sciences.* Cambridge: University of Cambridge Press, 1981.
Rosenzweig, Roy, and David Thelen. *Presence of the Past: Popular Uses of History in American Life.* New York: Columbia University Press, 1998.
Rüsen, Jörn. "The Didactics Of History In West Germany: Towards A New Self-Awareness Of Historical Studies." *History and Theory* 26, no. 3 (1987): 275–86.
Rüsen, Jörn. "Historical Consciousness: Narrative Structure, Moral Function, and Ontogenetic Development." In *Theorizing Historical Consciousness,* edited by Peter Seixas, 63–85. Toronto: University of Toronto Press, 2004.
Rüsen, Jörn. "Tradition: A Principle of Historical Sense-Generation and its Logic and Effect in Historical Culture." *History and Theory* 51, no. 4 (2012): 45–59.
Seixas, Peter. "Introduction." In *Theorizing Historical Consciousness,* edited by Peter Seixas, 3–24. Toronto: University of Toronto Press, 2004.

Seixas, Peter. "Historical Consciousness and Historical Thinking." In *Palgrave Handbook of Research in Historical Culture and Education,* edited by Mario Carretero, Stefan Berger, and Maria Grever, 59–72. Basingstoke: Palgrave Macmillan, 2017.

Stone, P., and R. Sharpley. "Consuming dark tourism: A thanatological perspective." *Annals of Tourism Research* 35 (2008): 574–95.

Straub, Jürgen, ed. *Narrative Identity, and Historical Consciousness.* New York: Berghahn Books, 2005.

Van den Akker, Chiel. "Antiquarianism and Historical Consciousness in the New Media Age." In *Sensitive Pasts. Question Heritage in Education,* edited by Carla van Boxtel, Maria Grever, and Stephan Klein, 59–72. New York: Berghahn Books, 2016.

Van den Heede, Pieter, Kees Ribbens, and Jeroen Jansz. "Replaying Today's Wars? A Study of the Conceptualization of Post-1989 Conflict in Digital 'War' Games." *International Journal of Politics Culture and Society* 31, no. 8 (2017): 229–250. DOI 10.1007/s10767-017-9267-5.

Veith, Jerome. *Gadamer and the Transmission of History.* Bloomington: Indiana University Press, 2015.

Wilschut, Arie. *Images of Time. The Role of a Historical Consciousness of Time in Learning History.* Charlotte, NC: Information Age Publishing, 2012.

Wineburg, Sam. *Historical Thinking and Other Unnatural Acts: Charting the Future of Teaching the Past.* Philadelphia: Temple University Press, 2001.

Winter, Jay. "Introduction. The Performance of the Past: Memory, History, Identity." In *Performing the Past. Memory, History, and Identity in Modern Europe,* edited by Karin Tilmans, Frank van Vree, and Jay Winter, 12–34. Amsterdam: Amsterdam University Press, 2010.

Index

Aboriginal, 105, 106, 108, 120, 142, 143, 146, 149, 150, 151, 195–197, 218, 219. *See also* Indigenous; First Nations; Native Americans
Academic historians, 2, 47, 121, 228
Adorno, Theodore, 175
Africa, African, 10, 164, 168
African American(s), 95, 105, 166–167, 214–215
Agency, 164, 166, 167, 168, 171, 172, 188, 208
Ahonen, Sirkka, 220
America, American, 5, 8, 10, 37, 39, 80, 81, 82, 91–100, 103, 105, 106, 107, 109, 111, 114, 121, 146, 148, 149, 151, 152, 169, 182, 203, 215, 217, 225
American Civil War, 82
American Revolution, 82, 154
American Samoa, 93, 94
Anderson, Benedict, 128, 213
Anglocentrism, 36
Anglophones, 150
Anglo-Saxon, 61, 117
Angvik, Magne, 5
Arabs, 82
Archaeology, 2, 21
Archives, 2, 93, 96, 105, 114, 132, 145, 178, 180
Argentina, 51, 84
Art groups, 116
Ashton, Paul, 115

Australia, 2, 4, 5, 6, 7, 8, 96, 100, 104, 109, 113–122, 129, 177, 187, 203, 226, 227
Australian Bureau of Statistics, 117

Bakhtin, Mikhail, 22
Balkans War, 79
Barton, David, 168
Barton, Keith C., 5, 8, 9, 35, 37, 156, 226, 227
Basso, Keith, 191
Beck, Glenn, 167–68
Becker, Carl, 121
Belfast, 25
Belgium, 7, 8, 46
Belonging, 7, 51, 53, 145–47, 154, 156, 207, 213
Bennett, Judith A., 91
Beren, Arthur, 96
Berlin Wall, 68, 76, 84
Biesta, Gert, 63
Biko, Stephen, 164
Billig, Michael, 84
Black Americans, 167, 168
Black consciousness, 164
Black Founding Fathers, 168
Black historical consciousness, 163, 164, 166, 167, 170, 172
Black history, 163–72
Black Lives Matter, 172
Black victimization, 166, 167, 172

Blackness, 164, 171
Black people, 164, 166, 167, 168, 169, 171, 172
Bora Bora, 93
Bosnia, 77, 78
Brawley, Sean, 94
Britain, British, 7, 23, 24, 33, 34, 36, 38, 39, 76, 77, 94, 95, 104, 148, 149, 151, 152, 153, 154, 195, 203, 213, 224
British Columbia, 189, 195, 106
Bruner, Jerome, 77
Bush-regeneration groups, 116

Canada, 5, 8, 51, 103–4, 106–8, 110–111, 114, 129, 142–146, 148–156, 186–87, 196, 203, 212–18, 226
Canadians and Their Pasts, 7, 103–11
Caribbean, 33, 36, 95
Carlin, John, 80
Carlson, Keith Thor, 190, 195
Carr, David, 144
Carretero, Mario, 8, 9, 212, 228
Catholic, 25, 146, 147, 151, 154
Centre for the Study of Historical Consciousness (University of British Columbia, Canada), 32, 212
Chakrabarty, Dipesh, 228
Chapman, Arthur, 7, 8, 9
Charter of Rights and Freedoms, 214
Chartism, Chartists, 33, 36
China, 7, 8, 9, 10, 52, 84, 125–139, 217
Chongqing, China, 126, 130, 137
Christianity, 63, 118
Citizenship, 38, 98, 99, 108, 126, 135, 136, 212, 213
Civil Rights Movement, 36, 166
Clarebout, Geraldine, 52
Clarke, Adele, 115
Clark, Anna, 7, 8, 227
Classroom, 5, 7, 8, 23, 26, 38, 49–53, 55, 56, 62, 64, 66, 145, 166, 169, 180, 187, 191, 194, 215
Coast Salish, 185–197
Cohen, Deborah, 98
Cold War, 68
Collective memory, 2, 23, 26, 34, 62, 64, 66–7, 109, 110, 113, 116, 127, 128, 144, 147, 152, 153, 200–2
Colonialism, Colonization, 1, 92, 93–5, 117, 119, 148, 149, 150, 151, 154, 181, 185–87, 189, 192, 194, 196–7, 209
Communism, Communist Party, 78, 84, 126, 133
Community, 3, 5–8, 19–28, 80, 96, 99, 106, 107, 109, 111, 113–19, 122, 128, 135, 137, 143, 152, 153, 186, 200–1, 204, 213, 218, 220, 226–7
Conservative Party (England), 37, 225
Constitution, 143, 168, 214
Cook Islands, 93, 94
Cornwall (England), 203, 207
Cross-cultural, 185, 192
Cultural hybridity, 203
Cultural Revolution, 126
Curriculum, 2, 4, 7, 8, 20–22, 33–4, 36–40, 56, 62, 63, 67–8, 103, 105, 139, 145, 154, 165, 166–170, 186–188, 195, 196, 216
Curriculum development, 2, 22

Dagbovie, Pero Gaglo, 169
Day, Mark, 35
Decolonizing, 186, 194
de Groot, Jerome, 121, 122, 228
Deloria, Vine, 188, 189, 193, 194
Democracy, 36, 37, 39, 54, 168, 171
Dening, Greg, 2, 114
Depaepe, Fien, 52
Devon (England), 203
Digital storytelling, 130
Dixon, Chris, 94
Dublin, 23
Dubois, W.E.B., 172
Dumas, Michael, 171
Duquette, Catherine, 4, 70
Durkheim, Émile, 201
Dutch Republic, 62

Easter Rising, 23
England, English, 5, 8, 20, 32, 34, 35, 37, 39, 104, 203, 204, 207–9, 151–2, 186
English Canadians, 142–3, 146–9, 151–2, 156
English National Curriculum, 34, 39
Enlightenment, 52, 106
Epistemology, 35, 48, 50, 51, 52, 55, 57, 65, 66, 69, 71, 105, 107, 163, 164, 165, 171, 172, 186, 192, 194, 195, 197

Ethnic identity, 1, 95, 116, 129, 135, 137, 144, 145, 180, 212–221
Ethnic minorities, 130, 137, 212–221
Eurocentrism, 36, 56, 57, 179
Europe, European, 5, 49, 51, 54, 56, 63, 78, 91, 93, 95, 106, 110, 117, 129, 151, 171, 179–82, 226
European ancestry, 148, 192, 208, 209, 215

Family history, 9, 100, 107, 108, 114, 119, 129, 131, 132, 136–7, 202
Fanon, Franz, 172
Fascism, 33
Fentress, James, 201
Fiji, 93–95
Finland, Finnish, 38
First Nations, 150, 151, 218. See also Aboriginal; Indigenous; Native Americans
Flanders, Flemish, 7, 8, 46–57
Founders' Friday, 167
France, 5, 128, 150, 152, 154, 217
Franco-Ontarian, 146, 150, 153, 214, 215
Francophone, Francophones, 8, 106, 144–54, 213
Friedländer, Saul, 182
French Canadians, 143–4, 152, 153, 157. See also Québec, Québecois
French Revolution, 52
FUER model of historical thinking, 65, 69, 70
Funkenstein, Amos, 127
Furedi, Frank, 34

Gadamer, Hans-Georg, 3, 127, 225
Gaeng, Michael, 96
Galloway, Brent, 190
Gee, James P., 220
Gender, 26, 91, 94, 117, 208, 209, 214, 216, 220
Germany, 4, 10, 84, 181, 203, 226
Glassberg, David, 114, 116
Globalization, 55, 219
Golden Age, 68, 152
Gove, Michael, 224
Greece, Greek, 82, 216
Green, Anna, 8, 9, 228
Gutmann, Amy, 220

Halbwachs, Maurice, 200–2, 208
Hall, Stuart, 215
Halpern, Jodi, 22
Hamilton, Paula, 115
Heritage, 2, 4, 6, 26, 34, 35, 39, 61, 63, 67, 105, 108, 114, 115, 136, 138, 201, 203, 227
Hewitson, Tony, 34
Hirsch, Marianne, 176
Historical culture, 2, 5, 6, 9, 34, 61, 66, 110, 114, 163, 165–6, 169–71, 228
Historical empathy, 121, 156
Historical evidence, 20, 21, 27, 28, 37, 39, 55, 62, 65, 68, 69, 97, 98, 104, 139, 181, 192, 193, 204
Historical interpretation, 2, 21, 23, 32, 33, 36, 39–40, 50, 62–3, 68, 69, 107, 125, 126, 132, 133, 152, 157, 165, 166, 171, 1857, 195, 202, 219
Historical knowledge, 2, 5, 6, 20, 24, 26, 48, 51, 54, 55, 62–4, 68, 70, 71, 114, 115, 138–9, 142, 145, 191, 192, 203, 208
Historical narrative, 51, 53, 55, 57, 69, 71, 93, 114, 116, 121, 122, 142, 144, 155–7, 179, 186, 190, 213, 219
Historical reasoning, 7, 61–6, 69–71
Historical societies, 6, 115
Historical thinking, 36, 56, 61–3, 65–71, 104, 139, 202, 203, 212, 214, 216, 219, 226
Historicity, 3, 6, 35, 69, 110, 114, 127, 165, 225, 226, 228
Historioglossia, 228
Historiography, 33, 36, 105, 113, 114, 117, 152, 178, 185, 202, 225
History and Memory (journal), 26
History didactics, 3, 38, 226. See also history education
History discipline, 7, 189
History education, 2, 4–8, 19, 22, 32, 34, 46–57, 61, 63, 66, 71, 76–9, 85, 114, 116, 125, 126, 129, 139, 142, 144, 155, 156, 164, 169, 214, 219, 227, 228
History educators, 76, 125, 126, 127, 128, 138, 139, 145, 156
History teachers, 20, 21, 27, 33, 36, 37, 47, 50, 51, 53, 63, 67, 132, 133, 165, 172, 181
History wars, 117, 121, 122

Holism, 188, 193, 195
Holocaust, 1, 8, 10, 92, 175–83
Holocaust education, 175–83

Iberian Peninsula, 82, 179
Identity, 3, 9, 10, 24–7, 34, 35, 38, 47, 79, 96, 98, 117, 126, 128, 137, 139, 142, 6, 155, 170, 180, 186, 187, 197, 206, 213–20, 226
Imagined community, 213
India, 36
Indigenous, 1, 3, 5, 8, 9, 10, 91–5, 97, 98, 100, 116, 117, 119, 185–97, 213, 220. *See also* Aboriginal; First Nations; Native Americans
Indigenous historical consciousness, 187, 188, 191, 193
Industrial Revolution, 64
Internet, 69, 108, 125, 145, 224
Intergenerational, 6, 200, 208
Intersectionality, 214
Interviews, 19, 26, 27, 53, 54, 64, 67, 92, 96, 97, 103–9, 116–22, 130, 137, 166, 176, 178–82, 203–6, 216, 219
Irish history, 20
Islam, 63
Israel, 5, 80, 181

Japan, 52, 93, 217
Jeismann, Karl-Ernst, 62
Jenness, Diamond, 195
Jewish, Jewishness, 175–83

K-12, 164–6, 169–72
Kammen, Michael, 6, 105, 106, 120
Kansteiner, Wulf, 66
Kilmainham Jail, Dublin, 23
King, Joyce, 172
King, LaGarrett J., 5, 8, 9, 227
Kiribati, 93–4
Kölbl, Carlos, 4
Konrad, Lisa, 4
Körber, Andreas, 4, 68, 226
Korea, 52
Köster, Manuel, 76
Kymlicka, Will, 213, 215

Language, 78, 103, 104, 107, 136, 146–52, 185, 186, 189, 190, 194, 195, 215

La survivance (survival), 152–5
Land, 152–5, 176, 185–97, 204, 207, 208, 224, 226
Latin America, 76, 84, 93
Leckie, Jacqueline, 92
Lee, Peter, 4, 32, 156
Létourneau, Jocelyn, 5, 8, 9, 144, 149, 212
Leuven Centre for Instructional Psychology and Technology, 52
Lévesque, Stéphane, 2, 5, 8, 9, 146
Levstik, Linda, 35, 37
LGBTI (Lesbian, Gay, Bisexual, Transgender, or Intersex), 118
Li, Na, 7, 8, 9, 227
Lieux de memoire, 110, 176
Logtenberg, Albert, 64, 65
Lorenz, Chris, 4
Lowenthal, David, 1
Lukacs, John, 3
Lynching, 166–7

Maiden of Deception Pass, 187, 190–2, 194
Māori, 97
Marker, Michael, 8, 9, 227, 228
Marx, Karl, 22
Massachusetts (USA), 39
McCully, Alan, 5, 8, 9, 226, 227
McKenna, Mark, 6, 120, 121
Media, 22, 67, 96, 125, 128, 129–132, 134, 138, 142, 144, 155, 165, 168, 170, 171, 224, 227, 228
Memorials, 1, 92, 100, 110, 119, 126, 133, 200
Memory, 1–4, 6, 9, 10, 22–3, 34, 35, 49, 62, 64, 66, 67, 77, 91, 92, 96, 100, 109–11, 113, 116, 121, 127–9, 133, 139, 144, 145, 147, 152, 153, 175–7, 181, 183, 200–9
Metaphysics, 186, 195–6
Métis, 151, 214
Mexico, 77, 79–85
Middle class, 169
Midway, 93
Moisan, Sabrina, 144
Monte-Sano, Chauncey, 169
Mothers' Darlings project, 9, 91, 92, 96, 98–100
Multiculturalism, 5, 213, 214, 217

Museum studies, 2, 77
Museums, 4, 6, 22, 34, 67, 69, 107, 108, 110, 113–5, 119, 121, 126, 128, 130, 132–5, 181, 227
Myth, 21, 24, 105, 121, 129, 149–53, 182, 186, 188, 190–2, 203, 228

NAACP, 167
Nakata, N. Martin, 192
Narrative, 2, 6, 7, 21, 22, 26, 39, 51, 53, 55, 57, 66–9, 71, 78, 79, 85, 91, 92, 93, 100, 104, 110, 114–22, 125, 127, 128, 138, 143–57, 163–71, 176–82, 186, 189–96, 200–209, 212–14, 220
Narrative competence, 143, 144, 155, 157
Nation, 1, 5–9, 20, 21, 25, 38, 49, 50–7, 66, 67, 68, 77–85, 92, 98, 100, 103, 107, 109–11, 113–22, 126–39, 142–56, 178–90, 186, 187, 200, 203, 208, 209, 213–20, 224, 227
National history, 49, 66, 107, 109, 115, 119, 135, 136, 142, 143, 145
National Slavery Monument, Amsterdam, 67
Nationalists (Northern Ireland), 20
Native Americans, 82. *See also* First Nations; Indigenous; Aboriginal)
Nazism, 33, 181, 182
Netherlands, 5, 8, 51, 61–2, 66
New Caledonia, 93, 94
New France, 143, 148, 150, 152, 153, 154
New Hebrides, 93. *See also* Vanuatu
New Zealand, 91, 93–7, 100, 208, 209
Newman, Richard, 168
Nokes, Jeffrey, 51
Non-racist, 170
Nora, Pierre, 1, 110, 128
Northern Ireland, 5, 8, 9, 19–29, 226, 227

Ontario, 106, 143, 145, 147, 148, 150, 153, 154
Ontology, 167
Oral historiography, 117
Oral history, 2, 93, 96, 100, 129, 130, 137, 200–204, 208, 209
Ortner, Sherry B., 192

Palestine, 5
Pandel, Hans-Jürgen, 68–70, 226

Passerini, Luisa, 200–2
Past-mindedness, 7, 115
Peck, Carla L., 5, 8, 9, 51
Pedagogy, 7, 8, 29, 33, 127, 166, 171, 176
Philippines, 93
Piaget, Jean, 76
Place, 9, 51, 77–8, 82, 100, 107, 115, 118, 119, 128–30, 137–8, 157, 165, 166, 167, 168, 177, 182, 186–97, 204, 208, 209, 213, 220, 228
Pluralist, 203
Portelli, Alessandro, 200, 201, 202
Positionality, 214
Postcolonialism, 1, 55, 203, 209
Postmemory, 176–77
Protestant, 23, 25, 147, 154, 169, 214
Pryor, Edward T., 214
Psychology, 28, 52, 77, 85, 201
Public history, 2, 3, 6, 103, 105, 107, 110, 115, 125–6, 128–30, 137–9, 201, 227

Qualitative methods, 5, 10, 24, 52, 53, 109, 117
Quantitative research, 5, 10, 49, 52, 106, 155, 129, 164, 202
Québec, Québécois, 5, 8, 106, 143–54, 213

Race, 94, 95, 98, 168, 172
Racism, 167–71, 196
Reconciliation, 186, 187, 196
Republican, Ireland, 25
Residential Schools, 186, 187, 196
Ricœur, Paul, 114, 146, 225
Riel, Louis, 146, 147, 151, 214
Rights, 36, 54, 85, 99, 142, 149, 151, 153, 156, 166, 106, 214, 218
Roman Empire, 84
Romani, 206
Rosenzweig, Roy, 5, 6, 7, 103, 105, 106, 107, 110, 118, 119, 120, 129, 201, 208
Rural, 108, 117, 145, 204, 206–9, 218
Rüsen, Jörn, 2–4, 7, 32–3, 35–7, 62, 63, 65, 67, 68, 71, 104, 106, 114, 128, 143, 165, 202, 212, 225, 226

Samuel, Raphael, 34, 203
Sapir-Whorf Hypothesis, 186
Savenije, Geerte, 67

School, 4, 5, 7, 19–28, 37–8, 46–8, 51, 54, 56, 61–2, 66, 71, 76, 103, 104, 105, 110, 113, 115, 116, 119, 121, 132–5, 139, 143–56, 164, 169–72, 175–82, 186–96, 212, 214, 216, 220, 221, 227
Schools Council History Project, 20
Schwarz, Bill, 208
Seixas, Peter, 4, 7, 8, 26, 32, 77, 114, 157, 163, 164, 201, 202, 212, 226
Serbia, 78
Settler(s), 143, 149, 152, 181, 185, 187, 189, 192, 194–6, 208
Shemilt, Denis, 145, 149, 155
Silence, 2, 93, 97, 98, 122, 165, 167, 168
Silverstein, Jordana, 9
Simon, Roger, 4, 7
Situational analysis, 115
Slavery, 1, 33, 36, 67, 68, 82, 166, 168, 171
Stó:lō, 190, 193, 195
Social media, 125, 126, 225
Solomon Islands, 93
South America, 10
South Pacific, 92–8
South Pacific Command, 92–4, 98
Southeast Asia, 93
Soviet Union, 84
Spain, 51, 76, 84, 179
Spanish Reconquest, 82
Spirituality, 186
Stolen Generation, 117, 120, 121, 227
Straub, Jürgen, 7, 202
Students, 5, 7, 21–9, 32–40, 46–57, 62–71, 77–9, 84, 104–5, 117–8, 130, 137, 139, 142–57, 162, 169, 178, 180–3, 188–97, 212–21, 226, 227
Survey, 5, 7, 24, 49, 103, 109, 110, 111, 115, 127, 129, 130, 131, 137, 138, 139, 146, 169, 203, 208, 215, 226

Taiwan, 129, 130, 136
Taylor, Charles, 220
Teacher educators, 22, 23, 29, 63
Textbooks, 1, 21, 50, 66, 82, 110, 145, 155, 156, 169, 170, 189, 217
Thatcherism, 34
Thelen, David, 5, 6, 7, 103, 105, 106, 107, 110, 118, 119, 120, 129, 201, 203, 206, 208
Thoreau, Henry David, 82

Thorp, Robert, 163, 165, 166, 170
Thünemann, Holger, 76
Trauma, 1, 99, 154, 177, 181, 186, 203
Truth and Reconciliation Commission, 186, 196
Tonga, 93, 94
Tosh, John, 7, 120
Treaties, 185, 194, 196
Trouillot, Michel-Rolph, 165, 170
Trump, Donald, 76–7, 79–81, 84, 85, 177, 225
Tuvalu, 93
Twitter, 224

Underwood, Victor, 190
Unionism (Northern Ireland), 20, 23, 25
United Kingdom (UK), 51
United States of America (US, USA). See America, American
University of Amsterdam, 62
University of Leuven, 46, 49
Urban, 117, 126, 145, 208, 213, 218
US Army, 95
US Fathers of Pacific Children (website), 97
US History, 5, 117, 166
US Navy, 91, 93, 95
US War Department, 95

Van Boxtel, Carla, 7, 8, 226
Van Drie, Jannet, 61, 64, 68
Van Nieuwenhuyse, Karel, 7, 8, 49
Vanuatu, 93, 94
Vernacular, 2, 3, 5, 6, 117, 121
Verschaffel, Lieven, 52
Vietnam War, 62
Visible minorities, 213
Von Borries, Bodo, 5
Vygotsky, Lev, 66

Wallis Island, 93
Wanhalla, Angela, 8, 9
Wells, Ida B., 167
Wertsch, James, 4, 22, 152, 153
West, Cornel, 167
West Germany, 84
The West, Western, 9, 10, 37, 49, 51, 52, 55, 56, 57, 63, 98, 106, 163–4, 169, 171, 172, 176, 185–8, 189, 190, 192–4, 197, 227

Western Samoa, 93, 94
White, 95, 117, 148, 164, 167, 168, 170–72, 215
White Supremacy, 167, 170
Whiteness, 170–71
Wickham, Chris, 201
Wildcat, Daniel, 188
Wils, Kaat, 7, 8, 227
Wineburg, Sam, 51, 104, 116, 143, 145, 169
Worldviews, 186
Womac, Patrick, 167, 168
Women, 91, 92–7, 100, 105, 108, 117, 143, 146, 148, 168, 179, 180, 206, 219

Woodson, Carter G., 172
Working class, 116
World history, 55, 56
World War I, 65, 92, 206
World War II, 25, 78, 92–3
Wright, Patrick, 34
Wynter, Sylvia, 172

Xenophobia, 80

YouTube, 228
Yugoslavia, 77, 78, 79

Zülsdorf-Kersting, Meik, 76

www.ingramcontent.com/pod-product-compliance
Lightning Source LLC
Chambersburg PA
CBHW072151100526
44589CB00015B/2177